Between Two Fires

Between Two Fires

Holding the Liberal Centre in South African Politics

John Kane-Berman

Jonathan Ball Publishers

JOHANNESBURG AND CAPE TOWN

Originally published in South Africa in 2017 by
JONATHAN BALL PUBLISHERS
A division of Media24 (Pty) Ltd
PO Box 33977
Jeppestown
2043

ISBN 978-1-86842-769-7
Ebook ISBN 978-1-86842-784-0

*Every effort has been made to trace the copyright holders and to obtain
their permission for the use of copyright material. The publishers apologise
for any errors or omissions and would be grateful to be notified of any
corrections that should be incorporated in future editions of this book.*

Twitter: www.twitter.com/JonathanBallPub
Facebook: www.facebook.com/JonathanBallPublishers
Blog: http://jonathanball.bookslive.co.za/

Cover by Michiel Botha
Design and typesetting by Triple M Design, Johannesburg
Printed and bound by CTP Printers
Set in 10,5/16pt Life LT Std

Contents

Abbreviations and Acronyms

AD	Appellate Division
Amcham	American Chamber of Commerce in South Africa
ANC	African National Congress
ARM	African Resistance Movement
Azapo	Azanian People's Organisation
BEE	Black Economic Empowerment
BI	Business International Corporation
BOSS	Bureau for State Security
BPC	Black People's Convention
Codesa	Convention for a Democratic South Africa
Cosatu	Congress of South African Trade Unions
CP	Conservative Party
DA	Democratic Alliance
EFF	Economic Freedom Fighters
FDI	Foreign direct investment
FM	*Financial Mail*
Fosatu	Federation of South African Trade Unions
FT	*Financial Times*
Gear	Growth, Employment, and Redistribution
HNP	Herstigte Nasionale Party
IFP	Inkatha Freedom Party (Previously Inkatha Yenkululeko Yesizwe)

Institute, the	South African Institute of Race Relations
Mail, the	*Rand Daily Mail*
NDP	National Development Plan
Nest	New Era Schools Trust
NP	National Party
NPO	Non-profit organisation
NUM	National Union of Mineworkers
Nusas	National Union of South African Students
PAC	Pan-Africanist Congress of Azania
PFP	Progressive Federal Party
PMC	Palabora Mining Company
Progs	Progressive Party
RAU	Rand Afrikaans University
RTZ	Rio Tinto Zinc
SAAN	South African Associated Newspapers
Sabra	South African Bureau of Racial Affairs
SACC	South African Council of Churches
SACP	South African Communist Party
Sactu	South African Congress of Trade Unions
SAIRR	South African Institute of Race Relations
SAR	South African Railways
Saso	South African Students' Organisation
Scopa	Standing committee on public accounts
Sprocas	Study Project on Christianity in Apartheid Society
SRC	Students' Representative Council
Swapo	South West African People's Organisation
UCT	University of Cape Town
UDF	United Democratic Front
UP	United Party
Wits	University of the Witwatersrand
YMCA	Young Men's Christian Association

Introduction

This memoir starts when I was five years old and I watched as my parents' home burnt down in what was widely, but wrongly, believed to be sabotage. It ends two years after my retirement as chief executive of the South African Institute of Race Relations (the Institute), the unashamedly liberal institution which was heading for bankruptcy when I was appointed. It is based mainly on what I wrote and said about South Africa during that time. I made more than 700 speeches, wrote four books on the country, and edited dozens. I also wrote hundreds of thousands of words in newspapers and journals both in South Africa and abroad.

So the memoir is the story of the intensification and fall of apartheid as I told it at the time – along with the story of the first 22 years of rule by the African National Congress (ANC), not forgetting its influential allies in the South African Communist Party (SACP). It's a personal story as well as the story of the Institute during the 30 years I was its head. And in many ways it's a contrarian story in that I was often at odds with prevailing wisdoms, whether about the demise of apartheid or the nature and aspirations of South Africa's new rulers.

The two decades prior to FW de Klerk's release of Nelson Mandela in 1990 were as fascinating a period as any in our history. These 20 years saw some of the most brutal features of apartheid, but also the beginnings of its disintegration. Although the dominating white politicians of that period, John Vorster and PW Botha, wielded enormous power, they were both impelled to make pragmatic compromises that in the end helped to undermine the very system they had been elected to implement. The political Right feared this, but correctly predicted that it would happen. It was the events of the 1970s and 1980s that made those of 1990 both necessary and possible.

Despite the immense harm that apartheid inflicted, South Africa embarked upon the post-apartheid era with great advantages, both political and economic. One of its many assets was the strength of vigilant institutions in civil society, pre-eminent among them the Institute, which had been founded in 1929. With the change of government and constitution in 1994, many people thought our work was done. Not so fast, I said: when parties committed to revolutionary methods and ideas come to power, liberal democracy is not the only possible outcome. In any event, the price of liberty, always, everywhere, is eternal vigilance. So the Institute has played as critical a role in relation to the present government as it did to the previous one. This has been more controversial, and politically more tricky, than our attacks on apartheid, and I was largely responsible for it.

I had enormously enjoyed student politics at the University of the Witwatersrand and I could easily have gone into parliamentary politics. But I was more interested in policy and ideas. I was also especially interested in the ideas driving policy. Unless one pays attention to these, one cannot understand some of the absurdities political parties get up to. The ANC, like earlier manifestations of the National Party (NP), is not a pragmatic party but an ideological one. It was fascinating to see – and record – how the NP eventually abandoned ideology for pragmatism. There is no evidence yet that the ANC will do so. Nor is there yet sufficient pressure on it to change course. Its racial policies, for example, enjoy ideological hegemony.

The first half of the book is broadly chronological. The second, especially after the change of government in 1994, is more thematic. The Institute dealt with various aspects of policy all at the same time, so I have separated them out by topic to make for easier reading.

The first three chapters deal with my home life, my ancestry, and my education. I was involved for most of my time at Wits in student politics. Even though the future looked bleak, this was the heyday of campus liberalism, much to the anger of Prime Minister Vorster. But it also saw the beginnings of the Black Consciousness movement inspired by Steve Biko. My time at Oxford was very different in that I spent most of it in libraries. Left to my own devices in my third and final year by a supervisor who abandoned me, I read a vast amount on South Africa that prepared me for the next phase of my working life.

This was 10 years in journalism, covered in chapters 4–8. I spent the first six years on the *Financial Mail*, a newspaper with a powerful liberal thrust and one not afraid to anger Mr Vorster. At Wits I'd felt the power of the spoken word in addressing packed mass meetings. Now I was able to use the written word to describe some of the worst cruelties and absurdities of apartheid, while also giving strong support to the emerging black trade union movement. I then had four years as a freelance journalist writing for newspapers in a dozen different countries. This gave me an international platform when the world was hungry for news from South Africa, then supposedly headed for race war and revolution. It was the heyday of PW Botha, reviled by so many but to whom I was happy to give credit for repealing the pass laws, whose inhumanity I had done much to expose. I eventually got bored and frustrated writing for foreign papers, however, and joined the South African Institute of Race Relations as its chief executive.

Chapters 9–15 deal with my time at the Institute. First and foremost I had to ensure the organisation's survival. This meant making some unpopular decisions. I made myself even more unpopular in some quarters by declaring that apartheid was on the way out when few people could see any light at the end of the tunnel. As if that were not bad enough, we broke a liberal taboo by criticising revolutionary violence at a time when others were playing it down. A chapter is devoted to the ruling party's continuing commitment to revolution, one deals with its racial policies, and one sets out a robust classically liberal alternative to South Africa's current policy direction, especially in the labour field. I argue the case for dethroning the state and enthroning the individual, and for revitalising the principle that the law should be colour-blind. The final chapter puts forward a set of practical ideas on how to bring about fundamental policy change.

This book is then to a large extent about power: its use, its abuse, its disintegration, and its acquisition. It's also about a lifetime in opposition to the abuse of power. I haven't theorised about power, but simply described how its use or misuse has usually hurt the most defenceless people. However, I have also joyfully described how the powerless have sometimes been able to turn the tables on the powerful. I myself never had any weapons, other than words. One of my favourite poems at school was Tennyson's 'Ulysses'. He says that, sword-like, he longs to shine in use, not be left to rust. I took the same view of freedom of speech. It was not merely a right, but a weapon to be used. And I spent much of my life using it, starting at school and then through university into journalism and the Institute. But speaking truth to power, as I tried to do, and enjoyed doing, was never enough. I seized opportunities to put forward alternative ideas. I did this in the apartheid era, and I regarded it as equally important to do it in the post-apartheid era as the country started once again to founder.

I worked hard. But no account of what I did would be complete without saying something about other interests. I'd read plenty about the Russian Revolution, but on visits to Russia I was far more interested in their paintings and their palaces than in visiting revolutionary sites. I've described some of these in the appropriate place. But I've also tried to describe some of the pleasure I got from reading, classical music, the London theatre, and travel to the Kruger Park and elsewhere. I went on pilgrimages to Commonwealth war cemeteries, among them the one at Alamein, where so many South Africans fought. And I went to Adolf Hitler's hideout in the Austrian Alps. How, I wondered, could such evil be plotted in such beautiful surroundings?

I have cited sources wherever possible. Sometimes the source is a published article in a foreign newspaper. However, I did not always receive clippings of my articles as published – assuming they were published! – so I have sometimes used instead the telexed articles as I sent them off prior to publication.

Although this book conveys mainly what I wrote and said, I sometimes use the term 'we' instead of 'I'. This is not a royal 'we', but rather conveys the fact that opinions expressed in the *Financial Mail* although written by me were expressed as the view of the paper. So also, opinions expressed by me while I was at the Institute were also expressed on behalf of the organisation. Sometimes the views expressed on behalf of the organisation were written not by me but by colleagues under my direction. Some of what I said or wrote appears in quotation marks, but some in the form of indirect speech. I've also sometimes simply conveyed my ideas directly rather than by referring to what I said at a particular time or in a particular place.

This book usually refers to the South African Institute of Race Relations as 'the Institute'. After I retired as chief executive the official name remained unchanged but the organisation was often referred to simply as the 'Institute of Race Relations' or as 'the IRR'.

My thanks are due to the Oppenheimer Memorial Trust for a generous grant which enabled me to write these memoirs. They are dedicated to Pierre Roestorf, who walked this journey with me while providing me with a wonderful home life.

CHAPTER 1

Home, school, army

Born in 1946, I grew up in a happy, comfortable, and politically conscious family. My father loathed the National Party. 'These people are simply inhuman,' he would say.

My earliest memory is of our house in Illovo, Johannesburg, burning down. It is 28 November 1951, my brother Peter's fourth birthday. He is ill in bed and I have been making a nuisance of myself, so my mother has sent me out into the garden. There, in my mind's eye, a man called Jack waves a languid arm up at smoke billowing from the thatched roof, and goes on with his digging. I scream.

Our borehole in this peri-urban area had dried up. When the fire engine came it had no water in it, and the house was quickly a smouldering ruin. As national chairman of the War Veterans' Torch Commando, my father, Louis, born in 1905, was a household name around the country. There was immediate speculation that the fire was sabotage because the Torch had been launched to fight the NP's plans to throw 'coloured' (mixed-race) voters off the common roll. 'Illovo home of Torch chairman burnt down' said the headline on the front page of one paper. Dad dismissed this, for the cause was a workman's carelessness with a blow torch while doing some waterproofing on the roof.

After the fire we lived in rented houses before moving to a house we built in the nearby suburb of Waverley. It had a double garage, open to the street. When they parked in the garage, my parents simply threw their car keys into the cubbyholes of their cars. Theft never crossed their minds. Once a week the cars were left out in the short driveway and the garage was used as a classroom for domestic servants in the neighbourhood. The YMCA provided a literacy teacher. After a year or two the government put a stop to this, using the laws that regulated what Africans might or might not do in supposedly 'white' suburbs other than work as domestic servants. The ban on the YMCA's literacy classes in our garage was a typically spiteful piece of what many people called 'petty apartheid'. My father always took the view, however, that there was no such thing as 'petty apartheid'. It was all inhuman. I was to spend a large part of my working life delving into the logic behind all these racial laws and exposing their consequences.

One of those denied literacy education when the YMCA night school was closed was Charlie Sikhakhane, who had worked for my father's parents since long before the Second World War. At the bottom of our garden in Waverley he grew 'weeds' that my father kept telling him to pull up and throw away, to no avail. One day the police arrived to search his room and the whole of our servants' quarters. Charlie's wife, Eva, who also worked for us, whispered to my mother that they must on no account be allowed to open a certain locked cupboard. Asked what was in it, my mother said, 'My husband keeps his tools in there and he takes the key to work.' This was ingenious because if my father had ever had any tools, he wouldn't have known how to use them. However, the police accepted the story and left. Charlie then produced the key, and he, Eva, and my mother loaded several suitcases full of dagga into my mother's car and drove off to dump them somewhere. My father was furious, pointing out that he, as an attorney, was an officer of the court, and that he was now being compromised because my mother was defeating the ends of justice in helping to get rid of the dagga. Charlie stayed with my parents for another 30 years or more. When we were little he had more or less *carte blanche* to discipline us if we were naughty. 'Daddy, Daddy,

2

Five brothers at our home in Waverley in about 1960.
From left to right, Michael, Charles, Brian, Peter, and me.

Charlie hit me,' we would wail when my father came home from the office. 'Well, I am sure you deserved it,' would be the inevitable reply before he went back to reading his newspaper.

Although the government prevented our garage in Waverley from being a classroom, I used it as a theatre. My brothers, friends, and neighbours were roped in to form a company called The Garage Players. We did bits of *Macbeth* and *Richard III*, the wig I used as Lady Macbeth doubling as my wig for Richard, in which role I did my schoolboy best to imitate Laurence Olivier in his great film. Jack Ralphs, my English teacher at St John's College, lent us the costumes from the school's wardrobe, but admonished me after watching my performance: 'You spoke too fast.' Not a great start for my theatrical ambitions. Our amateur lighting technician also managed to break the fittings, so the show, which included exhibitions of ballet, jiving, and Elvis Presley, went ahead by candlelight.

3

Proceeds of £6 12s 3d went to the African Children's Feeding Scheme. This was the only show our theatrical company managed, but we did put out three issues of *The Garage Players Newsletter* in 1959, an early sign that I was likely to go further in journalism than on the stage.

Every Sunday evening my brothers and I would be required to learn and recite poetry in front of the family, with a crown (five shillings) for the winner. My father, who was not religious, always used to talk about the beauty of the language in the Bible and other great works of literature. Perhaps that's why I've never liked the alternatives to the King James Bible. Contrast this:

> In the beginning God created the heaven and the earth. And the earth was without form, and void; and darkness was upon the face of the deep. And the Spirit of God moved upon the face of the waters.

With this:

> In the beginning God created the heavens and the earth. Now the earth was formless and empty. Darkness was on the surface of the deep. God's Spirit was hovering over the surface of the waters.[1]

An Anglican Prayer Book is likewise a poor substitute for the elegant phraseology of Thomas Cranmer's *Book of Common Prayer*, first published in 1549 and still in use in a few churches in Johannesburg.

Another clear memory of our time in Waverley was Sharpeville, when 69 Africans were shot dead on 21 March 1960 during a demonstration against the pass laws. As a newspaper addict, I always used to go down to breakfast before my father to snatch a few minutes with the *Rand Daily Mail* before he commandeered it. At the age of 14 I stared in horror and bewilderment at the photographs of all the bodies on the front page. Many of the dead, it later transpired, had been shot in the back. Shortly afterwards the Pan-Africanist Congress (PAC), which had organised the Sharpeville demonstration, and the African National Congress were banned. They remained banned for the next 30 years, forced to operate underground and in exile.

One of my classmates at St John's College was Nicholas Reeves, whose father, Ambrose Reeves, was the Anglican bishop of Johannesburg. Bishop Reeves made it his business to expose what had happened. *Inter alia*, he visited some of the victims at Baragwanath Hospital and later wrote *Shooting at Sharpeville*, a book which infuriated the government and outraged the vast majority of whites, who had been happy to believe the official account that the massacre had been a case of self-defence by the police.

No doubt reflecting the views of their parents, some boys at school made plain their hostility to Nicholas. His parents also received death threats, causing them to ask if he could come and stay with us, which he did, as all the tension at Bishop's House in Westcliff was making it impossible for him to do his homework. The Reeves family soon returned to the United Kingdom, Nicholas being the first of my friends to leave the country. Bishop Reeves became president of the Anti-apartheid Movement.

There were not many liberals among the St John's boys, although this was not true of the staff and least of all of the headmaster, Deane Yates. Yates made me secretary/treasurer of something called the St John's African Education Fund. It was set up to put an African student through university, the idea being that if each St John's boy paid in 10 cents a term it would be enough to finance the student, Clarence Ndlovu. My job was to get the boys to pay up, which sometimes elicited racist remarks, especially when Clarence failed some of his courses.

My experiences at school showed that support for the NP's policies went far beyond the Afrikaners. It was also to be found among the supposedly more liberal – and often more affluent – English-speaking section of the population, some of whom could be as racist in their language and attitudes as any member of an unashamedly right-wing party.

5

I also learnt that Afrikaners did not all support apartheid. I went along one day to Holy Trinity Church in Braamfontein to listen to a talk by Beyers Naudé, who had just founded the Christian Institute of Southern Africa to oppose apartheid. I went with Robin Margo, a friend from King Edward VII School, whose house was just down the road from ours after we moved from Waverley to Houghton. Robin and I later served together on the Students' Representative Council at the University of the Witwatersrand (Wits). We also worked together at the Institute for a short time.

St John's was an Anglican school. Chapel was compulsory. There was a sung mass on the first and last days of term, but on weekdays during term the service consisted of a hymn, a lesson, and a prayer every morning. Each day had a different prayer. One of these was 'for the right solution to all the problems presented by the native and coloured peoples'. I went along to one of the chaplains and complained. The 'problems' were not 'presented by the native and coloured peoples' but rather arose from the attitudes of whites towards them. The wording was later changed to a prayer 'for the right solution to all our racial problems'.

Father Neville Jarvis Palmer ('JP'), the senior chaplain, used to take parties of boys to Soweto once or twice a year. On the way we visited the Church of Christ the King in Sophiatown, whence many people had been forcibly removed to Soweto. It was partly about this that Trevor Huddleston had published *Naught for your Comfort* in 1956. Like Alan Paton's global bestseller *Cry the Beloved Country*, published in 1948, it helped put apartheid onto the international map, demonstrating the power of the written word.

These were not my first visits to Soweto, whose name was an acronym for South Western Townships. While still in prep school, I sometimes went with my mother on Saturday mornings to Chiawelo, one of the districts in Soweto, where she helped run a shop for Kupugani, a non-profit organisation selling foods to combat malnutrition. This was one of many charitable activities in which my mother, born Gabrielle de Maine in 1922, involved herself throughout most of her life – indeed, well into her eighties. Like my father, she was a member of the Liberal Party. She also raised money via an annual morning market for the Black Sash to help finance the advice centres it ran to assist Africans who fell foul of the pass laws designed to limit their presence in supposedly 'white' areas and so keep these areas as 'white' as possible.

St John's gave me experience in, and a taste for, journalism. I was appointed one of the editors of the school magazine, *The Johannian*, and given more or less a free hand with its content by the master in charge, Angus Rose.

One of my fellow editors was Michael Arnold, who many years later became the school chaplain. He won the Lawson Poetry Prize for a poem about British Prime Minister Harold Macmillan's visit in 1960 to South Africa, which Piet Cillié, editor of *Die Burger*, had described shortly after Sharpeville as the polecat of the world.[2] Macmillan shocked his audience of MPs and no doubt most of the rest of white South Africa by warning them of the wind of change, the powerful force of national consciousness that was rising in the African continent.[3]

Referring to Macmillan's own words, the poem was entitled 'The Winds of Change':

This gentle breeze doth purge the desert air
Embalming flowers with a fragrance fair
A fragrance such as rank hyenas know
A rancid stench a polecat would forgo
Yet fetid polecats are not quite the thing
About which educated citizens should sing
At least our newspapers would have us so believe
And why should press men trouble to deceive
When they with noted radio must compete
To noise abroad the newest and the fairest feat?

Not bad for a school magazine.

In sixth form in 1963 one of my classmates, Clive Nettleton, and I started a newsletter which we called *Sixth Sense*. We naturally specialised in publishing provocative and controversial stuff. There was no censorship, but circulation was restricted to prefects, matrics, sixth formers, and staff. On one occasion we gave Mr Rose an anonymous platform for a scathing attack on one of the school's hallowed traditions – its Gilbert and Sullivan productions. He wrote that G&S had a 'stranglehold' over the school's musical development. The headmaster carpeted Clive and myself, but he not did demand the name of the author.

I also started writing letters to the press. One of them was a parody of Mark Antony's sarcastic rabble-rousing speech in *Julius Caesar:*

> Friends, citizens, countrymen, lend me your ears
> I come to bury Freedom, not to praise her ...
> The noble Vorster
> Hath told you Freedom was a Communist
> If it were so, it was a grievous fault
> And grievously hath Freedom answered it
> And Vorster is an honourable man ...

My effort at parodied blank verse was published in the *Rand Daily Mail,*[4] in the midst of one of the security clampdowns by the minister of justice, John Vorster, to curtail political resistance. I enjoyed writing this kind of thing, and my parents encouraged me. So did Deane Yates. Alan Paton also quoted my parody in a lecture at Wits.[5] The so-called Rivonia trial of Nelson Mandela and others opened in October that same year and in due course led to their imprisonment, in Mandela's case for 27 years.

South Africa had passed another landmark only a month before that, when Solomon 'Looksmart' Ngudle, a trade unionist and member of the ANC, was found hanged in his cell at security police headquarters in Pretoria. Accused of being an organiser for Umkhonto we Sizwe, the military arm of the ANC, he was the first person to die in police custody while in detention under a law enacted earlier in the year to provide for detention without trial for up to 90 days.

Nearly 25 years later the Institute published a study of deaths in detention under the title *Behind Closed Doors*.[6] Several Institute fact sheets on detention had been banned so we distributed *Behind Closed Doors* as widely as we could before releasing it to the press so that any ban – none came – would be futile. By that stage 90-day detention had been superseded by 180-day detention and that in turn by indefinite detention without trial. Like banning orders, detention laws were designed to curtail resistance to apartheid. Instead they provided further focal points for opposition, as liberal critics predicted at the time.

Best known of all those who died in detention was Steve Biko, the fiftieth person known to have done so at that stage. A few years before he was beaten to death in September 1977 he took me to visit some of the 'dumping grounds' in the Eastern Cape into which people had been removed under the policy of ethnic cleansing pursued by the NP government and about which I was then writing for the *Financial Mail*. He did this although he was by then under a banning order.

In my sixth-form year I won a prize for an essay on Jan Hendrik Hofmeyr. He had been deputy prime minister for much of the war while General Smuts was up north. He was also the great liberal hope of the United Party (UP), though he was out of tune with his party, which shared many of the racial attitudes of the NP. Hofmeyr's liberal views had been blamed for Smuts's loss of power to Dr DF Malan's NP in the fateful 1948 election. Alan Paton was writing a biography of Hofmeyr, so I sent him my schoolboy offering, which he read carefully enough to pick up some contradictions.[7] Paton's book was subsequently launched at a function in our garage in St Patrick's Road in Houghton in 1964.

With schoolboy presumption I must have written to compliment him on it, because I received a letter thanking me for doing so. He said that most South African biographers failed to understand the nature of biography, which was 'not to make a point, preach a policy, help a party, or aggrandise a man – it was primarily to tell the life of a human being'. South African autobiographies, he said, were 'too terrible'. 'No one should write an autobiography, unless he is vitally interested in others beside himself.'[8] Many years later, when I was working for the *Financial Mail*, I sent Paton a novel to review. He sent it back and wrote, 'As a rule I don't review novels, but if I dislike the novel then I am doubly opposed to reviewing it. Just imagine for example what complications would set in if I were to review a novel by Nadine Gordimer unfavourably.'[9]

Still later, when I was working at the South African Institute of Race Relations, he wrote to complain about a 'mealy-mouthed' review we had published of a book on South African liberalism by a man called Paul Rich. He added: 'Don't take any notice of this letter. It is the work of a "crusty" old devil who never made it to the top. Good luck with the SAIRR. I don't envy you the job. When I come to power, Rich won't have long to live.' Paton's own review of the book was headlined 'Author Rich, Book Poor'.[10]

After completing sixth form I was called up by the army. Until then national service was only three or four months, but my intake was one of the first to go for nine months. Part of the reason no doubt was that Umkhonto we Sizwe, under Nelson Mandela's leadership, had launched its campaign of sabotage on 16 December 1961.

During my basic training at Potchefstroom, I was selected with two others from my regiment, the Transvaal Scottish, to go on an officers' training course at the Army Gymnasium in Voortrekkerhoogte outside Pretoria. We were told we would live in the officers' mess, each with his own room, and a batman to bring us tea in the mornings. This, of course, turned out to be nothing more than bait. We slept eight of us to a tent during the freezing Pretoria winter.

Part of our training was elaborate parade-ground work. But we also had lectures on military law, how to conduct courts martial and summary trials, mess etiquette, which glass to use for which wine should you ever be invited to a state banquet, and on 'promotion and maintenance of the desire to learn'. This last contained tips so sensible it is amazing they are not routinely used in every classroom and lecture theatre everywhere. First, we were told, when you go into a classroom to give a lecture, start with a joke or a funny story to get everyone's attention. Then explain what you're going to teach them. Then ask questions arising from what you've taught. Don't invite people to put up their hands with the answers. Wait half a minute and then call on somebody by name to stand up and answer the question. This would make sure that everyone would pay attention throughout the lecture for fear of being made to look foolish if they couldn't answer. The instructor would then be able to assess whether or not 'instruction has been assimilated'.

Some manoeuvres were held at Kakhuiskloof, west of Pretoria. This was a beautiful piece of hilly country, from which the distant lights of Johannesburg in the night sky were a magnificent sight. Our lectures on military law had included warnings against assaulting lower ranks. When we got to Kakhuiskloof we were told to forget everything we ever learnt about military law because it didn't apply to our instructors when we were in the veld. Other manoeuvres were along the Tugela River in KwaZulu-Natal in a week of drenching rain during which we came across many Boer War graves. The training was physically extremely tough – said to be the toughest after the training for the parabat battalion at Tempe, outside Bloemfontein. The reasoning was that infantry platoon leaders could not lead men into battle unless they had proved they could take it themselves.

Half our training during field manoeuvres was in conventional warfare, the other half in counter-insurgency, known as COIN operations. During the latter we were issued with sweets to hand out to any children we came across when searching rural areas and villages for 'terrorists' hiding out there. (These 'terrorists' were usually played by men from other regiments identified by the black tracksuits they wore.) We were also instructed to observe protocol. If you approached a village, you didn't just march in, but should send a small patrol ahead to ask to see the headman. He would probably invite you into his hut, where you should immediately squat down as a mark of respect. He was then likely to offer you something to drink. No matter how foul you suspected it might taste, either you or your second-in-command had to drink it, for refusal would be an insult. Polite or not, some of our manoeuvres were nevertheless intrusions into the tranquillity of some of these villages with their cattle.

Sometimes we went on route marches to supposedly classified destinations. When we got there, men with little ice cream carts packed with dry ice would be lying in the grass waiting for us. So much for military secrets.

At the end of all this, I was told I had failed the course. Something odd had in fact happened right at the start. Shortly before we packed up our kitbags and backpacks to leave Potchefstroom for Pretoria, one of my fellow trainees was told to stand by as he would be going instead of me. No explanation was given, and in the end I went as planned. But I later managed to get hold of my personal file. There I found a telegram from the army chief of staff to the commandant of the Potchefstroom camp wanting confirmation as to whether the 'above-mentioned ballottee' – one Kane-Berman – had been selected for the course. I could only surmise that this attention from on high was because I was my father's son. He had been on the reserve of officers after his time in the Western Desert and Italy during the war, but was purged from active duty during Torch Commando days.

After Voortrekkerhoogte I was posted to Lenz military camp opposite Lenasia, a few stops on the railway line after Soweto on the way to Vereeniging. While I was there, John Harris, a member of the African Resistance Movement (ARM) who had joined the Liberal Party as a cover, planted a bomb in the Johannesburg railway station on 24 July 1964. It killed 77-year-old Ethel Rhys and partially destroyed the face of her 12-year-old granddaughter, Glynnis Burleigh. Harris was subsequently hanged for this crime. A schoolboy by the name of Peter Hain read the lesson at Harris's funeral. Five years later, having emigrated to the UK, Hain organised a campaign to stop a planned Springbok cricket tour to that country.

The station bomb was the beginning of the end of the Liberal Party. Maritz van den Berg, who had been a leading member of the party and a friend of Harris, whom he visited in prison until the day before his execution, later wrote that his crime of 'premeditated murder' had dealt a death blow to the party.[11] Alan Paton, president of the party, said Harris was guilty not only of inhumanity and cowardice, but of 'putting a bomb' under the party.[12]

After the station bomb, raids, detentions, and arrests intensified. One of those detained without trial was Ernie Wentzel, an advocate who appeared for the defence in numerous political trials, and also a leading light in the Liberal Party. Ernie was instrumental in my joining the Institute as its chief executive 19 years later. He also became my first board chairman. Typical of Ernie was that he later got hold of his old cell door from the Marshall Square police station and installed it at his home in Sandringham. He would demonstrate how the warders or the police would bang on his cell door each morning, '*Kom, Wentzel, kom. Brekfis. Dink jy jy's in 'n hotel?*' And then Ernie would go into stitches of laughter, as only he could.

According to Ernie's widow, Jill Wentzel, Harris had begged Ernie, 'Please don't let them hang me.' Ernie declined to defend him as he was too close to Harris. Few others would take the case. Eventually, Harris's attorney, Ruth Hayman, went to call on Namie Philips, QC, who said to her in a lugubrious voice, 'Ruth, I know why you've come, and I will do it.' Namie's son David and I were together at Wits. On one occasion when the Harris trial came up during a lecture, David said in a stage whisper, 'Defended by Mr N Philips QC.' I could tell how proud he was of his father for taking so unpopular a case.

In the three months between finishing the army and enrolling at Wits at the beginning of 1965, I worked at Vanguard Booksellers in

Johannesburg. Owned and run by the redoubtable Fanny Klenerman, Vanguard gave jobs to several people who were subject to banning orders under the Suppression of Communism Act of 1950, which empowered the minister of justice to impose such orders on anyone he thought might be furthering the aims of communism. If you were banned you could not be quoted, enter premises where anything was published, or leave the magisterial district to which your ban confined you. There was no trial or appeal nor any obligation upon the minister to produce proof, give reasons, or explain what he meant by 'communism' as he wielded his pen. Most bans lasted for five years, and many were renewed more than once.

Among the banned people at Vanguard were Helen Joseph and Shantie Naidoo. Helen was the first person to be put under night-time and weekend house arrest, in 1962.[13] She had been prominent in various organisations and activities aligned with the ANC, and had also been one of the accused in the unsuccessful (for the prosecution) 'Treason Trial' which opened in 1958 and ended in 1961. Later she became famous for a book, *Tomorrow's Sun*, about people banished to remote parts of the country to take them out of political circulation.

Shantie, like her three brothers, had been involved in political and trade union activity. She'd been banned in 1963 and again in 1968. When she tried to leave the country some years later she was granted an exit permit by the minister of the interior, but refused permission by the minister of justice to leave the magisterial district of Johannesburg to travel to the airport. Eventually he gave her permission upon receipt of an undertaking from her that she would not involve herself in anti-South African activities abroad.[14] Before she left the country, I used to visit Shantie from time to time at the family home in Doornfontein. I gave her a pile of gramophone records to send to Robben Island to be played for prisoners, among them Indres, one of her brothers. The Naidoos were one of the last Indian families to have to leave this supposedly 'white' area in terms of the Group Areas Act and move to Lenasia, a township near Soweto demarcated as a group area for Indians and Asians.

Officials from the Department of Customs and Excise used to drop in to Vanguard to inspect shipments of new books. Anything suspect was embargoed for sale, and a copy sent to the Publications Control Board for vetting – and possible banning – before it could be released. On one occasion I remember one of the officials paging through *Is Sex Necessary?* by James Thurber and trying to decide whether it was pornographic or not.

Vanguard was a wonderfully pleasant experience from a racial point of view, in that everyone from Fanny Klenerman downwards was on first-name terms – although I always called her 'Miss Klenerman'. She was politically on the Left, and I assumed that Vanguard was named for 'vanguard of the proletariat'.

Before racing ahead to the years of university and beyond, let me round off my family history. My brothers and I spent nearly all our school holidays at Lowlands, a farm belonging to my grandparents, Noel and Gay (neé Brereton) de Maine, outside Barberton, a small town nestling at the foot of one of the mountains in the De Kaap Valley, so named because the first white settlers thought it as beautiful as the Cape. My father had been in the military camp there before going up North during the Second World War, and there he had met my mother on a blind date. This happened when one of my father's brother officers drove him to my grandparents' house and then went in on his behalf to ask my mother to join him at a dance in the town hall. 'What's the matter with him? Can't he come inside and ask me himself?' she demanded. Then in his mid-thirties, my father was both taken aback and impressed by this response from a matric pupil half his age. However, they didn't get married until nearly the end of the war, in which she also served, as a gunner, on Robben Island and Signal Hill in Cape Town, and on the Bluff in Durban.

At Lowlands I was never more content than when driving a 1945 Farmall tractor, from the age of about 10. My grandfather didn't really approve of this as he thought I would fall off and get run over, so tuition by one of the tractor drivers, Jack Twala, had to be clandestine. Across the road from Lowlands was the farm Verulam. There lived Bill and Doreen Carlin, one of whose daughters, Pamela, married Jonathan Ball.

Blue gums planted as windbreaks lined the fields where mealies, cotton, and tobacco were planted in rotation. Everywhere else was bushveld except where grass had been planted as fodder for the beef herd, a mixture of Afrikander and Sussex. As a little boy I used to think that the noise of the cicadas was coming from the millions of stars twinkling in the night sky. Often you would see the glow of veld fires on the surrounding mountains at night. When I wasn't driving the tractor or my grandfather around in his truck, I was riding a bicycle along the railway line which cut through the farm or pushing it up some of the surrounding mountains looking for a legendary ghost city where there had once been some gold diggings, these hills being where gold was first discovered in South Africa in 1884.

Although I thought Lowlands was just about the most beautiful place in the most beautiful setting in the world, I was never tempted to become a farmer. Lowlands was sold not long after my grandfather died in 1965. Two of my brothers, Peter and Brian, went farming, first in the Carolina district in the late 1960s and then at Arnot, halfway between Johannesburg and the Kruger Park, and where they have built up a great enterprise, Beestepan Boerdery. My youngest brother, Charles, later joined them. A fourth brother, Michael, taught at one of the schools on the farm. Though he had little formal training he was by all accounts an unusually gifted teacher. But he was also a drug addict. He committed suicide in 1999.

The schools were built by my brothers for the children of their staff, but in time there were enough places to accommodate children from neighbouring farms. Few of the neighbouring farmers were prepared to transport their workers' children to school, so my brothers sent out vehicles to fetch them every morning.

The project started with pre-primary schools, to which a primary school was soon added. My parents had gone to live on the farm after my father's retirement from legal practice in 1979 and the primary school was registered that same year. My mother soon took it under her wing.

Apart from fund-raising, apartheid policy had to be dealt with. It had forced the closure of the night school in our garage in Waverley all those many years ago. Now it put restrictions on farm schools. Under the pass and influx control laws, children of African farmworkers in the supposedly white parts of South Africa were permitted to study only at primary school. If they wanted secondary education, they had to take themselves off to one or other of the 'homelands'. Education was thus subordinate to the overarching policy of reducing the numbers of Africans in the white areas.

The local education authorities refused permission for post-primary grades to be added. Fortunately, I had got to know Sam de Beer, minister of education and training in the NP government. I arranged for my mother and my brother Brian to see him. He agreed that tuition could be offered up to matric. This was quite a breakthrough. The high school produced its first matriculants in 1993. In that same year the Johannesburg College of Education presented its 'rector's gold medal' to the 'Kane-Berman family and Beestepan Boerdery' for the establishment of the schools. At the end of 1993 Sam de Beer came to perform the official opening of the Beestepan Agricultural High School's new campus near my brother Peter's house.

After the ANC came to power, my brothers extended an invitation to one of its education ministers, Kader Asmal. I had been to see him when he was teaching law while in exile at Trinity College, Dublin. He now came to visit the high school. One of his entourage complained that some of the teachers were white. Sophie Mokoena, the African woman to whom the complaint was addressed, happened to be the chairman of the school governing body; she sent this official off with a flea in his ear.

17

Here was an interesting contrast: black parents did not object to white teachers, but black officials did.

What about my ancestry? My grandmother's father, Alfred William Brereton, born in 1862, had been an Anglican clergyman, and his wife, Daisy, born in 1868, was the daughter of Canon Charles Taberer of St Matthew's Mission in Keiskammahoek in the Eastern Cape. Brereton evidently became the first registrar of Rhodes University.[15] The family came from Cheshire in England, where their Elizabethan home is now a girls' school. Sir William Brereton, one of the four knights who murdered Thomas Becket at the behest of King Henry II in 1170, is claimed as an ancestor. My maternal grandfather was Noel de Maine, born in 1890, whose father came from Yorkshire and had been MP for Albany in the old Cape province.

My father's mother, Esther Stuart Kane, born in 1882, came from a Roman Catholic family in Dundee, Scotland. Family legend had it that she was somehow descended from Mary Queen of Scots, but my cousin Jocelyne Kane-Berman (later Ritchie) did all the necessary research and found this to be just that – legend. My father's father, Myer Berman, was born in Lithuania in 1877 whence he literally ran away to Germany as a boy to escape conscription. His elder brother was a corporal in the Russian army, the highest rank open to Jews, and had had a cross branded on his chest by Cossacks. With little formal education, my grandfather worked in brush factories in both Germany and England, before marrying my grandmother in London in 1902.[16] He eventually became a bookmaker at Tattersalls in Johannesburg.

My maternal grandmother made a name for herself as a young woman when a German submarine torpedoed the *Lusitania* off the coast of Ireland in May 1915 en route from New York to Liverpool during the First World War. Although it was also carrying munitions, this was a passenger liner and 1 198 lives were lost. An angry mob went on the rampage in Johannesburg. They were threatening to burn down the German church in Hillbrow, near where my grandparents lived. My grandmother rushed over and successfully pleaded with the crowd to spare the church. Eventually they cheered her.[17] She later became chief commandant of the Red Cross in South Africa. When she died in 1943, the prime minister, Field Marshal Smuts, said 'we have lost a great citizen'.[18]

The War Veterans' Torch Commando was founded in 1951, the year after Smuts's death, to oppose the Nationalists' plans to remove coloured voters from the common roll, where they had been registered since 1853. Under the Union Constitution, which had come into operation in 1910, franchise rights could be removed only by a two-thirds majority of both the House of Assembly and the Senate at a joint sitting. The African common-roll franchises had been removed in 1936. Plans for a limited franchise for Indians fell through in 1948.[19] Now it was the turn of coloured voters. Even though they constituted only a fraction of the total on the common roll, they were now to be put on a separate roll to elect four (white) MPs. The reason why they were to be thrown off the common roll was that they would vote against the Nationalists in various marginal seats.[20]

The Separate Representation of Voters Act of 1951 was passed by a simple majority, as the NP did not have two thirds. Challenged by four coloured voters, the act was declared null and void by the Appellate Division (AD) of the Supreme Court. The NP then put through the High Court of Parliament Act of 1952, in terms of which Parliament would be the final court of appeal on constitutional matters. A hundred Nationalist MPs – in fact the NP caucus – then solemnly constituted themselves as judges and overruled the AD. But the AD invalidated the High Court of Parliament Act as well.

The NP then passed the Appellate Division Quorum Act of 1955 to increase the size of the AD to 11 when sitting on constitutional matters. Extra judges were appointed. The NP also passed the Senate Act of 1955, entitling them to appoint enough senators to give the Nationalists the necessary two thirds at a joint sitting of both Houses of Parliament. These manoeuvres were also taken on appeal, but eventually, by 10 votes to 1, the AD upheld them. The coloured (and Asian) voters in the Cape were duly removed from the common roll in 1956,[21] though it took the government five years to do this. The single dissenting vote on the AD was that of Oliver Schreiner, who later became president of the South African Institute of Race Relations and chancellor of the University of the Witwatersrand.

The government's constitutional manoeuvring prompted a cartoon in the *Rand Daily Mail* by Bob Connolly depicting the Constitution with a mourning sash over it. A women's group established to defend the Constitution donned black sashes and stood in silent protest outside Parliament, the Union Buildings, and in many other parts of the country, including airports, whenever cabinet ministers were due to appear. This was the origin of the Black Sash, whose members were subsequently often to be found standing in silent protest against detention-without-trial and other laws, while also devoting a great deal of energy to helping pass-law victims.[22]

Although enacted by the British parliament, the Union Constitution was in fact a wholly South African document which the British rubber-stamped. The British had indeed ignored the objections of black South Africans who had gone to London to implore them not to hand independence to South Africa under a constitution which entrenched white minority rule.

Thwarted by the courts in their initial attempts to remove coloured voters from the common roll, the Nationalists labelled the Constitution an 'imperialist' document. The AD judges were 'old men' and 'five paid officials'. To submit to their attack on the 'sovereignty' of Parliament would be 'constitutional enslavement'.

All these arguments were refuted in various documents, among them a booklet written for the Torch by a Cape advocate, MM (Mick) Corbett. He accused the NP of behaving not only illegally, but also immorally and in 'gross bad faith' in violating the 'solemn compact' entered into at the time of Union. Said Corbett: 'Just as the humblest citizen must abide by the law, so the government must abide by the law.'[23] Later elevated to the Bench, Corbett became known for his advocacy of a bill of rights for South Africa. In 1989 he was appointed chief justice, in which capacity he delivered the Institute's Hoernlé Memorial Lecture in 1990. Four years later he administered the oath of office to Nelson Mandela when the NP formally handed over power to the ANC at the Union Buildings on 10 May 1994.

The NP's constitutional manoeuvring outraged tens of thousands of South Africans, not least ex-servicemen, Afrikaans as well as English-speaking. My father wrote that coloured soldiers had played a significant role in the Second World War as volunteers in the Desert and in Italy. Ex-servicemen were determined to rouse the electorate in resistance to the plan to remove them from the common roll.[24] Their franchise rights, and the constitutional clauses protecting them, should be regarded as 'inviolate and sacrosanct'.

At its height the Torch had 250 000 signed-up members, each paying a minimum subscription of a few shillings.[25] Alan Paton once said the Torch was the only white organisation the NP ever feared. The Nats had good reason to be frightened. The Torch forswore any form of violence and its members were never armed, but its leadership and about two thirds of its members were ex-servicemen, among them officers controlling most units of the Active Citizen Force. The Torch attracted up to 50 000 people to mass meetings outside the city halls in Johannesburg, Durban, Port Elizabeth, and Cape Town. Some of these, planned with military precision, were preceded by torch-lit processions from different parts of the city converging on the city hall. The torches were made of cotton wool doused in paraffin in tin cans, and were immediately dubbed *blikfakkels* (tin-can torches) by the Afrikaans press.

One night in October 1951 on the ninth anniversary of the Battle of Alamein, my father looked out over a sea of flaming torches outside the Johannesburg City Hall and declared to thousands of listeners, 'These are the lights of democracy – let them be a source of comfort to the people of this country, whatever their language, race, or colour. They convey a message to the people of South Africa in the name of those who fought and lived and in the name of those who fought and died.'

There were huge meetings in smaller centres all over the country too. Meetings were sometimes broken up – by Nationalists, according to my father. How did he know this? 'Who else would break up a meeting?' They had once broken up a meeting in Lydenburg, a small town in what is now Mpumalanga. 'So we immediately announced we'd have another meeting there the following week.' More than 500 cars in convoys from Barberton, Nelspruit, White River, and other places all over the Lowveld converged simultaneously on the town. 'You could not get into the town hall, nor could you get a gallon of petrol or a pint of beer in the town. It was *Nagmaal* so we were accused of desecrating that occasion, but we went back to assert that we had a right of free speech anywhere in the country.' This time there were no attacks. One man who tried to heckle was treated to drinks afterwards by Torchmen who admired his courage.

The Torchmen's practical assertion of the right of free speech impressed me enormously whenever my father mentioned it. More than 50 years later a judge who had been present as a young lawyer told me how proud he had been of my father and the Torch. Another ex-serviceman, to whom I proposed a toast at a small lunch on the seventieth anniversary of the victory in Europe in 1945, told me that my father had been an inspiration to him and many like him. Those who marched with the Torch have now nearly all died out.

Judges, civil servants, generals, and other army officers joined the Torch in such numbers that the government tried to prohibit this. Group Captain 'Sailor' Malan, a fighter pilot who had made a name for himself in the Battle of Britain, was the president, and my father the national chairman. The patron-in-chief was NJ de Wet, a former chief justice and officer administering the government.

The Torch had only one objective, which was to prevent the assault upon the Constitution and the removal of the coloured franchise. When it eventually failed thanks to all the NP's manoeuvring, the organisation disbanded. However, it had also been divided on strategy, my father wanting to call a 'national day of protest' – a one-day strike against unconstitutional action. This prompted the minister of justice, CR ('Blackie') Swart (later first state president when South Africa became a republic in 1961), to accuse him of invoking the aid of non-Europeans against the government, while Prime Minister Malan branded the Torch 'a most dangerous organisation' and announced that he was moving some military reserves to Cape Town.[26] There were also differences with the Torch's allies in the 'united front' it formed with the official opposition, the United Party, and the Labour Party. If the UP won the April 1953 election, the coloured franchise would be preserved and the *raison d'être* for the Torch would fall away. But the NP increased its seats in Parliament from 86 to 94, while UP representation dropped. A month after the election the Liberal Party was formed.[27]

At the time the Torch was mobilising white opposition, the ANC had launched its defiance campaign against unjust laws. To break this, the government passed the Public Safety Act of 1953, which provided for the declaration of states of emergency, detention without trial, and rule by decree. It also passed the Criminal Law Amendment Act of 1953 to provide for imprisonment and whipping of anyone breaking the law, or inciting anyone to break the law, as part of a political protest. The bills were introduced by Justice Minister Swart, whom my father described as a 'menace'. Said he: 'We were bitterly opposed to these two bills in principle,' but the UP leaders supported them because they never 'wanted to fight anything on principle'. The head of one of the smaller mining companies had said to him at a fund-raising dinner hosted by Harry Oppenheimer: 'During the war, Smuts imprisoned Afrikaners without trial and now you complain because the government wants to throw a few kaffirs into prison.'[28] But my father regarded the introduction of detention without trial as an ominous step that should be resisted from day one.

One liberal UP member – there were not many such – by the name of Helen Suzman approached my father with a view to getting prominent

Torchmen to join the UP to reform it from within. He told her that would be impossible. In fact it would be easier to reform the NP from within. In 1959, she and various other UP MPs broke away to form the Progressive Party. Unlike the Liberal Party, which was forced to dissolve itself in 1968, as we shall see below, the Progressive Party in various permutations survived into the post-apartheid era. Throughout the 1960s, the 1970s, and the 1980s it was the only real voice of liberalism in the South African parliament. Its successor, the Democratic Alliance, is now South Africa's official opposition.

Tragically, the decline of the Torch after only two years was as rapid as its rise. But it had captured the imagination of the country. My grandmother once told me that people used to stop her in the streets in Barberton, and ask excitedly, 'Do you think Louis will be prime minister?' But the loss of our house and nearly all its contents in the fire in 1951, along with all the (unpaid) time my father had spent on the Torch, meant that my parents were broke. Dad accepted a partnership in a law firm, Hayman, Godfrey, and Sanderson. But there was a condition: no politics. It was the end of any active political career – and in my view as great a loss to the liberal cause in the country as JH Hofmeyr's premature death in 1948.

The Nats did not forget the Torch, or my father, although they got the two of us mixed up. Many years later when I went to South West Africa to write a report for the Institute on the Ovambo strike at the end of 1971,[29] a Nationalist deputy minister by the name of HE Martins stated in Parliament that the Torch had become friendly with the ANC and others breaking down the colour bar, stirring up hatred against the Afrikaner, and 'encouraging anarchy, sabotage, strikes and even terrorism by means of liberalistic communism in South Africa'. The 'notorious Kane-Berman' who had been inciting all this was now 'again interfering in the Ovambo problem in South West Africa'.[30]

When the Torch folded it had R16 000 left in the bank. This was given to the Rand Cape Coloured Children's Health Fund. My father wrote that he thought this 'an appropriate gesture in view of the ineradicable hurt that the government had done [the coloured] community on the subject of the franchise'.[31] The fund had been started in 1932 to raise money to send children on holiday to the seaside. My parents served it as honorary legal adviser and honorary treasurer. Initially the children camped at the seaside but eventually the Transhaven Seaside Home at New Brighton Beach, Durban, was established. Many years later the Transhaven Seaside Fund wrote that my parents had played a prominent role in helping it to acquire the Durban property, which, Transhaven said, 'stands as a monument to their unselfish sterling services'.[32]

When my mother died at the age of 90 in November 2012 Transhaven sent a delegation to her funeral at St George's, Parktown. Ruth Spector, whose father, Frank Jacobs, had been honorary secretary of Transhaven for more than 30 years, and whose mother, Vera Jacobs, had also been a friend of my parents, wrote to me how her community had 'benefited so greatly from the brave and encouraging work both Louis and Gaby Kane-Berman did during the days of apartheid to actively support and encourage our hopes, ambitions, and dreams of political equality and personal dignity through an impossibly fraught time'.[33]

I was very proud of my parents. This went beyond politics. They were devoted to one another, and devoted also to their children. They'd made sacrifices to send five boys to St John's: it was, for example, very rare for them to travel abroad. My father had a reputation for absolute integrity, and my mother's charm and sweet nature were admired as much by my friends as by her contemporaries. She combined strength of character with a sparkling personality, and was always ready for an adventure. And although she didn't have a formal job, I soon learnt that making and running a beautiful home as well as bringing up five sons was a full-time job, even without all the charitable work she always had on the go.

Somehow, however, my mother also managed to find time to try her hand at painting, sculpting, making mosaics, and even welding. When she decided to wallpaper some of the rooms in our house, she did it herself. She had always wanted to study architecture, but the war intervened: she had to stay at home with her mother after her father joined the army again.

My father laid down strict rules, which of course he applied to himself as well as to us. When my mother came into the room we all stood up. Even when he was well into his eighties, he would struggle to his feet whenever one of his daughters-in-law entered the room. One of his rules was that we wore jacket and tie or cravat for dinner, which was sharp at seven every night. Being late or improperly dressed was out of the question. Some of my friends found this rather strange, but I could see the logic in it. Coming in every day after driving around the farm, my grandfather always changed for dinner. My grandmother always put on a long dress. In the army you would never dream of going in for supper without having showered and changed out of your fatigues, and polished up your buckles, badges, and boots. At Oxford a college official called the manciple inspected us every evening to ensure that we were wearing ties and gowns before he allowed us into Hall for dinner. My mother always took endless trouble preparing meals, so it was right that we should make the effort to dress properly.

So when my partner Pierre Roestorf and I were informed that we needed to take evening dress on board the Cunard ships on which we took four voyages, it did not bother us in the least. The ship's crew and other staff were always properly attired, and we didn't see why the passengers shouldn't rise to their standards. In any event, a decent martini almost demands a black tie. Dressing for dinner every night was quite fun, in fact. Very easy for the men, who could happily look the same night after night. But we rather pitied the women who had somehow to contrive to find a different outfit every night and therefore had to travel with extra luggage. One woman on a three-month round-the-world voyage told us that she had her evening gowns flown to every port shortly before the ship docked there.

Dressed for the occasion: Pierre Roestorf and me aboard the QE2.

If Dad's strict rules about dress and other things never bothered me, it was perhaps because he was much more liberal about everything else – except swearing. He never swore, and would not allow us to say even so much as 'bloody'. He was a keen sportsman, but it didn't seem to worry him in the least that I wasn't interested. There was one exception to this: he made us all take swimming lessons. He never tried to bully me into following him into law, or dissuade me from becoming a journalist or going to work at the Institute. He never tried to tell me what to think or what books I could or couldn't read.

One of the reasons I decided not to do law was that I saw how hard my father worked. He would disappear to his study five nights a week to complete what he been unable to finish at the office. This meant that my parents seldom went out during the week, missing out on plays and concerts they would otherwise have attended. Dad also sometimes worked on Saturday or Sunday afternoons, after playing tennis or golf. I thought, 'This is not for me.' In the end, both as a journalist and at the Institute, I worked almost as hard as he did. At one stage, before the advent of personal computers enabled me to do all my writing myself, I kept three secretaries at the Institute busy. I made time for holidays, and for reading. But I took the view that if I wasn't willing to work extremely hard, I shouldn't expect to be CEO. Everyone in my family had always worked hard as a matter of course, and I was no exception.

Throughout my time at the Institute, as in earlier years, my parents, who had themselves been members for many years, showed great interest in what I was saying and doing. I gave them copies of articles and speeches. When my father's eyesight began to fail, I blew these up so that he could read them. My mother occasionally thought I should tone things down, but my father generally thought one should not mince one's words.

After my father died in 1998 on the farm in his ninety-third year, my mother moved back to Johannesburg, where she made many new friends while also resuming contact with several old ones. As her health began to fade and she was unable to get out much, I used to visit her for half an hour almost every day en route home from work. Fortunately, I had been able to find a flat for her in a building in the same block as our house in Richmond Avenue, Auckland Park. We would have a drink together, whisky for me, brandy for her, a drink before dinner being a family tradition dating back to my grandparents.

Although many of my friends emigrated because the government had made their lives here impossible, or because they saw no future in this country, I never seriously thought of leaving. I don't regret that. So many of my mother's friends had to spend their twilight years visiting children

Parents Gaby and Louis Kane-Berman. I was very proud of them.

or grandchildren in various other parts of the world. I was always grateful that our family was never split up like this. I was also grateful that my brothers and I were able to club together to hire round-the-clock caregivers for her when she needed them over the last few years of her life. This meant she could remain in her flat surrounded by her own pictures, ornaments, books, silver, and other things instead of having to move into an institution. And we were fortunate to find wonderful women to look after her who could always be relied upon to arrive even in midwinter by taxi from Soweto or elsewhere at six in the morning when it was their turn for the day shift. Such people are the salt of the earth.

CHAPTER 2

Wits

I had a wonderful time at the University of the Witwatersrand. My meeting with the prime minister at the end of it was as fitting a climax as was getting my degree. My three-year majors were political science and law, with single years of English, Latin, and philosophy on the side. The star among my lecturers was Ellison Kahn, who taught us constitutional law. GHL ('Copper') le May was an entertaining lecturer in politics, but he didn't always show up. The man who taught us Roman law in third year was dull. He dictated, slowly, from a lever-arch file of notes we suspected he'd inherited. I skipped as many of his lectures as I could get away with, and was too busy with student politics anyway. Halfway through the year he set us a test. I figured that any fool could get 30 per cent, so I thought it best to fail with a bit of style. When he handed back the papers our lecturer called each student up to collect his paper as he read out the mark, starting with the top performer, who got 98 per cent or something. When it was my turn he said, 'Mr Kane-Berman, out of deference to your father, who is a distinguished member of the legal profession, I will not embarrass you by reading out your mark to the class.' It was a duck. Fortunately, class tests did not count towards the final results. For the end-of-year exams I photocopied a classmate's notes, crammed my head full of Roman law for a week, and scored a second.

My time at Wits was dominated by student politics, which was dominated by race.

Wits had been one of South Africa's two 'open universities', the other
being the University of Cape Town (UCT). They admitted students irrespective of race, but in 1959 the government passed the Extension of
University Education Act to put a stop to this for fear that racial mixing
at university would destroy the ideological foundations of apartheid.
Speaking the year before as minister of native affairs, Dr HF Verwoerd
had said that the government did not want 'non-Europeans' to be in the
same university as the young 'European' students of the day. 'We do not
want Europeans to become so accustomed to the natives that they feel
there is no difference between them and the natives.'[1] I always thought
this a most revealing remark, for Verwoerd seemed to be contradicting
the idea that whites were somehow superior to blacks, supposedly the
foundation of apartheid ideology. Crude racism abounded, but apartheid was also a far more comprehensive ideology. Social segregation
– sometimes dismissed as 'petty apartheid' – was intrinsic to it. So was
apartheid in education. In fact, as the Right argued, apartheid had to be
a case of all or nothing.

From 1960 onwards black students could be admitted to white universities only with ministerial permission in each case, and only for
courses not available at black universities, several more of which were
being set up in the African 'homelands'. By the time I started at Wits in
1965 it had only a handful of black students. Although the battle that
Wits and UCT fought against apartheid in higher education angered the
government, it won them the respect of their peers around the world.
Both of us held lectures to commemorate the fight against the 1959 act,
and to rededicate ourselves to reopening our universities.

Outside the Wits Great Hall was a plaque which read:

We are gathered here today to affirm in the name of the University of the
Witwatersrand that it is our duty to uphold the principle that a university

is a place where men and women without regard to race and colour are welcome to join in the acquisition and advancement of knowledge. And to continue faithfully to defend this ideal against all who have sought by legislative enactment to curtail the autonomy of our university. Now therefore we dedicate ourselves to the maintenance of this ideal and to the restoration of the autonomy of our university.

Noble words to describe a noble ideal. We invited distinguished academics and politicians to deliver these lectures. People came from the British Labour and Conservative parties, from Harvard Law School, and from Cambridge. The speaker in August 1967 was Lord James of Rusholme, vice-chancellor of the University of York. He was surprised at the strong liberal element he found in South Africa and told us it would be important for the country's future. The people I myself hosted were Alan Paton and Harry Walston, who had been under-secretary of state for foreign affairs in Harold Wilson's Labour government.

The National Union of South African Students (Nusas), to which Wits, UCT, and various other campuses were affiliated, held an annual Day of Affirmation of Academic and Human Freedom Lecture (which we called 'Day of Aff'). The man who delivered the lecture in 1966 was Robert Kennedy. Inviting him was my idea. However, being only a junior delegate to the 1965 Nusas congress at UCT, I suggested to Ian Robertson, more senior than I, that he put forward the proposal. This he did, only to be rewarded in May 1966 with a five-year banning order which prevented his serving out his term as Nusas president.

Wherever Kennedy spoke, there was an empty chair beside him on the platform to signify Robertson's absence, because one of the provisions of a banning order was that you could not set foot on a university campus or participate in a gathering of more than one other person. We made use of bannings to drive home on campus the fundamental importance of due process of law: that nobody should be punished except after trial in an open court with adequate defence, and that in the

Me, Robert Kennedy, Mark Gandar (partly obscured) and Robin Margo during Kennedy's visit to South Africa in 1966. Here was the brother of the late American president, the most powerful man in the world, taking our side.

absence of conviction in the courts everyone was entitled to a presumption of innocence. The slogan 'charge or release' was coined to sum up our stance and we printed stickers for display on campus and the rear windows of cars. Even students who were not particularly sympathetic towards Nusas were outraged at the thought that a student leader – or anyone else – could be punished without trial. By banning people such as Robertson, the government strengthened rather than weakened the liberal voice on campus, thereby scoring a goal against itself.

Kennedy's visit dominated the front pages of the newspapers for the week that he was in the country. Robertson reported how the American senator had visited him in his flat, putting his fingers to his lips as he walked in and then jumping up and down on the floor. Ian looked at him quizzically, but Kennedy explained that this would confuse the bugs. 'How do you know that?' Ian asked him. 'I was attorney general, wasn't I?' came the reply.

The Kennedys gave a great boost to everyone who opposed the government. They were mobbed in Soweto and wherever else they went. The people ruling South Africa loathed Nusas, but here was the brother of the late American president, the most powerful man in the world, taking our side, along with his attractive wife. I attended a reception for Robert and Ethel Kennedy at the home of Clive and Irene Menell in Parktown, Johannesburg, where a special performance of Alan Paton's play *Sponono* was put on for them. The senator's pockets were bulging with PT 109 tie pins, so named after the motor torpedo boat John F Kennedy had captained during the war. Mrs Kennedy kept fishing them out and handing them round. I still have mine.

Some years later, after I'd left Wits, Nusas contacted me in Oxford and asked me to help find a Day of Aff speaker. I rejected Nusas's own suggestion, James Callaghan, as he had recently put through legislation restricting (black) immigration into England from Commonwealth countries. So I invited Harold Wilson, who had recently been defeated by Edward Heath in the 1970 general election. Wilson wrote back suggesting we invite Denis Healey instead.[2] I'd heard Healey speak at Oxford. He had been defence secretary and was now shadow foreign secretary, and might one day be prime minister and therefore a potential Nusas ally. So I invited him. I remember mainly three things about his visit. One was that my parents hosted a lunch for him where – judging by photographs – one of the guests was Steve Biko. The second is that I don't think my father particularly approved of having this socialist in our house, because he thereafter referred to him as 'your friend in the crumpled suit'. The third is that I drove Healey in my father's old second-hand Rover 90 to visit Shantie Naidoo, the banned person I'd worked with at Vanguard. The Johannesburg motorway surrounding the city had only recently been built, and I got lost looking for the right exit for the Naidoos' house. In the end, of course, Callaghan might have been the better investment for Nusas because it was he rather than Healey who became prime minister.

Kennedy the great celebrity aside, the foreign figure who stands out is Robert Birley. Shortly after the Second World War he had been appointed educational adviser to the military governor of the British zone in occupied Germany. His achievement there, as *The Times* later said in his obituary, was to 'transform British policy from the illusory wartime conception of "re-educating Germany" to one of rediscovering the best in the German tradition and helping the Germans themselves to repair the spiritual damage the Nazis had done'.[3] That job over, Birley was appointed headmaster of Eton, from which he retired a year early to take up a visiting professorship of education at Wits for three years.[4] Thereafter Professor Sir Robert Birley, as he later became, and his wife, Elinor, jumped at every opportunity to return to South Africa.

Academic freedom, Birley once said, was something an Englishman like himself had always taken for granted. But when he came to Wits in 1964, he suddenly found himself at an institution which was having to fight for it. In a lecture I attended in my first year, he quoted Julius Ebbinghaus, one-time rector of Marburg University:

> One fact remains, unfortunately, all too true. The German universities failed, while there was still time, to oppose publicly with all their powers the destruction of learning and of the democratic state. They failed to keep the beacon of freedom and right burning through the night of tyranny so that it could be seen by the entire world.[5]

Birley saw the open universities in South Africa as waging a fight from which German universities had abstained. He used to say it would never have been possible to rebuild liberal education in Germany had there not been people who had lived through the Nazi dictatorship but refused to bow down before it. In a second academic freedom lecture he gave in 1970 to more than 1 000 students in the Great Hall, Birley quoted the words of a Jesuit priest, Alfred Delp, shortly before his execution by the Nazis in February 1945:

This is a time of sowing, it is not the time for harvest. It is God who sows, and in due course He will reap. I shall strive at least to fall as a fertile and good seed in the ground.

Birley then commented, 'History in years to come will not forget those who were the seed from which the harvest came. Nor will it regard the time of sowing as one of the less memorable periods in a country's story.'[6] We knew he was referring to us and it thrilled and inspired us.

Birley always warned against racial stereotyping and the idea of collective guilt. His biographer, Arthur Hearnden, described a classroom encounter in a Soweto school:

> The kind of question he was asked was, 'Is it true that the Nazis killed a great many Jews?', to which he would reply, 'Yes'. 'How many?' 'Well, the most conservative figure I can give you is five million.' Birley would then break the shocked silence by saying, 'If I give you a promise that when there is a massacre in the Congo I will never say that that is what blacks do, will you promise me that you will not say this is what whites do?' This would be followed by a solemn exchange of promises. Birley would then tell the story of the symbol of the 'White Rose' and how a small group of Munich students gave their lives to resist Hitler. This time the silence was expectant rather than shocked. 'Now, if I promise that I will not say this is what the Congolese do, but what some people in the Congo do, will you promise that you will not say this is what the Germans do, only what some Germans have done?' Again there would be a solemn exchange of promises.[7]

Nor did Birley stop at lectures. He joined student demonstrations on the pavement of Jan Smuts Avenue on the perimeter of the campus. He taught at various schools, including the famous Orlando High in Soweto, where he also helped to create one of the few libraries in black schools. That school's headmaster, Wilkie Kambule, later recalled how the Department of Bantu Education had demanded that Birley be kept away from the children as he was considered to be 'red'. Birley was denounced by the notorious anonymous voice on the SABC's 'current affairs' radio broadcast. He and Kambule ignored the threats.[8] I suspect Sir Robert half relished the thought of a headline in a British newspaper along the lines of 'Former Eton headmaster arrested for teaching in Soweto'. Of all the teachers I have ever met, Robert (and Elinor) Birley spent the least possible time in any ivory tower. My St John's headmaster, Deane Yates, about whom more below, was much the same.

Following the Extension Act, the number of African students at Wits dwindled from 72 in 1954 to four in 1968.[9] In 1970 there were five, along with 29 coloured, 163 Chinese, 133 Indian, and some 9 000 white students.[10] As we shall see below, the government wanted to exclude black staff as well. And it wanted to impose apartheid even within the universities by compelling them to recognise whites-only student organisations.

I witnessed a repeat of what had happened to the YMCA night classes in my parents' garage in Waverley. Ever since 1943 students at Wits had been running an African Night School for domestic servants, university employees, factory workers, and high school pupils. About 150 students were involved as teachers in this school, which had been started by medical students. It was now ordered to close, both under the Group Areas Act and because it was illegal to run a class for Africans across the colour line, a class being defined as more than one pupil per teacher. The forbidden classes were replaced by one-on-one tutorials. Another government own goal. By making it more difficult for blacks to get night-school education, the government helped to educate more whites about the wickedness of its policies.

During my first year I joined a society called the Political Forum. We invited representatives of various parties to speak on campus. Several came, but John Vorster, then minister of justice, refused because he was not prepared to accept an invitation from a student body affiliated to

Nusas.[11] Mr Vorster, it seemed to us, was obsessed with Nusas. After he'd banned Ian Robertson we held a mass meeting to protest. Ian was not at Wits, but at the University of Natal. However, we had elected him as our national leader and 3 000 of us marched in protest through the city against his banning. This, as it turned out, was the last march during my time as a student.

During my first year I was also elected to the Students' Representative Council. The man who got me to run was Alan Murray, then SRC president. He had been a few years senior to me at St John's. I had joined the university's choral society and got a part as a cowboy in *Paint Your Wagon*, a musical so dreadful it is difficult to believe it was the work of Lerner and Loewe, who gave the world *My Fair Lady*. Alan summoned me to the SRC office, told me never to waste my time on such trivia again, and more or less instructed me to put my name down in the forthcoming election. He later became – and remained – a dear friend until his death in 2013.

One of the reasons why the Wits SRC was so successful was that each year its leaders identified promising young students, persuaded them to run, and put them through various training courses run in conjunction with Nusas. One of the speakers at a course I took some of our students to near Pietermaritzburg was a young University of Natal lecturer by the name of Lawrence Schlemmer. He made a powerful impression on me with a talk that the Institute later published under the title *The Negro Ghetto Riots and South African Cities*.[12] Professor Schlemmer was later the first president of the Institute under whom I served.

Among the up-and-coming youngsters elected to the SRC when I was president was Charles Simkins, a physics student who had made a name for himself as an exceptionally bright member of the Science Students' Council. Charles subsequently did research for the emerging black trade union movement, for which he received a banning order. Not long after I had joined the Institute, he sent me the manuscript of a book based on a series of lectures on liberalism he'd given at the University of Cape

Town. The publisher David Philip had turned him down on the grounds that he had not expressed enough 'outrage' at the behaviour of the riot police and that this was 'no time to market books on liberalism'.[13] I jumped at this opportunity and we published the lectures in 1986 under the title *Reconstructing South African Liberalism*.[14] Charles subsequently became chairman of the board of the Institute.

We involved the university leadership in all our campaigns against government interference. When we had Paton to speak, our chancellor, Mr Justice Oliver Schreiner, read out the dedication on the plaque quoted at the beginning of this chapter. The vice-chancellor, Professor ID MacCrone, and his successor, Professor GR Bozzoli ('Boz'), also participated in all our academic freedom and Day of Affirmation lectures. They came to our social functions as well. Bozzoli used to plonk his decibel counter on the table next to his wine glass and calculate how long it would take for all the students to damage their hearing if the music wasn't turned down. His wife, Cora, was a hoot. She couldn't stand the Nats, as they were widely called, and saw no reason to conceal her views, least of all when she knew some government bigwig was within earshot.

Behind his desk MacCrone had a large photograph of the neo-classical facade of the university's central block which bore the words '*broeiplekke van liberalisme*'. Some or other minister or newspaper had intended this as an insult, but MacCrone, whose Oxford doctorate was on racial attitudes and who served as president of the Institute in 1968–69, wore the badge proudly. During my first year the university came under attack from various ministers, causing him to retort in a graduation address, 'I don't know whether this campaign is intended to frighten us or reduce us to silence, but I can assure these people that they would be better advised to save their breath to cool their porridge.'[15]

But we also had disputes with the administration. A member of the SRC contributed an anonymous piece of verse to the 'Loo Wall', a newspaper published on a notice board by the student Arts Faculty Council as its answer to the British magazine *Private Eye* and dedicated to deflating all those members of the university suffering from *pneumatic craniae*, or swollen heads. Entitled 'African and Witvel', this was a six-page parody of John Dryden's epic satire *Absalom and Achitophel* published in 1681. Our version contained the following rhyming couplet:

> The Boers till now to keep their nation white
> Ban blacks by day and sleep with them at night.

Following a suitably scandalised article in the Afrikaans Sunday newspaper *Dagbreek*, MacCrone ordered the offending parody removed from the Loo Wall. The editors, Clive Nettleton and David Said, were charged with causing racial ill-feeling within the university and so bringing it into disrepute. The professors responsible for the procedures were going to be prosecutor, judge, jury, and lord high executioner all rolled into one. However, one of them advised the editors that they were entitled to bring a friend to help with their defence, and added, 'If your friend happens to be a member of the Johannesburg Bar, then you choose your friends wisely.' They took the hint, and an advocate was engaged. The outcome was a warning, as the editors had previously settled the matter amicably with the Afrikaanse Studenteklub. Talk at the time was that the university in bringing the charges had brought itself into greater disrepute at the Bar than the offending heroic couplet ever could.

Social segregation was one of the biggest issues we faced. Looking back from today's perspective, where people of different races mix freely all over the country, all the legal restrictions on such mixing seem ludicrous as well as hurtful. The hostility that greeted attempts to circumvent them seem childish and bizarre. But sensing that social segregation could be the beginning of something worse, the SRCs of which I was a member took the view that wherever it was in our power we should ensure that those few black students who were permitted to attend the university should not be discriminated against while there.

We therefore thwarted attempts to establish racially segregated student societies on the campus. This led to accusations of 'liberal intolerance'. Our rejoinder was that whereas Nusas was banned on Afrikaans campuses, several anti-Nusas organisations operated freely at Wits and were indeed subsidised by the SRC on the same basis as all other clubs and societies. However, the condition was that they could not have a colour bar in their membership. There was enough apartheid around without our condoning it where we could stop it. We stuck to this position even though the government threatened to legislate to prevent black students from being members of, or attending the meetings of, any association of students of a different race.

We also decided that the popular dances organised by the Rag Committee should be open to all students. But we knew we couldn't do this without campus support, so we called a mass meeting to seek a mandate. The Right accused us of being 'totalitarian liberals'. The Left said we were being inconsistent in not enforcing integration upon sport. The Afrikaans press also weighed in. Having on one occasion rebuked us for trying to be replicas of Oxford and Harvard,[16] it now told us that by seeking to integrate Rag functions we were making it impossible for Afrikaans students to attend or for Afrikaners to contribute to Rag because of its *'bontpartytjies'* (*'bont'* meaning 'pied' or 'multi-coloured' and therefore supposedly beyond the pale). According to one editorial, the students at Wits were playing with fire, but in their state of liberal drunkenness preferred to forget that they were studying at an institution kept going through government help.

However, the mass meeting, held in May 1967, overwhelmingly endorsed our proposal. Only 170 out of the 1 200 students there voted against it. The SRC undertook to find a venue, since the campus itself was not a popular place for big student functions.[17] Every venue we approached refused, for fear of losing their liquor licences or violating the Group Areas Act or otherwise offending the authorities or their other customers. Eventually we found a venue in the south of the city. Our sense of triumph was short-lived. Somebody told the press. Headlines followed and that was the end of that venue. Eventually we found a private airfield on the way to Hartbeespoort Dam, where we pitched a tent, and the students stomped the night away in the dust. Not a single black student pitched, as we suspected they would not. There were very few on the campus anyway and there was no reason that those few should get involved in Rag activities, least of all if it meant jeopardising their study permits. Despite all the controversy – perhaps because of it – Rag that year raised a record amount of R82 000 for its various charities.

Social segregation helped to undermine Nusas, whose congresses were held on the various campuses in turn. White delegates stayed in residence, blacks elsewhere. This was bad enough. But in 1967 Rhodes University withdrew its permission for all the delegates to eat together. The congress then rejected a proposal to adjourn until an integrated venue could be found. This was too much for Steve Biko, who led the delegation from the 'non-European' campus of the University of Natal. He later wrote that this was 'perhaps the turning-point in the history of black support for Nusas'.[18] Not long afterwards he launched the South African Students' Organisation (Saso) and other Black Consciousness groups. This actually happened after I'd left for Oxford. Although it has been suggested that white liberals saw this as a slap in the face, I never did. I thought the rise of Black Consciousness was a healthy and necessary development. In any event, as Biko wrote, there was still plenty of work for white liberals to do in changing attitudes in their own community.[19]

One of the reasons there were not many more black students in Nusas was that the organisation was effectively banned on most black campuses. Its branches therefore operated clandestinely, and delegates sometimes came to Nusas congresses using pseudonyms. One Indian campus was forced to disaffiliate. The atmosphere on Afrikaans campuses was often just as hostile, and Nusas branches there were usually small. It certainly took more courage for Afrikaans and black students to associate with Nusas than was the case with English-language campuses, where we could operate freely. Various attempts were made to establish a whites-only national student federation linking English and Afrikaans campuses in opposition to Nusas 'with its foreign ideologies and risk of being manipulated by pro-communist elements', but we successfully thwarted these.

One such attempt was made by Professor Owen Horwood, vice-chancellor of the University of Natal. In 1968 he hosted a meeting for various SRC presidents. I suspected he might be up to something, egged on by the government. So before agreeing to go, I got an undertaking from him that the representatives of the black campuses would also be invited. A colleague and I drove from the airport in Durban to pick up Johnny Masindane from the nearby residence of the 'non-European' section of the University of Natal, only to discover he had not been invited after all. We urged him to come anyway. But when we walked in with him the president of the SRC of the University of the Orange Free State withdrew from the meeting, while his Stellenbosch counterpart accused me of trying to jeopardise English–Afrikaans dialogue by instigating Johnny to talk at the conference.[20]

To counter allegations that affiliation to Nusas did not enjoy campus support, I called a referendum. The students decided by a 30 per cent majority in a 60 per cent poll to retain affiliation – 3 368 pro-Nusas votes and 1 783 against.[21] Total Wits enrolment then was 8 610.[22] Nusas had been on the defensive for some years because of the involvement of one of its previous presidents, Adrian Leftwich, in sabotage as a member of the African Resistance Movement (ARM). Although Nusas disowned those who had turned to violence, the government exploited all of this for a smear campaign. So our referendum result was a significant repudiation of its efforts. In fact, it was a mighty slap in the face to John Vorster himself.

In the 1970s, after I had graduated, Nusas and several of the SRCs moved to the Left. Nusas also embraced socialism and denounced liberalism, angering such people as Alan Paton and Helen Suzman. The former criticised Nusas for 'intellectual stupidity' in seeking to 'radicalise' itself at the cost of campus support. The latter – never one to mince her words – was 'furious' when a Nusas official called for a student boycott of the 1977 general election.[23] The government intensified its pressure against the organisation, with bannings and prosecutions. Steve Biko and other Saso leaders also came under attack. Saso was banned in 1977. In 1991, following the lifting of the bans on the ANC and other organisations, Nusas dissolved itself after 67 years in existence.

The end of Nusas was a tragedy for liberalism. As the *Sunday Times* once said, 'Nusas is one of the most enlightened and courageous bodies we have ever had in South Africa' – and a 'voice crying out against injustice and inhumanity'.[24] For many years Nusas and its affiliated SRCs were a liberal kindergarten, from whose loss South Africa has not recovered, for there is no longer a powerful liberal voice on our campuses.

Nusas was also important beyond the campuses. Opening the organisation's 42nd annual congress at the University of Natal, Durban, in July 1966, after Ian Robertson had been banned, Alan Paton told us: 'Keep up your courage, Nusas, so that others can keep up theirs.' The wider liberal community was even more embattled than we were. The government was threatening to impose segregation on political parties. Opposition newspapers – especially the outspoken liberal *Rand Daily Mail* – were under attack. There had been a fierce clampdown on black resistance. Vorster's government seemed impregnable. Liberals on and off the campus reinforced one another. The South African Institute of Race Relations, the Black Sash, the Liberal Party, the Progressive Party, Nusas, the affiliated SRCs, the Christian Institute and sympathetic newspaper editors formed a sort of liberal caucus, which often met in a flat in Killarney belonging to Jean Sinclair, then president of the Black Sash.

We were all well aware that we represented a tiny minority of the voting population. Most English-speaking people had long since turned a blind eye to all the injustice around them. Many of them hated the *Rand*

Daily Mail for trying to open their eyes. The students, we said, were filling a gap left by most of their parents. We saw ourselves as trying to preserve an island of sanity in a sea of racial madness.

For the second time in a row, in fact, Helen Suzman had been the only Progressive Party (Prog) MP to get elected to Parliament. Before throwing myself more or less full-time into student politics I'd worked for her as chairman of the youth branch in her Houghton constituency. The Houghton Young Progs, as we called ourselves, did a third of all the canvassing and took responsibility for plastering the constituency with posters. I also got Harry Oppenheimer to write a message to the voters of Houghton for our newsletter urging them to vote for Helen.[25]

A group of us went to one of the opposing candidate's public meetings to ask nasty questions and do a bit of heckling. Helen forbade us to do it ever again: don't turn his dull campaign into something newsworthy, she said. When the opposition started pulling down our posters, Max Borkum, Helen's campaign manager, instructed me, 'Tell them I'll be issuing my men with wire cutters.' Several times we slept in shifts with baseball bats in our campaign office at 38 Ivy Road, Norwood, after tip-offs that the opposition was coming with hosepipes to flood all the ink on our canvass cards. Knowing we were sometimes sleeping there, Helen and Max occasionally arrived after dinner to share a bottle of Scotch with us. Helen scraped in on 30 March 1966 with a majority of 711 votes, up from 564 in the 1961 election.[26] After her retirement from Parliament in 1989, Helen Suzman, as we shall see, accepted my invitation to become president of the Institute.

During this election campaign three of my colleagues and I attended a meeting addressed by John Vorster at Helpmekaar, an Afrikaans high school near Wits. The hall was full of uniformed students from the Goudstad teacher training college and other institutions singing lustily as if with one voice. When Vorster, then still minister of justice, police, and prisons, walked in, it was the first time I'd set eyes on him. He looked exhausted and at the end of his speech said, 'I feel tonight like

the United Party is going to feel when it gets the results of the election.'
A vote of confidence in the National Party was then called. 'All those
against, stand up!', ordered the chairman of the meeting. The four of us
got warily to our feet. Vorster looked at us, then looked across in the
direction of Wits, then looked back at us, declaring, 'Well, we all know
where you come from!'

Six months after the 1966 election, Dr Verwoerd was assassinated.
I was one of a small delegation from Wits present at his state funeral
in the amphitheatre of the Union Buildings. Some 28 years later, Pierre
Roestorf and I were in the same amphitheatre to witness the inauguration
of Nelson Mandela as president after the first post-apartheid election.
Sitting near us, barely noticed, was the widow of Chief Albert Luthuli,
one-time president of the ANC who, despite having been banned, was
elected as honorary president of Nusas in 1962, a post he held until his
death in 1967.

Even after he had taken over from Verwoerd as prime minister,
Vorster still seemed to have time to indulge his loathing of some of the
English-language universities and their opposition to his government's
racial policies. Students in Paris and elsewhere made headlines in 1968.
But so did we, though for different reasons and with a great deal more
restraint.

The drama opened at UCT on 14 August 1968. Around 300 students
at that university staged what the *Rand Daily Mail*'s front-page headline
the next day described as South Africa's first 'sit-in'.[27] The issue was the
UCT council's decision to rescind the appointment of an African UCT
graduate, Archie Mafeje, to a senior lectureship in social anthropology.
The appointment was revoked after the government had threatened to
take action against the council – Helen Suzman told me that the government had told the council it would if necessary reconvene Parliament
to legislate to put a stop to the appointment of Africans to the staffs
of white universities. While waiting to take up his new appointment,
Mafeje was doing research at King's College, Cambridge.

By wonderful coincidence we at Wits were holding our annual Richard Feetham Academic Freedom Lecture on the day that the news of the UCT sit-in broke. Lord Walston began his lecture by saluting Wits 'not only for its learning but also for its liberalism'. He was proud, he said, 'to be among students who are such valiant upholders of those traditions'.

Nearly 2 000 students crammed into the Great Hall. According to the *Rand Daily Mail*, they gave 'thunderous applause' to my pledge of support for the students at UCT, whose council, we said, had been 'browbeaten and bludgeoned' by the minister of national education, Senator Jan de Klerk. There were calls for a protest march. Sir Richard Luyt, vice-chancellor of UCT, was summoned back from a conference he was attending in Australia.

Prime Minister Vorster then weighed in. Speaking at Heilbron in the Orange Free State, he said there were a handful of people in South Africa who wanted to 'transplant' the troubles of Europe and the United States to this country, but that he would not allow this. If university councils and the 'parents of the children at these universities' did not put a stop to the agitation at Wits and UCT, 'I will do it myself and I will do it very thoroughly'.[28] In the meantime, plans for a march went ahead. Neville Curtis, deputy vice-president on my SRC, announced that the Johannesburg City Council had given the go-ahead and promised a motorcycle escort. Then Vorster weighed in again. He telephoned the mayor of Johannesburg and told him he would take swift action if the council allowed the march.[29] The mayor withdrew his consent. Police vans drew up outside the university. My SRC announced that we were not prepared to expose our students to violence, and we called off the march.

Between 1 000 and 2 000 students then mounted a placard demonstration on the pavement along Jan Smuts Avenue outside the University. They were excited. They were also getting angry as students in the temporary premises of Rand Afrikaans University on the South African Breweries site across the road were pelting us with eggs, paint, stones, and half-bricks. A few of our own students tried to incite violence, and we had to deal swiftly with them. We also had to deal with *agents provocateurs* who joined our demonstration – some of them young women with iron bars wrapped in newspapers – who also tried to incite violence. We suspected that some of the provocateurs were off-duty police. To isolate them we asked all students participating in the demonstration to wear academic gowns borrowed from the men's and women's residences. But getting our students to control their anger was becoming difficult. We decided that I would lead a convoy to Pretoria to seek a meeting with Mr Vorster to object to his interference in university affairs.

Just as we were about to leave, Robert Eales, a friend and former SRC treasurer, pulled me aside and said, 'You can't go to Pretoria, you must stay here and control our students.' So I asked Neville Curtis to lead the convoy instead. One of those who went with him was Johnny Myburgh, chairman of the house committee of one of the men's residences, who later became a judge. They were intercepted by traffic police and told they could not enter Pretoria, but some of them only pretended to turn back, and found another way to the Union Buildings. There they encountered the prime minister on the way from his office. He refused to accept our petition and the newspapers carried a photograph of him admonishing Neville with one hand and holding a cigarette in the other. I had in the meantime asked the SRC secretary, Mrs Zena Blackstock-MacFarlane, to phone ahead as a courtesy to warn the prime minister's office that we were sending over a petition. A message came back that he would see me on 30 August – 10 days away.

Not all our students got through safely. Young men, some of them wearing University of Pretoria blazers, ambushed them, bashed dents into their cars, shaved their heads, kidnapped them, and took them off to hostels where they were dragged through hot and cold showers and then polished all over. According to the *Rand Daily Mail*, the minister of police, Mr SL Muller, looked on while some of this was happening.[30]

48

One of the students attacked, Peter Laubscher, said, 'We were in the grounds behind Union Buildings when a mob surrounded us. There were about 25 uniformed policeman standing about. I appealed to one who told me to go to the captain. The captain followed me to our car, but the only time he intervened was when a Pretoria student tried to start our car. I said, "I demand protection from these hooligans." He said he was going to leave us and he did.'

We held another mass meeting the next day, at which I paid tribute to our students for the magnificent and disciplined protest they had staged. They were outraged at the attack on their colleagues while the police stood by. The atmosphere in the packed Great Hall was electric and our students gave me a standing ovation. The issue now was no longer one just of Mr Mafeje's race, or of university autonomy – it was whether there was a right to dissent in South Africa. Newspaper editorials endorsed this point.

Back to Jan Smuts Avenue. RAU students had by now been joined by some from the Goudstad teacher training college. Cars arrived with their boots full of eggs to throw at us. The counter-demonstrators also stole fruit and vegetables off lorries taking them to the Johannesburg market and threw those as well. Our students were being provoked beyond endurance. They far outnumbered the counter-demonstrators and my main concern was to stop them from charging across the road and beating the hell out of the counter-demonstrators. I tried several times in vain to get the police to stop the attacks on us; I knew that the moment our students did retaliate, the police would beat us up and then arrest us. Some of the police stood nearby, just watching while the RAU missiles were hurled at us.

I asked Helen Suzman to try to get the police to intervene, but they gave her the runaround too. Eventually she came and joined the demonstration. We supplied her with one of the posters to use as a shield against the eggs and whatnot. Meanwhile some of our own right-wing opponents on the campus brought round a petition for us to sign attacking the Russian invasion of Czechoslovakia, then under way. We dismissed this as a childish ploy to divert attention from what was going on in South Africa under their very noses.

In the meantime, Sir Richard Luyt was on his way back from Australia. We decided to go and meet him at Jan Smuts Airport to show him the strength of feeling among South African students at the UCT council's capitulation to government threats. I also thought that getting our students to the airport would be one means of avoiding the bloodshed that now seemed inevitable on Jan Smuts Avenue. Vorster was having none of this either. Speaking at a civic banquet in his honour in the Johannesburg City Hall, he said no demonstration would be allowed at the airport 'under any circumstances'. We replied that we weren't going to demonstrate, but merely to greet Sir Richard. Some 300 of us went out to the airport.[31] We struck up 'We shall overcome', and I welcomed him through a loudhailer, watched by police who did nothing to stop us, despite the prime minister's threat. We sang 'Die Stem' and watched in amusement as the police shuffled awkwardly to attention. Sir Richard then flew off to Cape Town.

In the meantime, the UCT students called off their sit-in. We also decided to call off the Wits protest, which had been going on for nearly 10 days. We had obtained strong support from many outsiders, as well as from academics and the University. Some of the support came from unpredictable quarters: the Hell's Angels, a team of motorbike riders, rang one day to say they had been put out by a report that they were coming to attack us. It was not true, and they were sending a delegation to support us. We had also secured major news coverage in South Africa, often at the top of front pages. We had featured in numerous foreign papers, including a supporting editorial in *The Times* of London.[32] Better to stop while we were riding high than watch the protest peter out as students had to start returning to their books. Also, my year-long term of office as president of the SRC was about to end. And I was going off to a compulsory weekend army camp.

The prime minister then issued another threat, this time from Vereeniging. If order was not restored at Wits and UCT by 11 am the following Monday, the police would do it at 11.05 am. A great country like France had almost been brought to its knees because of student and labour unrest, but this would not be tolerated in South Africa. 'I know Mrs Helen Suzman will hit the sky – but she has always been very flighty,' he added.[33]

During my absence that weekend at the army camp, my SRC issued a statement telling Mr Vorster his threat was pointless and ridiculous. We had already decided to end our protests and there was no disorder at Wits for him to deal with anyway. We had exercised the utmost restraint and complete observance of the law, despite rough treatment by hooligans while the police stood by.[34]

Some students demanded that we continue with our demonstrations despite our decision to call them off. A few staged a sit-in in my office. An editorial in *Wits Student* denounced us as 'sellouts' for not 'defying' the prime minister. But neither I nor my SRC was willing to allow ourselves to be provoked by Vorster into an act of reckless bravado. This was my first run-in with the Left, an experience that was to be repeated when I took over the Institute.

A few days later it was the turn of the minister of police, SL Muller, to enter the fray. Speaking in Potchefstroom about our demonstrations, he read out a list of South African students who were Jewish. Some of his best friends were Jews, he added in the standard giveaway preface to anti-Semitic remarks, but a large percentage of listed communists were Jews. He appealed to the Jewish community to use their influence to get their young people to respect authority in South Africa. Mr Mafeje, the minister went on, had a politically suspect past, and he had a better job in London anyway.[35]

I was alerted to this attack by an official of the South African Jewish Board of Deputies, who rang to urge me not to react too strongly. I was in no mood for such advice. My SRC issued a statement that it was 'an old, unsubtle, and completely predictable trick for the Government to make Jews the scapegoat for things they disapprove of. There were a lot of Jewish students involved in the protest and they have every reason to be proud of [this].' We also said that I would raise the matter with the prime minister at our meeting with him the next day.

Our delegation, Mark Orkin, Neville Curtis, and I, duly set off for the Union Buildings. The prime minister received us less than graciously. The first thing he said was that we would probably misrepresent him to the press, so he assumed we would not object if he recorded the meeting. When Vorster asked why we wanted to see him, I said we were worried that the ceiling of tolerance had been lowered. At this, he more or less exploded and told us that what we had been doing would not be tolerated. He had agreed to see us only in order to tell us this first hand. When we asked him to explain exactly what it was that would not be tolerated he said if we didn't know that we weren't worth our salt as student leaders. The police had no time to waste protecting marches by irresponsible students. Sit-ins and pickets were 'communistic'. If the university authorities didn't stop us, he would. There would not be any more protest marches in any city in South Africa as long as he was prime minister. Demonstrators here were being influenced by students in France and Germany, including 'Danny the Red', the German anarchist who had played a prominent part in the Paris revolt in 1968. Referring to Adrian Leftwich, the Nusas president arrested in 1964, he said he didn't like locking up students to rot in jail. I raised Muller's attacks on Jewish students, but Vorster brushed this aside, telling me to speak to Muller himself. He also told us that he would take steps to ensure that SRCs recognised whites-only student organisations.[36] If necessary he would legislate to enforce this.

A delegation of three students complaining about our refusal to recognise segregated student organisations was received by Vorster straight after he'd seen us. They made much of the fact that he'd given them

Mark Orkin (left), me, and Neville Curtis leaving the Union Buildings after a meeting with John Vorster in August 1968. The prime minister received us less than graciously.

tea, which had not been given to us. Vorster, Neville, and I had chain-smoked our way through the meeting.

Our meeting with the prime minister was front-page news in newspapers around the country, along with photographs of Mark, Neville, and myself leaving the Union Buildings. One headline said he'd referred to us as 'little pink liberals'.[37] I told the waiting journalists that there had been no common ground between Vorster and ourselves. Mark Orkin later told them that he had interrupted us at least 25 times to tell us that what we had been doing would not be tolerated.

Not long after this unpleasant but instructive experience, I was off on the 'boat train' to Cape Town to board the *Edinburgh Castle* for Southampton. I left with mixed feelings. A number of people from Wits and other campuses had written letters asking me to run for the presidency of Nusas, and I was keen to do so. But my father had set his heart on my going to Oxford as a Rhodes Scholar, and I didn't have the heart to resist him. My parents had endured plenty of anxiety during my time at Wits without ever complaining, even though I knew they were terrified I would be banned. I suspect they received far more threatening phone calls than they ever told me about. So it was off to Oxford. Despite accusations that student politicians neglected their studies, just about all of us got very good degrees, and many of us won Rhodes Scholarships – Alan Murray, Robin Margo, David Phillips, Charles Simkins, Mark Orkin, and myself.

I didn't actually win the scholarship first time round. Only one Rhodes was available for the Transvaal, and I was beaten by David Phillips, author of the Loo Wall parody. I told the selection committee I didn't mind having lost to him. Rex Welsh, the general secretary of the scholarships in South Africa, invited me round for lunch and urged me to apply again the following year, and the second time round I was successful. I heaved a great sigh of relief, mainly because I had been worried about how much Oxford would cost my parents.

My failure to win the first time round led to a restructuring of the South African scholarships. Apart from four earmarked for particular schools and an extra one for Natal, each of the four provinces had one. But the Transvaal had far more graduates than the Free State and it was felt that reserving a scholarship for that province meant there were too few for the Transvaal. So the four provincial scholarships were replaced in 1973 with four that went to 'South Africa at large'. This region was later widened to include Botswana, Lesotho, Swaziland, and South West Africa/Namibia.

No sooner had I deposited my bags in my cabin on the *Edinburgh Castle* and gone on deck to explore the ship, than the ship's intercom summoned me back to my cabin. There awaited three or four men in white uniforms who described themselves as customs officers doing a spot check. They did a thorough search, read various papers, and took away a tape-recorded letter I was carrying for a friend.

Also summoned on the intercom was Jean Middleton. Convicted several years before with Bram Fischer and 12 others for furthering the aims of communism, she was leaving the country on an exit permit after having been released from the maximum security prison for white women in Barberton, the town outside which my grandparents farmed. She recalled how the Anglican priest in the town used to arrive at the prison every Sunday with an offer to serve Holy Communion. As good communists they all refused, but he kept on coming back. One Sunday he'd absolutely refused to take no for an answer, and they attended his service. He proceeded to pray for the late Dr Verwoerd, the first news they had of the assassination in September 1966, for political prisoners were usually denied newspapers. Thereafter Jean and the others regularly went to Father Tom Langley's service, during which he kept them up to date with what was going on in the country.

When I wasn't playing Scrabble with Jean, I was playing poker with about eight other students also on their way to Oxford. We declined to join in any of the deck games, so were labelled as wet blankets and spoilsports. On the last night before we reached Southampton there was a fancy dress dance which we felt we had better enter. One of our number, Colin Bundy, who later became vice-chancellor of Wits, drew the short straw and arrived at the dance dripping wet in a blanket. He won first prize.

Thinking back on my time at Wits, it is easy to understand John Vorster's fury. In the midst of our demonstrations I received a letter which said that 'so long as there is opposition to racialism and the clampdown on human freedom and expression, the government has not won. I think [it] realises this. That is why it fears you so much, and wants to destroy you.' The writer was Raymond Tucker, who later became honorary legal adviser to the Institute.[38]

The imposition of segregation on the open universities was a logical extension of the NP's policy of applying apartheid to every nook and cranny of national life. They had been trying to stamp out racial mixing at the open universities for years. As far back as 1951, Prime Minister Malan had said that the 'mingling of European and non-European at the two largest universities would have to be eliminated as it was directly opposed to the principle of apartheid'.[39] After the passage of the Extension of University Education Act of 1959, it was only with the greatest reluctance that a handful of black students were given permits to attend Wits and UCT.

But here were thousands of students holding out for racial mixing. This was not just a question of wanting a different policy. It implied a fundamentally different kind of society. There weren't many people still doing this. The NP had passed the Prohibition of Political Interference Act of 1968, which compelled racially mixed political parties to segregate themselves. The Progressive Party had reluctantly complied by shedding all its black members (a decision which my Houghton Young Progs branch opposed, to the annoyance of some of our seniors). The Liberal Party, grievously damaged by the African Resistance Movement and the station bomb, crippled by bannings, its commitment to non-violence betrayed by some of its own members, had reluctantly decided to close down rather than expel its black members.

I was present in April 1968 at the party's last meeting in Johannesburg, in Darragh Hall, which adjoined St Mary's Cathedral. Alan Paton went out of his way to say that what was right for the Liberal Party was not necessarily right for others, which I took as a sign that he understood the Progs' decision to keep going. I can still remember Paton's putting on his fiercest look and saying in that growly voice of his, 'Man was not born to go down on his belly before the state!' He added: 'I read that Mr J van der Berg MP, speaking in Parliament, prophesied that in ten years' time it would be an offence to oppose separate development. That may or may not come true, but one thing will be true, and that is that in ten years' time it will be a still greater intellectual offence to believe in it.'[40] On its dissolution, the Liberal Party gave its remaining funds to the Institute.[41]

Yet just as the government was extending this form of apartheid, it was starting to relax apartheid in sport. In 1967 the very same John Vorster had reiterated that no mixed sport would be allowed between black and white South Africans, but that Maoris could be included in New Zealand All Black rugby teams touring to play against the Springboks. The alternative would have been calling off a tour that was due in 1970 (and which took place with three Maoris in the visiting team).[42]

This tiny chink in the colour bar was widely dismissed as cosmetic. But 11 NP MPs were strongly enough opposed to it to refuse to support a motion endorsing Vorster's action at the party's Transvaal congress in 1969.[43] Three of them were expelled from the party, and one resigned to avoid expulsion. They went on to form the Herstigte Nasionale Party (HNP), under the leadership of Dr Albert Hertzog. No doubt they felt that Vorster was now suffering from the same 'unbridled liberalism' of which he had been accusing us.

The HNP did not survive into the post-apartheid era. A right-wing Conservative Party (CP) was launched in 1982, giving the NP a huge fright by winning a crucial by-election in 1992 in the midst of the constitutional negotiations leading up to the 1994 election – a reverse which FW de Klerk swiftly dealt with by calling a referendum among the white electorate, 69 per cent of whom gave him a mandate to continue with constitutional reform.[44] Like the HNP, the CP has effectively ceased to exist. The white Right, if it can be called that, now has only four seats in the National Assembly, held by the Freedom Front Plus. The United Party, having been turfed out by the white electorate in 1948, eventually dissolved itself in 1977. It was replaced that same year as the official opposition by the Progressive Federal Party (PFP), which absorbed most of its liberals. Having also absorbed some of the remnants of the old NP, the PFP now exists as the Democratic Alliance (DA). With 22 per cent of the seats in the National Assembly elected in 2014, it constitutes the official opposition. Although ideologically rather a mess, it is the closest thing South Africa has to a liberal voice in Parliament.

Despite the fact that the Liberal Party was forced to dissolve in 1968 after only 15 years in existence, liberalism was never extinguished. It had taken root in the country long before Alan Paton and others established the party in 1953. Its cradle was the Cape, under renewed British rule from 1806. Milestones in the history of Cape liberalism include commitments to a free press and an independent judiciary adopted in 1827. Another milestone was the abolition of slavery in 1834.[45] Yet another was the establishment by the British government in 1853 of a local legislature to be elected on a common voters' roll under a colour-blind constitution.[46] Although non-racial, the franchise was confined to men and subject to economic and educational qualifications – which were subsequently raised as more people met them.[47] When the British granted self-governing status to the Cape in 1872, the colony incorporated British institutions that included the rule of law, freedom of speech, and equality before the law. At the national convention of 1908, which led to the establishment of the Union of South Africa in 1910, attempts by Cape liberals, English-speaking and Afrikaners alike, to extend the non-racial franchise were rebuffed and they settled for the compromise of confining it to the Cape. But it was to be protected by the two-thirds requirement stipulated in one of the entrenched clauses of the Constitution. However, as we saw in the previous chapter, all common-roll franchises were finally abolished by the NP in 1956.

For the Liberal Party, this was not the end of the matter, for it was determined to restore a common-roll franchise. Echoing Cape liberalism, the party initially proposed that the franchise, although colour-blind, should be limited to persons with the requisite education, property, or income qualifications. Even this limited franchise had little appeal to the white electorate. It was also resented by many blacks. In 1960 the party embraced universal adult suffrage. The Liberal Party also called for an independent judiciary with the power to enforce an entrenched bill of rights against the 'encroachments of the state'. It further advocated redistribution of land, recognition of all trade unions, abolition of the colour bar in industry, and even the appointment of a 'public protector'. Finally, it wanted the repeal of all apartheid laws.[48]

Commitment to universal adult suffrage on a common roll was a momentous development for South African liberalism. It did not come easily. Professor RF Alfred Hoernlé, a German-born philosopher who was president of the Institute from 1934 to 1943, observed that the classical doctrine of liberalism did not contemplate how it would work in a multiracial society such as South Africa.[49] The classical thinkers had no first-hand experience of such a society. South African liberals had to feel their way. Some experimented intellectually with total racial separation. Most recognised that this was economically impossible. Although often dismissed as idealists and dreamers, liberals were South Africa's true realists in recognising that one could not impose a straitjacket of political apartheid upon an industrialising economy. They were also pioneers in that they broke with the established view among whites that the main challenge in the country was how to reconcile the two white groups, rather than to find ways of incorporating blacks into a common society.

South African liberalism was also distinguished by its crusades against apartheid. This was fought as much by liberal newspapers as by the Liberal and Progressive parties and other liberal organisations, among them the Institute and Nusas. Liberal businessmen such as Harry Oppenheimer helped to make this possible. Liberals fought not only racial laws but also all the security legislation designed to curtail opposition. In 2006, Mosiuoa Lekota, then minister of defence and chairman of the ANC, said that many people had forgotten that in the darkest days of apartheid, liberals had given people hope when there seemed to be none. They had shown blacks that there were some whites who did not wish them away.

Although the Liberal Party adopted universal adult suffrage in 1960, the Progressive Party did not do so until 1978.[50] The fact that these parties ever supported a qualified franchise at all still rankles with many black people, and helps explain continuing hostility to liberalism.

Whereas other parties simply denied blacks the vote, the qualified franchise somehow implied that liberals were willing to give it with one
hand but take it away with the other. Although I worked for Helen
Suzman and held a junior position in the Progressive Party, I thought
a qualified franchise was defensible only on pragmatic grounds. Whites
would never support a universal franchise, but there might just be
enough support for a qualified franchise to ensure that Helen could be
returned to Parliament, which of course she was, by the slenderest of
majorities. However, I always rejected as spurious the argument that
there was some sort of connection between the ability of voters to make
supposedly wise political choices on the one hand and their educational
or economic status on the other. The notion of 'a vote for every civilised
man and a chance for every man to become civilised' was sometimes put
forward as the reasoning behind the qualified franchise in the Cape. But
I never thought either property or education guaranteed even common
sense, let alone 'civilisation'.

CHAPTER 3

Oxford

My time at Oxford was very different from that at Wits. For a start I was no longer a BMOC (Big Man on Campus), as we were sometimes called, but more or less a nobody. I ran in no elections, sat on no councils, and played no political role. I had no debates other than in tutorials or with colleagues over glasses of college sherry or port (£1 a bottle) in the middle common room to which graduates invariably repaired after dinner. My fortnight on the *Edinburgh Castle* had slowed me down from 90 miles an hour at Wits to about 20 knots, or whatever was the speed of the ship. It was remarkably pleasant.

I joined the Oxford Union and went to one or two debates. After all the excitement at Wits the issues seemed trivial. You couldn't go to hear visiting speakers unless you joined the club hosting them, so I joined the Labour Club to listen to Denis Healey and others. I also joined the Oxford University Conservative Association to listen to Enoch Powell, who packed the town hall in January 1969 after having been refused the union as a venue. Powell was an MP and former Conservative minister who had been sacked from Edward Heath's shadow cabinet in 1968 after making a speech in Birmingham in which he prophesied that uncontrolled immigration might lead to bloodshed. Militants in Oxford had vowed to break up his meeting there, so the town hall was cordoned off by 200 policemen to protect his right of free speech and the rights of those who wished to hear him. Powell's language made him a political untouchable. But his experience showed how difficult it was – and still is – to talk about race except in politically correct terms.

Almost everyone expected Harold Wilson, who had won the general elections in 1964 and 1966, to become the first prime minister to pull off a hat trick by winning in 1970 as well. But Heath defeated him, much to my disgust as a Wilson man. In rapidly deteriorating stages of sobriety, the Oxford Tories celebrated all night long, bellowing out 'Land of Hope and Glory' across the city. Heath's premiership ended in ignominious defeat after only four years when he took on the coal miners after they had brought Britain to a standstill, causing the government to proclaim a three-day week as the country ran out of power. He called an election on the issue 'Who governs Britain?', but the voters decided that whoever governed Britain it wasn't going to be Mr Heath.

Edward Heath was not the first British prime minister to fail at trade union reform. Wilson himself had failed when in 1969 his left-wing employment secretary, Barbara Castle, tried to introduce compulsory pre-strike ballots and other measures to curtail union power. I followed with fascination the saga of how Wilson's right-wing home secretary, James Callaghan, successfully led a revolt against Wilson and Castle and their policy paper 'In Place of Strife'. Perhaps it was poetic justice that Callaghan's own government was destroyed by union power fewer than 10 years later, paving the way for Margaret Thatcher.

I have been lucky enough to do all my formal education in glorious surroundings. St John's had beautiful buildings and gardens in a matchless setting on the Houghton Ridge. It had a wonderful sense of light and space. So did the lawns and other open areas overlooked by the neoclassical façade of the Wits central block. Oxford had no central campus, its 23 men's, five women's, and five graduate colleges being interspersed with shops, pubs, hotels, churches, and other bits of the city and the university. Architectural styles, among them Gothic, Renaissance, and Classical, span some 800 years. Towers, domes, and spires dominate the skyline. Lots of friends from Wits or St John's came to visit me and I walked them through the various college quadrangles and gardens, and along the river past the college boathouses. To stroll through Magdalen's deer park or Christ Church Meadow – off limits to 'very dirty persons', according to a sign at the entrance – after a lecture was always a delight. In summer Oxford was ablaze with flowers, some in beds, some in window boxes, some in baskets hanging from lampposts. We sometimes had tutorials on the lawns in college gardens or in punts on the river. Some colleges put on plays or concerts in their own gardens or beside their own lakes during the long summer evenings – serious competition for spending the evening in your college library. In winter, buildings and grounds bedecked with snow would be as beautiful as the summer flowers until the snow turned to sludge. Somehow the beauty always outweighed the cold. Summer and winter, every church bell in the city seemed to ring for most of Sunday.

One of the other things that was so striking about Oxford was how easy it was to find the books you needed. Quite a lot of what we were told to read by some of the Wits politics lecturers was unavailable in South Africa. But the main Oxford library, the Bodleian, stocked everything published in the UK and vast numbers of other books. Each college also had its own library, and then there was also Blackwell's, the renowned, though always overheated, bookshop. I bought as much as I could, including material banned in South Africa. Blackwell's also had a music shop; there I stocked up with boxed sets of all of Beethoven's symphonies, concertos, and piano sonatas and much else to play on the gramophone the Wits SRC had given me as a farewell present.

The warden of Rhodes House, who was *in loco parentis* to all the Rhodes Scholars in Oxford, was a former history don called ET ('Bill') Williams. During the Second World War he'd been General Bernard Montgomery's intelligence officer. In his memoirs Montgomery wrote that Major (later Brigadier) Williams 'gave me the idea which played a huge part in winning the battle of Alamein' in October 1942. This was to separate the Italians from the Germans, who were 'corsetting' them, and then smash through the weaker Italian forces. Montgomery wrote that the best intelligence officers were civilians, as they had the best brains and the most fertile imaginations. Williams – later Sir Edgar Williams – had 'stood out supreme among them all'.[1] My father had been at Alamein as General Dan Pienaar's assistant divisional signals officer. After the battle he brought home his numbered copy of the 'most secret and personal' orders for Operation Lightfoot issued a few days in advance for such things as wireless deception, the laying of smoke-screens from aircraft, and how to requisition air support.

As a graduate I was entitled to do a postgraduate degree at Oxford. Instead I chose to read for another undergraduate course, the PPE (philosophy, politics, and economics). Though this is normally three years, the fact that I was a graduate meant I could do it in two.

The method of instruction was very different from that at Wits. Lectures at Wits were all-important, and you could be penalised if your attendance was poor. Tutorials were rare, and the numbers in the class were large. At Oxford one of my tutors paged lazily through the university's schedule of lectures for the coming term, only to toss it aside with the words, 'There don't appear to be any lectures in Oxford worth going to this term.' During my three years there I nevertheless went to plenty of lectures, some of them by famous writers and academics such as the historian AJP Taylor, the philosophers AJ Ayer and Herbert Hart, and Isaiah Berlin, author of the famous essay 'Two Concepts of Liberty'. Ayer on one of these occasions said, 'Of course we were all appalled by the invasion of Czechoslovakia. But what could we do? We're philosophers, not lifeboat men!' Taylor wasn't lecturing on anything particularly relevant to my courses, but I went because he was so famous and because I'd also read his controversial study on the origins of the war.

Although I spent more time in lectures than in tutorials, the tutorial system is the heart of undergraduate teaching in Oxford. This is possible only in a university rich enough to have loads of teaching staff. Taking full advantage of it was one of my main reasons for choosing an under-graduate course. In my first year in our weekly economics and politics tutorials there were no more than half a dozen students. In philosophy there were only two of us; and Ken Davis, a Cornell graduate, and I took it in turns to write the weekly essay the tutor required.

Occasionally one might fall asleep listening to the other man's essay. This happened one winter's evening when Donald MacNabb, senior phi-losophy tutor of Pembroke College, was acting master and therefore due to host Harold Macmillan, chancellor of the university and also titular head, or 'visitor', of the college, who was coming to dinner. The occasion was to be marked by a ration of beer to all of us dining in Hall, while Macmillan was entertained by the dons in evening dress at High Table using the college's fabulous silver collection. Protocol required that Mr MacNabb await the former prime minister at the entrance to the college.

A couple of hours before Macmillan was due, MacNabb, a specialist on the great Scottish philosopher David Hume, was holding his weekly philosophy tutorial for Ken and myself. He had switched on his bar heater and poured all three of us the customary glass of sherry. I forget whether it was Ken's or my turn to read the week's essay, but no matter: all three of us fell asleep – until there came a knock on the door. Enter the head porter with the news that 'Mr MacNabb, sir, Mr Macmillan is waiting for you in the lodge.'

For three of my eight PPE papers I was the only student in the weekly tutorial. This meant I had to write an essay every week throughout those courses, and either hand it in to the tutor beforehand or read it out to him during the tutorial. This was about the most privileged tutor-intensive education one could get. It was tough going, because you invariably didn't finish your essay until 4 o'clock in the morning and the tutorial was only a few hours later. But I loved every minute of it.

One paper was on political theory since Hobbes, the second on the history of the British labour movement since 1815, and the third on

British political and constitutional history since 1865. You had one eight-week term in which to master each of these, starting with a long reading list. My eight-week reading list on the labour movement contained the titles of 87 books on trade unionism, socialism, politics, and industrial relations, along with volumes of documents and biographies of some of the leading figures. Armed with your list you would head for one of the libraries or for Blackwell's.

You would then produce your essay. 'Why was the progress of independent labour representation in parliament so slow before 1906?' 'What were the major strengths and weaknesses of the Labour Party from 1906 to 1929?' 'Discuss the idea that the general strike of 1926 was British trade unionism's last fling with syndicalism.' Your tutor would then critique it: 'Very interesting but somewhat off the point,' or some such. For my work on the labour movement I was farmed out to a tutor in Ruskin College, which runs courses for trade unionists.

In political theory we had to knock off about a dozen people, among them Mill, Rousseau, Hegel, and Marx, in eight weeks. My tutor, Zbigniew Pelczynski – who also taught Bill Clinton – had done his own doctorate on Hegel, which I had read at Wits. So I wrote essays on such topics as the distinction Hegel drew between the state and civil society. Some essays required you to get on top of three people in a single week: 'Compare Burke's and Bentham's (plus Mill's) theories of representation.' Then you would get questions in the 'final honour schools', as the exams were called, along the lines of: 'How Marxian is the concept of permanent revolution?' 'Has anarchism a coherent theoretical foundation?' 'Did 19th century theorists of democracy greatly overestimate the political consciousness of the ordinary man?' 'Have any of JS Mill's critics given convincing reasons why a liberal need not fear majority rule?'

Unlike at Wits, where exams were spaced out, leaving time for last-minute cramming, my Oxford exams were crammed together – eight three-hour papers in four or five days, the dress code for which was subfusc, in other words gown, dark suit, mortar-board, and white bowtie and shirt. If you hadn't worked steadily during the preceding two years, you were done for. So the only way to prepare for 'schools' was to inspect the cattle and daffodils in Christ Church Meadow, go for a punt on the river, or play squash with Ken Davis or John Platt, the college chaplain.

The course that I loved was the one on British political and constitutional history. The essay topics could not have been more interesting. Among them: '"Plundering and blundering": Do you agree with this description of Gladstone's first government?' 'Account for the predominance of imperialism in British politics for the last 20 years of the 19th century.' 'Discuss the suggestion that the Labour victory of 1945 was already inevitable by the outbreak of the Second World War.'

'Plundering and blundering' was Disraeli's description of his great rival. Among other things, Gladstone's first government had dealt with the disestablishment of the Irish church, attempted to curb Irish landlords' abuse of their powers, abolished the practice of purchasing commissions in the army, thrown open the civil service to competitive entry, reorganised the judicial system, and put through the Education Act of 1870. You had a week to read up on all these issues before you could assess his handling thereof. Great pressure, but also great enjoyment, not least their sparkling performances in the House of Commons.

Birley – who was at that stage teaching at the City University in London – took me to the House of Commons not long after I'd arrived in Oxford. His plan was to ensure that potentially influential people were kept abreast of what was happening on South African campuses. The small group he got together in a committee room included Sir Edward Boyle, a former Conservative education minister who had once done a Richard Feetham Lecture at Wits. Another person who came was Shirley Williams, then a junior Labour minister but later one of the 'gang of four' Labour notables who defected in 1981 to found the Social (now the Liberal) Democratic Party.

Birley was determined to do all he could to support the fight for academic freedom in South Africa. From time to time he hosted a lunch for a dozen or so South Africans in Oxford at the Randolph Hotel. On one of these occasions he called on us all to stand and drink a toast to Mark Orkin and others at Wits who were standing up to the government.

Knowing how important support from people like Birley was when we were embattled at Wits, I organised telegrams of solidarity from South Africans at Oxford for Laurence Gandar and Benjamin Pogrund of the *Rand Daily Mail*, who were on trial in South Africa under the Prisons Act, of which more below. Gandar sent me a pile of letters responding personally to each and every signatory and asked me to distribute them.

Harry Walston also maintained the interest awakened during his visit. I once spent the weekend at his farm outside Cambridge. One of the other guests was George Brown, who had been foreign secretary and deputy prime minister in Harold Wilson's cabinet. He had resigned after falling out with Wilson for the umpteenth time. The conversation across the dinner table was hilarious, not least because of stories that Brown told about Wilson's failings and power struggles in the cabinet. I had an argument with Brown over an arms embargo against South Africa – I was in favour but he wasn't.

I also supported the sports boycott against segregated South African teams. One of the other South Africans at Oxford, Eddie Webster, and I wrote a letter to *The Times* in November 1969 criticising the Oxford rugby club for fielding a team against the visiting Springboks the following month.[2] We got another 20 South Africans to sign the letter, which caused some of them to be attacked back home in the Afrikaans press. One of those so attacked was Johann Maree, who later married Helen Zille. Many of the signatories of the letter were refused renewals when their passports expired. I was among these, and was without a passport for several years. Then I was given a passport for only a year at a time, until eventually I managed to get a five-year passport. Limited renewals, which were referred to the security police for clearance, were presumably designed to keep me on some sort of leash.

A Springbok cricket team was due in England in 1970. When Peter

Hain organised his campaign against the tour, there were threats to throw glass onto the pitch. I wrote home that I supported this. But my parents were having none of it. They wrote to me that they thought the cancellation of all sporting tours would help bring people in South Africa to their senses, but that they were most emphatically against any kind of demonstration that was not peaceful.

The police federation was among those who welcomed the British government's decision to call off the tour in the face of threats of violent disruption. I had an exchange of views about the tour in the pages of a South African journal called *New Nation* with Blyth Thompson, leader of South Africa's National Alliance Party. He accused me of being a 'malcontent whipping up bitterness and hatred'. One of the questions I asked was, 'How many schools in Soweto have cricket fields or a cricket coach?'[3] Fifty years later this question can still be asked, for 'transformation' in sport focuses on racial quotas for teams but pays little attention to grass-roots development of black sport.

One of the South Africans I got to know in Oxford was Wellington Tshazibane. Birley wrote to me one day to tell me that Wellington would soon be arriving at Wadham College; would I please look him up and show him around. He had at one stage taught Wellington and thought him one of the best mathematical minds he had ever come across. I think Birley had got Wellington a scholarship to Wadham. As frequently happened with Africans in particular, he was then refused a passport and offered instead a one-way exit permit. This he declined to accept as he did not want to leave his mother, so Birley used his influence as an ex-headmaster of Eton to get Wellington a passport.

Wellington and I played bridge together from time to time. He also played chess but I never dared take him on. One day he changed his field of study and told me that he needed to learn how to make bombs. After I returned to South Africa I lost contact with him. In December 1976, after he had himself returned to the country and got a job with De Beers, he was picked up by the security police at Rand Airport under Section

6 of the Terrorism Act. Within 48 hours he was dead. His family were told he had hanged himself. The police said that he'd been held in connection with an explosion at the Carlton Centre.[4]

Other Oxford friends included a Malaysian, an Indian, and a Mauritian. The last of these was in fact Chinese. He teased me to write to my parents that I was 'socialising with a coloured person'. I also wrote to them that I was embarrassed that I couldn't invite them to South Africa without subjecting them to apartheid humiliation. One English friend, Peter Farthing, did come on a visit some years later. He could barely contain his excitement at seeing an elephant in the Kruger National Park, jumping around in his seat like a schoolboy to get a better view until the magnificent animal was out of sight. Peter had a car in Oxford, so we sometimes took off for afternoons and evenings at the Royal Shakespeare Theatre at Stratford-upon-Avon. I could hardly believe that such cultural riches were only a couple of hours' drive away.

While I was at Oxford a number of black Americans there took up the issue of whether South African Rhodes Scholarships were open to blacks. There was never any prohibition in Rhodes's will against blacks: he had indeed stipulated that race should neither qualify nor disqualify a candidate, and the first black American Rhodes Scholar was in fact elected in 1907, only five years after Rhodes died. However, there had never been a black South African Scholar. I was approached by some South African friends who had applied for but failed to win Scholarships. They were hesitant about pressing the matter of black Scholars themselves lest they be accused of sour grapes, so I agreed to take it up. My Wits colleague Charles Simkins, who was also in Oxford at the time, and I wrote to Rex Welsh, the general secretary of the Rhodes Scholarships in South Africa. On my return to the country Rex invited me to lunch, and we put together a list of blacks and women to invite onto the selection committees. One of its members was Desmond Tutu. A new constituency – Botswana, Lesotho, South West Africa/Namibia, and Swaziland – was set up to widen the catchment area for black students. We advertised in papers such as the *Times of Swaziland*, and I also went to Windhoek in 1977 to meet local notables, including officials of the South West African People's Organisation (Swapo), to try to find more black applicants.

Choosing blacks was in fact easier than choosing women. The initial attempts by the Rhodes Trust to open the Scholarships to women were rejected by the then British education minister, Margaret Thatcher, on the grounds that Rhodes's wishes should be respected. Eventually the Trust was able to throw the Scholarships open to women in 1976 by seeking a ministerial order in terms of the Sex Discrimination Act passed by the Labour government in 1975.

Once I'd finished my PPE, I had a third year of my Rhodes to spend in Oxford. I intended to study for a doctorate on the administrative controls to which black South Africans were subject, among them the pass laws. Refusal by the Department of the Interior to renew my passport interfered with this, and it proved too cumbersome to transfer the registration to Wits. In any event, I soon got so absorbed in work at the Institute and then on the *Financial Mail* after my return to South Africa that I abandoned the doctorate. Instead, in 1978, I published a book on the Soweto revolt which incorporated some of the ideas I'd been thinking about for the doctorate in Oxford.[5]

In the end I spent my third year at Oxford reading. Some of what I read was material banned back home. All of this reading and extensive note-taking in those beautiful surroundings before going off to dinner with some of my friends every night – and no exams at the end of it – was about as enjoyable a 'gap year' as one could hope for. I spent much of my reading time in the Radcliffe Camera, the great rotunda in the middle of Oxford which houses part of the Bodleian Library. It features prominently in a popular television series: whenever Inspector Morse or his successor, Inspector Lewis, are trying to think through a particularly difficult murder mystery, they seem to seek inspiration by pacing round and round the Radcliffe.

Rhodes House had a large collection of material on South Africa, and it was there that I read a doctoral dissertation entitled 'The Drift from the Reserves among South African Bantu'. It was a remarkably liberal and enlightened piece of work. Written in the early 1950s, this thesis had involved four or five months' fieldwork into family disruption in the Nkandla reserve in Zululand. Its author was none other than Dr Piet Koornhof, one-time secretary of the Afrikaner Broederbond, and a man who spent much of his career as a minister enforcing some of the very laws whose effects he had so eloquently described. I sent my mother some quotes from the thesis to pass on to the Black Sash in the hope that they might assist it in its battle against the pass laws. For example,

> In his account of working-class life in England during the first half of the 19th century, Friedrich Engels drew a picture of slums, poverty, family disintegration, illiteracy, vice, and lawlessness which can be duplicated very nearly from the description of African conditions in the union today.

And:

> Nowhere in the world ... does there exist a system of executive despotism similar to the executive administration of native affairs in South Africa.

'Executive despotism' was exactly what I intended to look into for my doctorate and what I described in great detail in my Soweto book. This system was also one of the matters I wrote about at the Institute when I returned to South Africa, and then later on for the *Financial Mail*. Koornhof in the late 1970s and early 1980s was in fact responsible for drawing up legislation to tighten up the pass laws. He became South Africa's foremost practitioner of the very 'executive despotism' he had described. I sent the quotes from his thesis to Helen Suzman to use against him in Parliament. In the end, the laws proved unworkable and, as we shall see, PW Botha repealed them in 1986.

My parents and I had much correspondence about whether Gandhi-style passive resistance could work in South Africa, where I suggested such strategies had failed. I also expressed scepticism about the ability of laissez-faire liberalism to solve the problems of poverty – a view which is still widely held in South Africa, though no longer by me. While I was at Oxford there was also much debate as to whether or not economic forces would undermine apartheid. I was one of the sceptics. I argued that industrial development and apartheid had grown up together. While apartheid was being undermined to the extent that the flow of blacks to the so-called 'white' areas could not be reversed, and also by the employment of Africans in supposedly 'white' jobs, there was no sign that business favoured recognising black trade unions. Business was also able to rely on the 'massive coercive apparatus of the state'.[6]

I arrived back in South Africa in the middle of 1971 convinced that Peter Hain's efforts were responsible for the more liberal statements now coming out of sports officials. Economic sanctions also seemed to be the only means the outside world had of doing anything about apartheid. On the home front we needed radical redistribution of wealth, accompanied if necessary by nationalisation. Liberals who were suggesting that apartheid was crumbling were clutching at straws.[7]

The next 20 years proved me wrong. Coercion was tightened, but in the end it failed. Most of business reacted with hostility towards black unions, but in the end they could not avoid dealing with them. The colour bar was removed from labour legislation from 1979 onwards. While my Soweto book described executive despotism in great detail, my *South Africa's Silent Revolution*, published 12 years later, chronicled the disintegration of that same system.[8] In fact it described the very crumbling process I had been sceptical about.

Just as they had seen me off to Oxford on the *Edinburgh Castle*, customs officials welcomed me back to South Africa at Jan Smuts Airport by confiscating a number of books they found in my luggage. One of these was Alan Paton's novel *Too Late the Phalarope*. Another was a collection of Nelson Mandela's writings which I sheepishly fished out of my raincoat pocket when asked if I had anything further to declare after the officials had found everything else. Nor were the customs men taking any chances. One of the publications taken off me was a periodical called *Problems of Communism* issued by the US embassy. Most of the banned books I bought in Oxford had been sent home by sea, and arrived safely. *Problems of Communism* was inspected and 'found to be not objectionable'.

Some of the books confiscated at the airport were subsequently banned. However, on the strength of letters from my tutors in Oxford stating that I needed them for study purposes, they were released to me on condition I used them for study purposes only, kept them under lock and key when not in use, and didn't lend, display, or sell them. One of the books to which these conditions applied was Helen Joseph's *Tomorrow's Sun*. I also had to pay 90 cents for 'rental of a state warehouse for three months' while the books were in the custody of the customs officials.

Having been banned after being taken off me, the Mandela book was in a different category. Jannie Kruger, chairman of the Publications Control Board, told me that to the best of his knowledge Mandela's writings were prohibited. No person could possess a publication containing them without the consent of the minister of justice. Before I could apply for a permit I should therefore obtain that minister's consent.[9]

Not long after my return from Oxford I met Pierre Roestorf, with whom I have shared all my life since then. In 2013 – 41 years after we'd met – we entered into a civil union, the ceremony being performed by Edwin Cameron, who'd been in the army with Pierre and whom I'd met through the Rhodes Scholarships. Pierre worked at the SABC as a lighting designer and for two years at South African Airways as a cabin steward so that he could see the world. We later spent a lot of time travelling, of which more in later chapters of this memoir.

Two of the books I read at Oxford were *They Thought They Were Free* by Milton Mayer[10] and *The Nazi Seizure of Power* by William Sheridan Allen.[11] They made a deep impression on me at the time, because I could see parallels between Nazi Germany and South Africa. The most striking parallel was that of how people could become conditioned over time to accept what they might not immediately be prepared to accept. I wrote several articles on this theme on my return to South Africa[12] and also later spoke about it on various campuses.

Having played no public role at Oxford, I was delighted to be back on campus and speaking as freely as I had in my own student days at Wits. A talk I gave in November 1976 at the invitation of the SRC on the Durban campus of the University of Natal was overshadowed by the bannings in the preceding two weeks of some 25 young people, most of them students or former students, many known to me and some of them personal friends.

In their efforts to justify bannings, apologists for the government usually took the line that 'the minister wouldn't have banned him if he hadn't done something wrong' and 'there's no smoke without fire'. So I reminded the Durban students of the famous remarks of Pastor Niemoller:

> In Germany they first came for the Communists, and I did not speak up because I wasn't a Communist. Then they came for the Jews, and I did not speak up because I was not a Jew. Then they came for the trade unionists, and I did not speak up because I was not a trade unionist. Then they came for the Catholics and I did not speak up because I was a Protestant. Then they came for me – and by that time there was no one left to speak.

White South Africans had been corrupted by conditioning. Apartheid was the beginning of it: we were born into and lived in separate worlds and most whites were oblivious of the horrors being inflicted upon blacks and seemed not to care anyway. Whites were not inherently evil: they had just become accustomed to detention without trial, reports of torture, stories about malnutrition, forced removals, and the like. I then quoted from the Milton Mayer book about the Third Reich:

> What happened in Germany was the gradual habituation of the people, little by little, to being governed by surprise; to receiving decisions taken in secret; to believing that the situation was so complicated that the government had to act on information that people could not understand, or so dangerous that it would not be revealed for national security reasons. ... To live in this process did not mean that one noticed it. Each step was so small, so inconsequential, or on occasion so regretted, that unless one were detached from the whole process from the beginning, unless one understood what the whole thing was in principle, what all these 'little measures' that 'no patriotic German' could resist must someday lead to, one could no more see it developing than a farmer sees his corn growing – until one day it is over his head.[13]

Conditioning of the Germans had started off with what might aptly be called 'petty apartheid' in the form of throwing Jews out of social clubs, boycotting Jewish shops, then moving them to separate areas. The result of this process of separation was that the Nazis could then create whatever stereotypes they chose, and on the strength of these do what they liked to the Jews. It took only a million or so racist fanatics and hoodlums to run the Nazi machine. Apart from those in the army, all that the rest of the populace had to do was to mind their own business, pay their taxes, go to church, listen to the radio, and so on. With their passive acquiescence, the dictatorship could do its work without restraint. There were no gas chambers in South Africa, but we did arrest 1 000 people a day under the pass laws, uproot them from their homes by the tens of thousands, and then dump them destitute on the veld.

Conditioning started with language. When the government talked about people as 'superfluous', it reminded me of 'another country not that many years ago which also decided that people were superfluous – six million of them'.

I went on to suggest how white students could resist conditioning. They should continue to defend the rule of law, even in the face of bannings and detentions. They could work to assist black trade unions, which in fact Nusas had started to do. They could pump alternative ideas such as majority rule into the public domain. Equally important, they should build up contacts and friendships across the colour line. White students, in short, should support the black demand for freedom.[14]

And I recited to them the words of Professor Julius Ebbinghaus that Birley had used so often:

> One fact remains unfortunately all too true. The German universities failed, while there was still time, to oppose publicly with all their power the destruction of learning and the democratic state. They failed to keep the beacon of freedom and right (or justice) burning through the night of tyranny so that it could be seen by the entire world.[15]

These speeches went down very well. More controversial were some I gave at Wits and UCT some 13 years later, when I was running the Institute. They were both graduation addresses.[16] I referred in both to a notorious incident in 1986 when violent disruption of a lecture he was giving at UCT forced Conor Cruise O'Brien, the Irish politician, diplomat, writer, and academic, to cancel his remaining lectures there and at Wits.[17] Although O'Brien was a prominent member of anti-apartheid organisations, he had infuriated some on the Left by describing the academic boycott of South Africa – broken most prominently by Birley – as a 'Mickey Mouse affair'. Nor was he the only speaker denied a platform, for the same had happened to Helen Suzman and Mangosuthu Buthelezi, among others. Intolerance on the part of the state or the Right, I said, did not entitle anyone to use 'physical violence or the threat thereof to put the campus out of bounds to controversial speakers'. Richard Luyt wrote to congratulate me, as did Harry Oppenheimer, then chancellor of UCT.[18] But a prominent Wits professor told me that some of the academics sitting behind me on the stage of the Great Hall looked as if they were ready to lynch me as I spoke.

When O'Brien was denied a platform on campus, I decided that somebody had to step into the breach and offer him one. So on the spur of the moment I tracked him down and invited him to talk in the Rheinallt Jones Memorial Hall in Auden House, the Institute's building in Braamfontein, Johannesburg. Our hall, which could seat 200 people at a push, had proudly hosted dozens of speakers from right across the political spectrum. If no one else would offer O'Brien a platform, we would. Unfortunately, he was leaving South Africa within a day or two. But it would have been nice to strike a blow for free speech by hosting him.

CHAPTER 4

Truth to power

When I worked for Helen Suzman in the 1966 election one of my colleagues was Mark Gandar, whose father, Laurence Gandar, was editor of the *Rand Daily Mail* (the *Mail*). I visited their home in Riviera Road, Killarney, quite often, sometimes stayed with them, and went on holiday with them to Southbroom on the Natal south coast. They were keen on horse-racing and we went one day to the Durban July.

Laurence Gandar had been appointed editor in 1957. Most of the English-language newspapers in South Africa supported the official opposition, the United Party. When Helen Suzman and several others broke away in 1959 to form the Progressive Party, Gandar switched his paper's support to the Progs. More than that, he used it to expose the horrors of apartheid. This was not what most of his white readers wanted to find in their newspaper every morning, and both circulation and advertising revenue declined.

Joel Mervis, who was at the time editor of the *Sunday Times*, later wrote of Gandar:

'His crusade against race discrimination and injustice was conducted with an intensity and on a scale not matched by other major newspaper in South Africa. What he wrote and published jolted and irritated many South Africans, but it needed saying and he had the courage to say it loud and clear. At home he was reviled. The outside world on the other hand saw him as a fearless champion of justice, and granted him the highest awards in the gift of newspapers and journalists.'[1]

In July 1965 the *Mail* published a series of horrifying articles on conditions in South African prisons. I felt physically ill as I read them. They were based largely on information supplied to one of the paper's senior journalists, Benjamin Pogrund, by a one-time political prisoner, Harold Strachan (who was at one stage married to my shipboard companion Jean Middleton). Prosecuted under the Prisons Act, Gandar and Pogrund were unable to convince the judge that they had taken adequate steps to verify what they had published – even though their counsel, Sydney Kentridge, argued that the procession of prison warders paraded in court to contradict them had committed perjury. For the board of South African Associated Newspapers (SAAN), owners of both the *Mail* and the *Sunday Times* and of many other publications, this was the last straw.

I was horrified to learn from Mark one day that his father had been fired. In fact he had been 'elevated' – in Mervis's words – to editor-in-chief.[2] In that capacity he wrote dozens of blistering front-page leaders, but the running of the paper was entrusted to a new editor, Raymond Louw. Gandar himself then retired from the paper altogether in 1969. Though he was reviled as much as was Ambrose Reeves, to my parents and myself Gandar was a brave man and a martyr. He gave moral and intellectual leadership, but the white community was too smug to follow him.

In the end, according to Mervis, the loss-making *Rand Daily Mail* threatened the future of the whole SAAN group and in 1985 the 83-year-old paper was closed at the behest of the Anglo American Corporation, the ultimate shareholders. *Business Day* was launched in the same year to take its place.

Pogrund one day came to visit me in Oxford, and suggested that after leaving there I should join the *Mail*. On my return I was also offered a job by the Study Project on Christianity in Apartheid Society (Sprocas). Jointly sponsored by the South African Council of Churches and the Christian Institute of Southern Africa, Sprocas produced a series of reports in the early 1970s designed to promote 'urgent and radical change' in the country. I also had an interview at Wits, but nothing came of that. My old school friend Clive Nettleton was assistant director at the South African Institute of Race Relations, and he was largely responsible for persuading me to apply to join its research department – although the Progressive Party tried to poach me when they heard of this. The report I wrote for the Institute on the strike by Ovambo contract workers in South West Africa at the end of 1971 led to a meeting one day over lunch at the fine Pot Luck restaurant in Braamfontein with JDF Jones of the *Financial Times* (*FT*), and Graham Hatton, assistant editor of the *Financial Mail* (*FM*), who offered me a job. I turned him down but several months later phoned to ask if there was still a job available. I went for an interview with the editor, George Palmer, got the job, and handed in my notice to the Institute after only about 18 months there.

Thus by a somewhat roundabout route began my 10-year career in journalism. Ironically, the man who had conceived of the idea of the *FM*, which was launched in 1959, was Laurence Gandar, who had spotted a gap in the market while he was working for Anglo American before joining the *Rand Daily Mail*.[3] When my father one day happened to mention to Mervis that I was joining the *FM*, Joel wanted to know why I didn't come and work for him on the *Sunday Times* instead of languishing in 'obscurity' on the *FM*, whose articles carried no by-lines.

Many years later Pierre and I found ourselves on the same tour to Moscow and St Petersburg as Joel and Osna Mervis. Though both in their eighties they were wonderful travelling companions, game even for trips up and down the long escalators on the Moscow underground, which move at breakneck speed. Joel and I cracked a bottle of vodka together at midnight on a beach in the Gulf of Finland to witness the midnight sun.

No sooner had I joined the *FM* than I was assigned the labour beat to replace Bob Nugent, who was leaving the paper to do his LLB – which in due course took him to the bench of the Supreme Court of Appeal. Very soon I was writing leading articles and cover stories. I had never had any formal journalistic training, but with Graham Hatton as my mentor I did not need it because I learnt on the job like an apprentice. He was both a brilliant economist and a fine writer. He could demystify economics as no one else could, and he could produce articles of outstanding quality and clarity at top speed. We were also on the same liberal wavelength politically, and lunched often at Chez André, the unpretentious but superb restaurant near our offices in the Carlton Centre.

George Palmer had a formidable reputation both as an intellectual and as an editor. He too was a liberal. He had no truck with notions that a financial paper should stick to business and economics and avoid politics, though many people thought that. There were of course quite a lot of conservative writers on the *FM*, and some of them thought the paper had become too 'political' – later starting *Finance Week* in opposition to us. Palmer occasionally toned down some of my articles, but otherwise he allowed me as much freedom as I could reasonably have wished for. We were all proud to be working for him, and the atmosphere on the *FM* was as intellectually stimulating as Oxford tutorials. I was permitted also to accept speaking invitations around the country.

We worked under pressure but also had plenty of fun. I would often chain-smoke my way through a box of Ritmeester Juniors at home until the small hours of Wednesday morning bashing out a leader on my Hermes Baby typewriter for a deadline a few hours later. After putting the paper to bed late on Wednesday night we would repair for dinner at the Koffiehuis in the adjoining Carlton Hotel. Except for an editorial meeting on Thursday morning invariably followed by a long liquid lunch

While on the Financial Mail. *My time at the* FM *in the 1970s gave me the chance to chronicle the National Party's attempts to reconcile the irreconcilable – economic necessity and political ideology.*

at Chez André, the rest of the week would be a write-off so I usually found myself cramming a week's work into the first three days of the following week. The *FM* normally ran three leaders each week, and one week I pulled off a hat trick by writing all three of them.

Given its prestige, the *FM* could not easily be banned. But sometimes when I wrote elsewhere what I'd written in the *FM*, the publication was banned. One student newsletter was banned partly because my contribution was found by the Directorate of Publications to be in character with my 'somewhat deviationist articles in that supposedly capitalist weekly on black trade unions'.[4]

My brushes with the security police were limited. On one occasion after visiting a mine compound at City Deep one night without authorisation I was summoned to security police headquarters on the ninth floor of John Vorster Square. The summons had no legal force, but I thought it best to go anyway rather than tempt the police to come and get me. It was obvious that mine security automatically reported any strange visitors to the security police. They seemed satisfied with my explanation that I'd actually driven in by mistake when seeking out some workers in a coal yard who had gone on strike, but then taken the opportunity to look around at the dreadful conditions under which mineworkers were living. On another occasion I was summoned to the ninth floor to explain an article I had sent to the *Sunday Times* in London reporting that the police in Soweto had incited residents of hostels to attack schoolchildren in 1976. I told them that the source of the report was a speech given by Chief Mangosuthu Buthelezi, president of Inkatha Yenkululeko Yesizwe (later renamed the Inkatha Freedom Party). In this, he had lambasted the police. I knew, of course, that the security police controlled my passport, which had been withdrawn in 1972. I was granted a new passport in 1975 to go to France to write a survey for the *FM*, but until about 10 years later my passports were valid for only a year at a time. Every application, Helen Suzman informed me, was referred to the security police for their approval.

Not long after I joined the *FM* I almost landed it in court. *The Guardian* of London had published articles about starvation wages allegedly paid by British firms in South Africa, and these became a talking point in both countries. Palabora Mining Company (PMC), of which Rio Tinto Zinc (RTZ) held 39 per cent, was one of those against which allegations had been made in respect of the wages at its copper mine at Phalaborwa on the western border of the Kruger National Park. PMC had commissioned an independent panel to investigate. I heard that 4 000 copies of their report had been printed, but that the company was trying to stop distribution.[5] One of the members of the panel was Beyers Naudé of the Christian Institute, so I went to see him. He had stacks of the forbidden fruit in his office, and conveniently absented himself for a minute or two to enable me to help myself, which I did.

I wrote it up. *FM* policy was that if you wrote an article criticising somebody you should send or read it to them and give them a chance to reply. I did this. Soon a messenger arrived from a law firm with a demand from PMC that we undertake not to publish. Palmer sent me off to see our attorney, Kelsey Stuart. He briefed Colin Kinghorn and we were due to appear at midnight that same day before Mr Justice Gert Coetzee, from whom the companies were seeking an interdict for breach of copyright. Our defence was to be that copyright was held by Professor Wolfgang Thomas of the University of the Western Cape, principal author of the report. I had been in touch with him and knew that he had no objection to publication. While we were preparing for the hearing, Walter Felgate, a senior official at PMC, came to see us to argue against publication, bringing Beyers Naudé with him. Beyers and I could barely avoid winking at one another as we sat together in the editor's office.

In the meantime, we set up an alternative page of the *FM* in case the interdict was granted and we had to throw my article out. I also tipped off the newsdesk of the *Rand Daily Mail*. At the eleventh hour our attorney phoned to say PMC had abandoned the interdict, so we went ahead with publication, as did the *Mail*, while two Afrikaans newspapers also picked up the story.[6] This of course ensured far greater publicity for whatever PMC was trying to hide. Beyers had asked me to keep him informed. When I rang at midnight to tell him that PMC had abandoned the interdict, he burst out laughing.

A few days later, I saw some men in dark suits going to George Palmer's office and his secretary told me they were from the mining company. This got me worried. I had not been on the *FM* for six months, yet I'd incurred legal expenses and nearly landed us in court. I was not told anything but a few days later came a letter from Palmer promoting me to labour editor and putting my salary up from R350 to R500 a month.

The *FM* was widely read not only in business but also in government. We knew too that it was one of the few papers political prisoners were allowed to read, although apparently Jackie Bosman's striking and often provocative covers were sometimes torn off. Under Palmer and Hatton it was a uniquely powerful platform for liberal ideas. Moreover, as a weekly it gave you time to research your articles more thoroughly than did a daily newspaper with its tighter deadlines. This meant that although the *FM* never hesitated to express forthright opinions, it was able to back them with plenty of hard factual data. 'Seek truth from facts' applied as much there as it did at the Institute.

My time at the *FM* in the 1970s gave me the chance to chronicle the National Party's attempts to reconcile the irreconcilable – economic necessity and political ideology. The NP was simultaneously trying both to loosen and to strengthen apartheid. It was also trying to shift the basis of discrimination from race to nationality. We were relentless in exposing each twist and turn of this saga, both the absurdity and the inhumanity.

Nobody incorporated the contradictions better than John Vorster himself. He had started to relax apartheid in sport with his concession about Maoris in 1967, but in the same year he had tightened up the country's security laws by introducing indefinite detention without trial under Section 6 of the Terrorism Act. Now he relaxed the ban on strikes by African workers[7] and reminded employers that blacks were also 'human beings with souls'.[8] However, he then served banning orders on young whites working in the black trade union movement, among them David Hemson, who had worked with me on the report on contract labour in South West Africa, and Halton Cheadle, who later helped to draft the Labour Relations Act of 1995.[9]

Vorster signalled that Africans could start moving up the jobs ladder, and agreed that they could be trained for higher levels of skill. He reintroduced long-term leases for African householders, and told hotels and theatres they could desegregate. He endorsed a statement condemning racial discrimination, but when the press speculated that he was going to introduce major political reform he slapped them down and trumpeted defiance.

When he promised the party faithful that there would be no majority rule he was greeted with thunderous applause. Did he really believe that? Did his labour minister, Marais Viljoen, really believe that the white workers of South Africa would ensure that the NP would 'govern this country for all eternity'? Vorster seemed to think he could make concessions to reality where he had to, but then seal these off in watertight compartments. Did he ever have a moment of doubt? Did he ever worry that one concession might lead to the next? Perhaps in the end he was just another *après-moi-la-deluge* man.

So, probably, were most of his supporters. As he shed Afrikaner support to the Right, he picked it up among English-speaking whites. Their traditional home was the United Party. However, its increasing fecklessness as the official opposition was no match for the seductive blend of toughness, humour, and pragmatism epitomised by the man I often heard Helen Suzman ironically describe as 'our golf-playing joke-cracking *verligte* prime minister'.

By the end of the 1970s Vorster had been destroyed by what was usually known as 'Muldergate' or the 'Information scandal', when the *Rand Daily Mail*, the *Sunday Express*, and other newspapers exposed his government's secret funding of *The Citizen* newspaper using public money. 'Muldergate' – named after the minister of information, Dr Connie Mulder – was a forlorn attempt to counter the terrible image South Africa earned abroad for its apartheid policies. Did the *FM* contribute to that poor image? The government certainly thought so. *The Citizen* reported the secretary for information, Dr Eschel Rhoodie, as saying that many of the most twisted and poisonous reports on South

Africa overseas were based on reports from our own press, 70 per cent from the *Rand Daily Mail* and 20 per cent from the *FM*.[10] Since the *Mail* published six times a week and ourselves only once, this was quite a compliment to our influence.

Although my beat started off with labour, it soon spread to influx control, forced removals, citizenship, social segregation, and the upheavals in Soweto in June 1976. I drew on this material to write a book on the Soweto upheavals which came out during my time at the *FM*.[11] I spent about six and a half years on the paper, first under George Palmer and then under Graham Hatton after George left in March 1977 for a job on *Business Week* in New York. Graham then resigned the editorship in June 1979 to take up a job in London with Business International. Stephen Mulholland took over from him. By now I was number three on the paper as senior assistant editor. However, Steve and I did not see eye to eye politically, so I resigned a few months after his appointment to become a freelancer. When I resigned, Sheena Duncan of the Black Sash wrote to me that the *FM* 'was so much more than just a business and economic survey' and that it had been responsible 'for initiating much new thinking and for fostering a much greater understanding of the real issues in South Africa'.[12]

Re-reading some of what we wrote at the time makes me realise the extent to which the *FM* was not only engaged in a battle of ideas but also playing a leading role in that battle. We were waging it on two fronts. The first was business. Even though this was our biggest target market, we were critical of business for not taking a much bolder stance on political issues, especially black rights. And we did not hesitate to tell business what it should be doing. With a handful of well-known exceptions, business then was as timid as it is now. Indeed, it is something of a miracle that there is any support at all for the free-enterprise system among South African blacks. Not only was it largely closed to them except as customers and labourers, but business did little to try to persuade the government to open it up. Such criticisms of apartheid as it did voice in public were carefully qualified. And indeed business also practised discrimination over and above what the law required. Even a person as strongly opposed to socialism as Buthelezi said to us that he did not want to hear about the supposed benefits of a free-enterprise system which was closed to blacks.[13]

The second target market for our ideas was government. We knew that they were reading us. They were trying to make all their policies fit together into a coherent ideological and – so they thought – morally justifiable framework. But we didn't let them get away with anything. We exposed all the contradictions. We forced them to look at pictures of some of the horrors and humiliations they were inflicting upon black people. We made use of the violence in 1976 to say that there was no alternative to negotiation, that oppression wouldn't work. We made sure that the views of black leaders were fully canvassed and reported. Even when people and organisations were banned and could not therefore be directly quoted, we quoted people likely to reflect their views. What lent weight to our opinion was our thorough knowledge of the complexities of apartheid laws, our insights into how policies actually worked on the ground, and our ability to deploy telling statistics to back our arguments.

Many years later, in an article written for the *FM*'s fortieth birthday in 1999, Steven Friedman reflected on his time at the paper.[14] He had been there for four years, most of them working under me. I had encouraged him to join the *FM*, and recommended to Palmer that he be hired. Friedman wrote:

> Though the 1970s was a time when most businesses were happily cohabiting with apartheid, the *FM*, journalistically devoted entirely to the concerns of the business community, was often ahead of all other publications both in identifying the costs of apartheid and in taking a stand against it … [Palmer] was a liberal who understood that South African business would be poorly served if the *FM* did not offer it adequate coverage of the

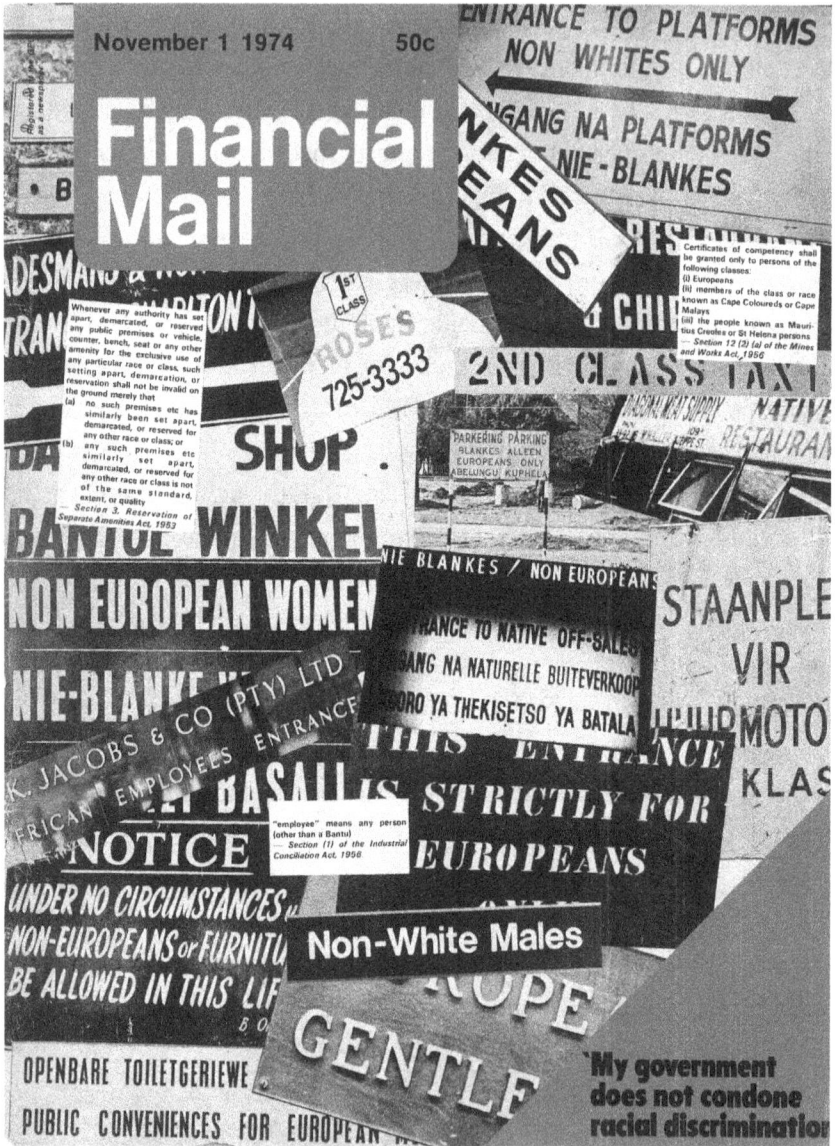

Financial Mail, *1 November 1974: Pik Botha's assertion that the government did not condone racial discrimination was too good an opportunity to miss.*

Photo courtesy *Financial Mail.*

tensions in society – or warn it of their consequences. On many occasions, he seemed well aware that the FM was telling its readers things they did not wish to hear. But he seemed convinced that they ought to hear them.

Friedman also wrote that the scope the *FM* offered for quality labour and political journalism did not rest purely on denouncing apartheid's moral effects. The daily newspapers, even the most liberal among them, routinely misunderstood the nature of government initiatives, but it was 'almost invariably the *FM* which analysed them accurately' and was able often to point out, based on painstaking research, that 'the emperor had no clothes'.

> So the *FM* during the mid-1970s was not just a crusader: it was a source of quality which offered by far the most accurate account of the non-business events of the time. And it was for that reason that left-wing intellectuals or exiled political activists read it – and academics cited it in their articles probably more than any other publication. If you wanted to understand South Africa during those years, you had to read the *FM*.

John Vorster was one of our readers. As we shall see in chapter 6, his office objected strongly to a cover story I wrote on forced removals. He also attacked another cover story, this one ridiculing the speech by RF ('Pik') Botha when he made his debut as South African ambassador to the United Nations in 1974. Addressing the Security Council, Botha declared, 'My government does not condone racial discrimination.' This was too good an opportunity to miss. I sent our photographer out to take photographs of some choice apartheid signs, such as one in a Doornfontein block of flats reading 'UNDER NO CIRCUMSTANCES MAY NON-EUROPEANS OR FURNITURE BE ALLOWED IN THIS LIFT. BY ORDER'. Juxtaposed with Pik's quote and supplemented by several other photographs of signs and quotes from discriminatory laws, this made a wonderful front cover. Inside I wrote:

> Discrimination is at the very heart of our society. It governs every facet of our lives, from the cradle to the grave – and even beyond, since even our cemeteries are racially segregated. It is enforced where we live, where we work, where we play, where we learn, where we go when sick, and on the transport we use. Not only does government condone it; it systematically pursues it, preaches it, practises it, and enforces it. It is enshrined in our constitution, written into our laws, and enforced by our courts.

I then went on to give chapter and verse, commenting that our ambassador's words would be 'immortalised not because of noble sentiments or shining truth, but because they will surely rank among the most breathtaking falsifications ever presented to the world body'. To this Palmer or whoever edited my article added, 'unless they are followed by, and were intended to presage, some real action at home – and fast'.[15]

Even though this was intended to soften what I said, Vorster lashed out. Speaking in Zeerust and Bloemfontein, he said patriotism demanded that one should not write in this way because South Africa was fighting for her very existence. If editors carried on like this, the new press code the government had been discussing with the newspaper owners would not be worth the paper it was written on. Some of these editors appeared to be in rebellion against their directors. Nationalist sources were reported as saying that Vorster was waiting for just one newspaper to overstep the mark and he would proceed with legislation – already drafted – to curb the press.[16] The *FM* ignored the threat.

Later I had a bit more fun with Pik Botha, who had by now become foreign minister. He had said he was not willing to die for an apartheid sign in a lift. 'No one would wish him to die for that,' I said, but 'we should ask him what he is prepared to die for. An apartheid sign over the House of Assembly? Or the Group Areas Act? Or the pass laws? Or the power to lock people up without trial? Or to strip black people of their citizenship?'[17]

Vorster himself used the *FM* to have some fun at the expense of Colin

Eglin, whose Progressive Federal Party, successor to Helen Suzman's Progressive Party, had become the official opposition after the general election in November 1977. We put Eglin on the front cover and published an open letter to 'Dear Colin' giving him some unsolicited advice just before he introduced his first motion of censure during the new parliamentary session in January 1978. Vorster got up to congratulate him on his election to the leadership of the official opposition, and then said he'd read Eglin's speech in the *FM* the previous day. He proceeded to read out bits of my article that Eglin had used in his speech, and commented, 'The whole tone of the article was that of a master giving his servant instructions as to how to act. It shakes the worthiness of a political party in this house to its foundations when a publication like the *Financial Mail* can issue such instructions to its leader.'[18]

Although we had clearly infuriated him on several occasions of which we knew – and no doubt on other occasions of which we knew nothing – it was clear that the prime minister had continued to read us. And we helped to change South Africa. We did so by connecting all the dots to produce profound analysis of policy, telling the truth about its impact even if most whites didn't want to listen, and playing a crusading role in putting forward ideas to extricate the country from the dead end up which the NP was leading it.

CHAPTER 5

Injustice and absurdity

The injustice of apartheid was matched by its absurdity. One of the absurdities was the legal position of African trade unions. Unions representing white, coloured, and Indian workers could be officially registered and were entitled to bargain with employers over wages and other matters. African unions, although never actually prohibited, could not be registered. This despite the fact that by the beginning of the 1970s Africans constituted nearly 71 per cent of the country's workforce.

By the end of the 1970s, however, African unions had won their battle for the same rights as other unions. The *Financial Mail* did more than any other paper to argue the case for statutory recognition. We were also the first paper to support the emerging independent African trade union movement. We took the view that these unions were more likely to be representative of African workers than the 'parallel' unions for Africans that some white unions were trying to establish in order to control African unionisation. I wrote most of the early material on trade unions, but Steven Friedman took over when he joined.

I was fortunate to be given the labour beat just when things were hotting up on that front. In the first few months of 1973, more than 61 000 African workers went on illegal strikes affecting 146 establishments in various industries in Durban.[1] One of the first leading articles I wrote for the *FM* argued that the law prohibiting strikes by African workers was a 'dead letter'.[2] To general amazement, the labour minister, Marais Viljoen, recognised this and tabled legislation to remove the prohibition, which dated back to 1942. Only a few weeks later I was marvelling that a Nationalist government had legalised African strikes. Who would ever have thought it? It was a liberalising measure totally out of keeping with the normally intransigent response of Vorster's government to any attempts by blacks to rock the boat.

The bill legalising African strikes was on the statute book within a month. However, declared Viljoen, it was not a first step on the road to the recognition of African trade unions.[3] No? The bill proved to be exactly such a step. It had created a new absurdity: African workers would now have the right to strike, but not the right to negotiate. This put the ball into the employers' court. There was no law to stop them from negotiating with African unions, and we urged them to do just that. So did the chairman of the Anglo American Corporation, Harry Oppenheimer.[4] My old friend from Wits, Alan Murray, was working in the industrial relations department at Anglo. So was Bobby Godsell, who later became chairman of AngloGold Ashanti. He and I lunched frequently, and several times he arranged for Oppenheimer to invite me to Anglo for discussions over lunch.

Other businessmen were calling for a lead from the government. But we told them they should rather give a lead to the government by themselves recognising unions.[5] We invited some of the black union leaders to a conference in our boardroom. Getting six black unionists to attend took six phone calls. Finding six employers willing to sit round a table with them and have the proceedings recorded and printed was more difficult. But we succeeded in showing our business readership – and the government – that it was actually possible for black unions and employers to sit round the same table without the skies falling in.[6]

We applauded Raymond Ackerman, chairman of Pick 'n Pay, for saying that 'businessmen should stop hiding behind the government's skirts in failing to open up opportunities for blacks even when they could legally do so'. His own company, however, was among those refusing to recognise Emma Mashinini's Commercial, Catering, and Allied Workers Union.[7]

The *FM* helped mobilise international pressure for the recognition of African unions. We urged American companies to set up a chamber of commerce in South Africa and start addressing union rights for Africans.[8] In 1977 the European Economic Community adopted a code of conduct for European companies in South Africa. Through our connection with Bill Vose, labour attaché at the British embassy in Pretoria, we had a hand in drafting this, particularly its clause that all employees should be free to choose the type of representation they wanted, including unions.[9]

In July of that same year (1977) the government appointed a commission of enquiry into labour legislation under the chairmanship of Professor Nic Wiehahn.[10] The commission reported back at the beginning of February 1979, following which Africans were given the same statutory trade union rights as other workers had long enjoyed. The changes came into effect from 1 October that year. This was shortly after I had left the *FM*, but I kept writing about them for other papers.

The Wiehahn reforms were the most important victory so far against South Africa's racial legislation. It was won firstly by the black unions themselves. It was impossible not to be moved by the determination shown in meetings of workers and shop stewards that I attended. Sometimes a dozen shop stewards would crowd into my office at the *FM* to tell me their side of the story in disputes with employers. Also important in the battle for union rights was that companies started to defy the government and sign agreements with unions, although they sometimes did so only after unions demonstrated shop-floor support during strikes. Within 10 years of the outbreak of strikes in Durban in 1973 at least 200 agreements had been signed or were being negotiated between unions and employers.[11] After a 10-year battle, black trade unionism had finally taken firm root in South Africa's factories.[12]

Appropriately, the most important and symbolic break with the past was in mining. I recorded its significance in *The Economist* in June 1983: 'For the first time since gold-mining began in South Africa nearly 100 years ago the pay of black miners has been negotiated by a trade union rather than decided by the mining companies.' The man who signed the agreement with the Chamber of Mines was Cyril Ramaphosa, general secretary of the National Union of Mineworkers (NUM).[13] Few people outside the mining industry had heard of Ramaphosa, but I had been to visit him as he started organising in the early 1980s. When he told me that he'd been given access to some of the mine compounds to recruit members, I was so surprised I didn't believe him. I knew that whatever Anglo or other head offices might have said, making things happen on the mines was unlikely to be easy since mine management could be hostile to 'liberals' at head office. So I rang around to check. Ramaphosa had indeed been given access.

Of those who supported the union struggle throughout the 1970s the *FM* was the most influential. While the unions struggled in the factories, we led the fight in the realm of ideas. Not only did we encourage the unions with moral support and generally favourable publicity, but we helped to soften up both business and government opinion for what we knew, thanks to leaks from some of the commissioners, the Wiehahn Commission would recommend. This turned a momentous step into a non-event.

One of the factors that made it possible for us to support the emerging unions was that their struggle was not violent. Even though companies claimed that workers were intimidated into supporting strikes or joining unions, such coercion was limited. When one employer in Pinetown claimed that a union official had intimidated his employees, I wrote this up in the *FM* and she promptly sued him, calling me as a witness – although the case was dismissed on a technicality. There was little of the violence that has come to characterise strikes in later years in which almost 190 workers have been killed, mostly for failing to support strikes.[14] Unions were also much more cautious about using strike action than is the case today, because strikes did not have the legal protection they now enjoy.

Although some of their officials no doubt had ties with banned organisations, including the South African Congress of Trade Unions (Sactu), which was aligned to the ANC, most new unions were politically non-aligned. This was seen as essential to growth, as Durban was the cradle of the new union movement and Buthelezi its most influential political supporter. However, in 1985 the largest union grouping, the Federation of South African Trade Unions (Fosatu), rebranded itself as the Congress of South African Trade Unions (Cosatu) and threw in its lot with the ANC, the SACP, and Sactu. Sactu had in fact succeeded in establishing itself in some circles abroad as the only true representative of workers in South Africa. On one occasion Alec Erwin, then general secretary of Cosatu and later an ANC minister in the first post-apartheid government, wistfully said to me during a strike, 'We get the solidarity telegram from the international union federation here at our office in Pinetown, Sactu in Lusaka gets the money.'

Although we never discussed it, two friends of mine, Jeannette Curtis and Pindile Mfeti, were probably linked with Sactu. I'd written up their work in running a training organisation for trade unionists in the *FM* and given them some curtains for their office in Bree Street in Johannesburg. Jenny, whom I'd known at Wits, and her six-year-old daughter, Katryn, were killed in Lubango in Angola in 1984 by a letter bomb apparently intended for Jenny's husband, Marius Schoon.[15] Pindile, of whom more in due course, disappeared without trace in 1987.

My job as *FM* labour editor went beyond unions. I also wrote a great deal on the industrial colour bar, a more complicated issue. Five problems had to be overcome. First, the minister of labour had the power to reserve specified jobs for whites. Second, white unions and employers could agree to do the same and get him to proclaim their agreement as legally binding. Third, white workers feared competition from blacks.

Fourth, apartheid ideology held that Africans could not do skilled work in the so-called 'white' area, but only in the homelands. Fifth, prejudice on the part of employers sometimes kept blacks out of jobs even where there were no legal restrictions.

Policy notwithstanding, change was taking place. The Department of Labour reported a shortage of 20 000 artisans and 5 000 apprentices. Shortages meant that more and more African and coloured workers were being employed in jobs that the law barred them from. No doubt many labour inspectors turned a blind eye to violations in exchange for a case or two of Scotch from desperate employers.

It was not easy to keep track of how the colour bar was being eroded. Employers were reluctant to clarify for fear of provoking union or government reaction. Union officials were also reluctant to explain the significance of colour-bar relaxations to which they had agreed. They would sometimes do so only if you promised not to print the detail. Arrie Paulus, leader of the Mine Workers' Union and a man with a reputation as a reactionary, told me his members would kill him if they realised how many parts of their jobs he'd given away in negotiations with employers. Paulus once also told me that apartheid was like a piano: the black and white notes were entirely separate, but when played together could produce perfect harmony. His building in Braamfontein had two lifts, one marked 'whites only' and the other 'multi-racial'. Paulus refused to talk to other newspapers, whether English or Afrikaans, because they always condemned him as a racist. He spoke to us because we merely reported what he said, without passing judgement.

The main factor forcing the erosion of the industrial colour bar was that 'the white, coloured, and Asian labour surplus has finally dried up for the first time in the country's history, and growth will now depend on Africans to an ever larger degree'. In the end 'economic rather than political factors' would be decisive. This turned out to be true, but political factors kept getting in the way. It was bizarre that these factors made it so difficult to tap the country's most important and abundant resource, the people born there.[16]

In October 1973 Prime Minister Vorster made a historic speech to the Motor Industries Federation:

> The government is not prepared to force workers in the white parts of the country to make concessions in respect of traditional work patterns if they feel this would undermine their job security. On the other hand, the government does not stand in the way of changes in traditional work patterns which allow non-whites to move up into job categories for which they will require higher skills and in which they can earn higher wages than previously, provided these changes come about in an orderly fashion and with the concurrence of the trade unions.[17]

In a nutshell, Africans could move up the jobs ladder provided the white unions agreed.

The following year the government budgeted for tax allowances for employers who trained Africans. Training could be done on the job or at industrial training centres that were opened in 1975. But it was limited to operator or semi-skilled jobs. African artisans were still officially a no-no. In fact, the Department of Bantu Education planned to scrutinise training curricula in the new centres to ensure that Africans were not trained for jobs closed to them by the industrial colour bar. This was another example of how the apartheid system was sometimes quite bizarre: here was the department responsible for African education making sure Africans didn't get too much of it.[18]

Even so, progress was being made. In steel and engineering, Africans were moving up the jobs ladder from labouring jobs to middle-level jobs and would soon be knocking on the door of artisan status.[19] Sometimes, as in building, progress was made and then reversed. Coloured workers had been granted permission to be bricklayers and plasterers in 1971, but the permission was withdrawn when the shortage of whites eased.[20]

A building contractor was prosecuted after an inspector caught him using an African to paint a second coat on a wall.[21]

In motor repair, African 'repair shop assistants' could not be trained as mechanics, but they could take over all but the most skilled parts of mechanics' jobs.[22] Coloured and Indian workers were sometimes also barred from certain jobs. Ronnie Webb, general secretary of the Motor Industry Combined Workers' Union, told me, 'It's a case of dog eats dog.' His union, which represented coloured workers, had no choice but to keep Africans out of apprenticeships as long as the white union kept coloured workers out. 'We are inundated with applications from matriculated youngsters whose sole desire in life is to become motor mechanics. But we can't assist them.'[23] These heartbreaking stories, we knew, were the tip of an iceberg. And it was tragic to see coloured workers and their union leaders, themselves victims of apartheid laws, practising discrimination against other victims of these laws.

Since Vorster had insisted that the movement of Africans up the jobs ladder should have the concurrence of the white unions, I went off to see some of their leaders. Wally Grobler of the Artisan Staff Association on the South African Railways (SAR) said, 'The SAR is a vital industry and must be kept going. So blacks have to be upgraded. The black man is knocking at the door all the time. We can't wish him away.'[24] His union had already opened up 1 000 jobs. The Footplate Staff Association on the SAR was engaged in negotiations likely to open up even more jobs.[25] Public sector unions sometimes had a more liberal attitude than some of their private sector counterparts.

One of the latter was Gert Beetge of the 7 000-member Blanke-bouwerkersvakbond (white building workers' union), with whom I used to lunch in Pretoria from time to time. He told me that Vorster was seeking a confrontation with the unions and did not know 'how close the revolt is'. A recent inspection of building sites in Johannesburg had found contraventions of job reservation on 63 per cent of them. 'The jobs free-for-all means the white man is being undermined as never before – by blacks brought in at lower wages.'[26] Beetge told me he had demanded a meeting with the labour minister to protest against the change of policy. He flew to Cape Town, only to be taken by the minister straight to Vorster's office. Vorster had berated him, told him that the changes were necessary in the interests of the country, and that nobody would stand in his way. 'It was then,' Beetge told me, 'that I realised John Vorster and his liberal friends had hijacked the [Afrikaner] Broederbond.' At the time I dismissed this, only to realise later that there was more than a little truth in it.

When it came to apprenticeships and artisan training, even the more flexible unions were against opening up to Africans. The Artisan Staff Association said there was fear of wage undercutting if this were to happen.[27] Lief van Tonder, president of the South African Typographical Union, told me: 'One big grievance of the unions is a tendency to pay blacks only basic prescribed minimum wages, which are much lower than the wages actually paid to white artisans. This is why there is this tremendous resistance among whites to giving blacks a place in the sun. We can only try and educate our members to accept the inevitable. But at the moment any employer who tried to recruit an African apprentice would have unrest on the shop floor.' However, he added, it was a foregone conclusion that in time we would have African apprentices.[28]

The government itself was starting to get a bit tougher with the white unions. Back in 1973 Prime Minister Vorster had said black movement up the jobs ladder would be permissible only if they agreed. Now the government said that if white unions continued to block the training of Africans as artisans, it would override their vetoes.[29] Following further recommendations of the Wiehahn Commission, Africans could now be registered as apprentices, and 491 were so registered by the end of 1981, against zero only two years previously. The apprenticeship route was now open to all, Sam van Coller, director of the Steel and Engineering Industries Federation of South Africa, told me.

There was of course a catch and yet another absurdity: apprentices had to supplement their practical training with theoretical instruction, but the technical colleges were still open only to whites.[30] Moreover, the backward school system for blacks was as serious a problem as the lack of industrial training. The motor industry said there was no longer any bar to the promotion of blacks but most weren't competent to be promoted. The country needed 1 000 new engineers a year but was training only 700. Public service staffing, said the director general of manpower, had gone from 'semi-chaos' to 'complete chaos'. It seemed to me that the skill shortage from financial director to boilermaker would take 'at least a generation' to rectify.[31] Written in 1981, this proved to be wildly, tragically, optimistic. One generation has passed. At least another will be necessary. Maybe longer.

It was of course easy to dismiss white unions as racist reactionaries, which many liberals did. But in the end the 'revolt' against reform of which some of them spoke was largely confined to the ballot box. There its main beneficiary was the Conservative Party launched in 1982 by Dr Andries Treurnicht to resist reforms in the political arena.

Even where there was no white union resistance to erosions of the industrial colour bar, there could be problems. Top Centre, a subsidiary of the Truworth's clothing chain, wanted to appoint Africans to manage its shops near the Johannesburg station and elsewhere catering for African consumers. I went to see Josie Katzenellenbogen, chairman of the company. The African salesmen they'd been putting through managers' courses had been 'terribly enthusiastic' and the company wanted to expand this to all its stores. However, when Top Centre sought registration of its course and attendant tax concessions, they received a letter telling them that it had been decided at ministerial level that the appointment of 'Bantu' shop managers in white areas could not be allowed. This was a golden opportunity to train 'Bantu' to manage shops in the homelands.[32]

The author of this letter was Michiel Botha, minister of Bantu administration and development. It showed that the attitudes of white unions were not the only problem in moving blacks up the jobs ladder; the government itself was an obstacle. This was because Africans in the supposedly 'white' area of the country could be only 'temporary sojourners' there.

Often sheer prejudice on the part of employers kept blacks out of jobs, although the employers claimed they did not themselves object but that their customers would. One five-star foreign-run hotel in Johannesburg did not allow African waiters to take orders in its restaurants, even though there was no law to stop this. White foreigners were used instead.[33]

Social desegregation nevertheless gathered momentum. When I joined the *FM* the only restaurant to which one could normally invite a black person was at the international departures lounge of Jan Smuts Airport. There I used to go with Constance Ntshona, a successful Soweto businesswoman who became a friend. She was a free and lively spirit, who always told me she was not going to let any of 'this apartheid nonsense' get her down. She was the very opposite of the subservience that white township officials expected, and they did not quite know how to handle this self-confident and articulate woman who addressed them by their surnames. She kept a battered station wagon for chores in Soweto, but a Mercedes at a friend's house in Houghton, which she used when she came to dine in the 'suburbs'. She nevertheless decided to emigrate to the US. Shortly before she left, the Carlton Hotel was desegregated and she demanded that I take her to lunch at its plush Three Ships restaurant. 'I just want to see how shocked everybody is going to be, John, when you walk in with this kaffir on your arm!' When Constance died in New York in 2006 at the age of 80, I used my column in *Business Day* to 'salute a truly free spirit'.[34]

Desegregation, though limited, occurred so smoothly that the *FM* wrote that 'white voters are more ready to go along with social integration than is sometimes supposed'. As was invariably the case with limited relaxations of apartheid, removing one barrier merely exposed the one behind it. In 1978 the government decided to open performances at 26 theatres to all South Africans. I went to talk to Michal Grobbelaar, director of the Civic Theatre in Johannesburg. He was not prepared to open his theatre unless his liquor licence was amended to enable him to serve drinks to black as well as white patrons in the theatre bar. So, we said, the government should open the bar as well.

Although I had long since abandoned my theatrical ambitions, not that they amounted to very much anyway, I knew the Civic Theatre quite well. It had been designed by a friend of my father's, Manfred Hermer, who took me on a tour of it. He showed me how everything worked, from set changes to replacing the hundreds of light bulbs above the auditorium. On that stage I saw superb productions of Robert Bolt's *A Man for All Seasons*, Verdi's *La Traviata*, and Prokofiev's *Romeo and Juliet*. I still remember the thrill of seeing *King Kong*, the jazz opera in which Miriam Makeba made her name, in the Wits Great Hall, with music by Todd Matshikiza. When I got my matric results early in 1963, my parents took me as a reward to see *My Fair Lady* with Diane Todd as Eliza Doolittle at the Empire in Commissioner Street. Sunday observance laws kept theatres and cinemas closed on Sundays, but the Alexander Theatre in Johannesburg got round this by running a Sunday club, and we went to plenty of plays. Until it shut most of its theatres, Johannesburg staged lots of fine productions of wonderful plays, many of them with first-rate local actors. Richard Haines, who played the part of Salieri in the brilliant local production of *Amadeus*, could have graced any stage anywhere, including those in London, where I must have seen several dozen plays during my student, *FM*, and Institute days. One of the attractions of these plays was that they weren't about South Africa, so that I could enjoy them as theatre without thinking about politics back home.

On my first trip to London in 1967, I went with my grandmother to a couple of performances at the Aldwych Theatre on the Strand. One of these was of Henrik Ibsen's *Ghosts*, with Peggy Ashcroft in one of the leading roles. Sitting in the row in front of us was a man who worried me throughout the first act. He looked familiar, but I couldn't place him: had he been one of my lecturers at Wits, or a friend of my parents? At the interval a couple of people thrust their programmes at him. That was one way of finding out who he was, so I did the same. It came back with the signature 'Paul Scofield'. He looked so familiar because he'd been on stage the night before in the same theatre playing Macbeth. On that same trip I saw all the great theatrical knights in performances at the Old Vic: Laurence Olivier, John Gielgud, and Ralph Richardson.

Several years later, Pierre and I saw Gielgud and Richardson in Harold Pinter's *No Man's Land,* in which these two great masters performed a verbal duet for two or three hours. We later saw Gielgud at the age of 90 in one of the Shaftesbury Avenue theatres. Part of the marvel of these theatres – and of theatres anywhere – is the sheer professional mechanics of it: great names appearing night after night as part of their job. To see Alan Rickman, or Alec Guinness, or Joan Plowright, or Maggie Smith, or Derek Jacobi, or Vanessa Redgrave, translated from global celluloid onto a few planks right there in front of you in an ancient theatre giving a flawless performance each time never fails to excite. The finest production of *Hamlet* I ever saw had Daniel Day-Lewis in the title role.

But part of the attraction of London theatres is that there's so much great acting talent at work every night on the part of people you've never heard of and who have probably never been in front of a Hollywood camera. Some who have been in front of cameras with great success have in my view failed on the stage: Charlton Heston in *The Caine Mutiny* was so wooden I could not understand how he got the part in the first place. Fortunately, we experienced only a few other duds. We were with our friend Peter Farthing at the theatre in the Barbican for a Royal Shakespeare Company *King Lear.* The seats had cost a fortune but at the first interval we looked warily at one another with a common unspoken thought: do we really need to endure this dreadful production a moment longer? No! We wasted the money for the tickets but that's no reason to waste the rest of the evening! So it was out of the theatre, into a taxi, and soon tucking into roast beef and Yorkshire pudding at Simpson's-in-the-Strand, preceded by their excellent martinis.

Two things stand out about our most recent visit to Shaftesbury Avenue. One was that we made a mixup with the bookings and were expecting to see Schiller's play *Mary Stuart.* Instead I was disgusted to find that we were confronted with *Mary Poppins.* It was one of those Disney productions where no expense is spared, including getting Mary Poppins to float around the auditorium hanging from her umbrella: it was enchanting. The following night we saw RC Sherriff's celebrated *Journey's End,* set in a trench on the Western front in the First World War. This had a young woman in a nearby seat weeping most of the way through, perhaps a more appropriate reaction to this play than anything else.

We went to a number of magnificent concerts in London and Amsterdam. Once in the latter city the main work was Shostakovich's fifth symphony played by the Leningrad Philharmonic. After its powerful great finale the audience demanded an encore. When the orchestra struck up a Boccherini minuet the audience burst out laughing as they could scarcely believe that the musicians who had deafened us with the Shostakovich could play anything as delicate as the Boccherini. This concert was also memorable in that the conductor announced that while it was being given Leningrad was changing its name back to 'St Petersburg'. But our greatest musical experience was a visit to Leipzig in 2011 for a Gustav Mahler festival on the centenary of the great composer's death. All 10 of his symphonies, one each night, were played by orchestras flown in from around the world, among them the New York Philharmonic, the London Symphony Orchestra, the Royal Concertgebouw from Amsterdam, the Bavarian Radio Symphony Orchestra, the Vienna Philharmonic, the Tonhalle-Orchester Zürich, and the Staatskapelle Dresden, which had been founded in 1548.

We were also loyal supporters of the Johannesburg Philharmonic

Orchestra throughout its short life from 2000 to 2015. Exactly why the JPO folded has never been fully explained. But it put on some wonderful concerts, playing many of the usual favourites but also plenty of lesser-known and more adventurous works. Conductors and soloists came from many different countries, and, judging by their names on the programmes, so did many members of the orchestra. Sitting in the Linder Auditorium during some of these concerts, it always struck me that music was the greatest international language. Here were a Japanese piano soloist on a German piano, an American conductor, and a Bulgarian orchestra leader producing magical sounds written by a Finnish composer, with black and white South Africans scattered throughout the orchestra all following the same composition but without being able to understand each other's languages. One of the most memorable concerts was a performance of Handel's *Messiah*, using three different choirs. Each part of the libretto was translated into one or other of South Africa's 11 official languages. That made the occasion as exciting as one many years earlier in a Royal Albert Hall packed to the rafters.

CHAPTER 6

A permit for everything

Although I generally avoided plays with an overtly South African political theme, one we did see was *Sizwe Banzi is Dead*. This was written by Athol Fugard in conjunction with the two actors who played the leading roles, John Kani and Winston Ntshona. Its first performance was in 1972, and we saw it in the church hall at St Martin's-in-the-Veld in Rosebank, Johannesburg, which was a venue open to all races. The play had been inspired by Fugard's experiences as a clerk in a Bantu Commissioner's Court trying offences under the pass laws. I had also witnessed the proceedings in some of these courts. At the time we saw the play I was working at the Institute combing police reports for information on prosecutions and sentences for pass law violations.

I knew about these laws from an early age. The people shot down at Sharpeville in 1960 had been protesting against them. One night when we lived in Waverley my father went out in his pyjamas with his ceremonial army sword to confront police who wanted to inspect our servants' passes. I'd read up on the influx control system at Oxford. Now on the *Financial Mail* I was writing about how the pass laws were used to enforce that system. Today it would be called ethnic cleansing. Its purpose was to consolidate white political power. These laws were thus the linchpin of the entire apartheid edifice.

Influx control had a brutal logic to it. The idea was to keep the number of Africans in the 'white' areas to the minimum compatible with the needs of employers. This would prevent whites from being outnumbered by too great a margin. Influx control had two prongs. One was to ensure that Africans already in the cities were actually needed for work there, preferably without family members. The other prong was to limit the number of Africans moving from the homelands to the cities to the bare minimum. If they moved to town or to a white farm or to a mine they could do so only as 'migrant workers' on year-long contracts and they could not bring spouses or children with them.

Shortly after becoming prime minister in 1958, Dr Verwoerd had predicted that the flow of Africans to the cities would be reversed by 1978. A Nationalist minister, Blaar Coetzee, had promised to ensure that this was accomplished.[1] Few people had taken the idea seriously, but I made use of Institute research to show that the proportion of the African population living in 'white' areas had dropped from 63 per cent in 1960 to 54 per cent in 1970. 'It's clear,' I wrote, that the government is in 'deadly earnest'.[2]

The overriding idea was that the 87 per cent of the country outside the 10 ethnic homelands defined by the Land Acts of 1913 and 1936 was the 'white area'. Africans there were only 'temporary sojourners' who would 'return' to the homelands once their labour was no longer required in the 'white' area. Their families, or those too old or sick to work, were 'superfluous appendages'. Of course, most of the people living and working in the supposedly 'white' area were not whites but Africans. The official term was 'prescribed' area. However, the *FM* often referred to this 87 per cent of the country as the 'common area'. This was to signal our view that describing it as 'white' was misleading. But we also wanted to show that we regarded that part of the country as the homeland of everyone, not just the whites. By choice of terminology we conveyed our repudiation of the whole nefarious design to balkanise the country. Later at the Institute I ensured that all our population figures included Africans who had lost their South

African citizenship, even though official data excluded these millions of people.

Administration of the influx control system needed an army of bureaucrats all over the country, usually headed by a regional 'Bantu affairs commissioner'. Enforcement required the police. Every African above the age of 16 was required to carry a 'pass', officially known as a 'reference book'. This was an internal passport indicating what rights of residence or employment you had. You were required to produce it on demand to the police, who would inspect the various rubber-stamps inside it – just like a visa in a passport, except that this didn't happen only at border posts but at your home or place of work, on the street, at the bus stop, or wherever the police chose to accost you.

Most prized stamp of all was one showing you had been born in the prescribed area. Continuous lawful residence there for 15 years, or continuous lawful employment there for one and the same employer for 10 years, were other prized qualifications. Lower down on the scale was a stamp indicating your one-year employment contract as a migrant worker. The relevant qualifications were set out in Section 10 of the Bantu (Urban Areas) Consolidation Act of 1945.

To obtain the relevant stamp you had to produce a birth certificate, or proof of residence, or proof of employment. If you didn't have the right stamp you were liable to arrest and 'endorsement out' to one or other homeland. In other words, you could be deported in your own country. A friend described one day how she'd visited the main pass office at 80 Albert Street in Johannesburg to obtain the right stamp for someone. An official on duty called to a colleague, '*Ag*, please, get my Section 10 stamp out of my handbag'. This summed it all up: an African's entire life was governed by a rubber stamp that a white bureaucrat kept in her handbag.

The pass laws got so much bad publicity that the Nationalists were starting to feel guilty, or perhaps just embarrassed. Every time a new minister was appointed he would promise to see what he could do about them. One example was Punt Janson, deputy minister of Bantu administration, who sprang to national prominence when he promised to 'humanise' the pass laws. Shortly after I joined the *FM*, he said he was willing to look at suggestions as to how to counteract 'whatever evils' they might contain. Pass arrests were then averaging 1 690 a day.

The problem was not how 'humanely' the pass laws were implemented, however, but that they existed at all. The Black Sash had produced a study based on reports from the women who ran its advice offices in Johannesburg, Cape Town, and Durban in efforts to assist people who fell foul of these laws: 'In terms of the law, Africans need permits to seek work, to work, to reside, to rent a house, to live with a husband or wife, to have their children living in the same house, to visit relatives for a weekend, to change jobs, to move to another place, to be on the streets after curfew where this applies, to obtain a pension. A black man can only be born and die without a permit from the white authority.'³

A few years later we published an attack on the pass laws from an unusual quarter, a former chief magistrate of the Transkei and Bantu affairs commissioner for the Northern Transvaal, Vic Leibbrandt. He and my father had been friends since their schooldays and he was now retired:

> No amount of influx control legislation has succeeded in keeping Africans from seeking and obtaining work in cities throughout the Republic ... Most of the people coming in from the homelands are law-abiding citizens. If a man has not obtained the necessary documents to look for work, I don't think it's right that he should be put into prison for a technical offence.⁴

The fact that pass offices were the first buildings to be destroyed in the riots in Soweto in 1976 showed how Africans hated these laws, Leibbrandt concluded. Perhaps some people in the government were beginning to realise this. A business delegation reported back after a meeting with the minister of justice, Jimmy Kruger, towards the end of

1976. Kruger – the man who later said he had been 'left cold' by Steve Biko's death in police custody – had told them that failure to carry a pass should not be a criminal offence. He referred to Africans who spent the greater part of their lives in prison because they did not have passes. Every time they were released they were arrested within a week and thrown back into prison. This was a tremendous burden on the police and the country. Kruger had evidently suggested that convicted pass offenders should be given the choice of jail or signing a contract to go to a training centre for a year.[5]

Kruger's views did not stop his policemen from staging pass raids. I witnessed one of these a few days after Soweto exploded in June 1976 when I went one afternoon to visit Graham Hatton at his home in Craighall, Johannesburg. As I got out of my car a young African sprinted past hotly pursued by two or three policeman. He leapt over Hatton's fence, tore through the garden, and disappeared over the next fence followed by the cops. I couldn't believe my eyes. Soweto was in flames, the country perhaps on the brink of revolution, and here were the police hunting down pass offenders in the suburbs. They caught the man, handcuffed him, threw him in the back of the van along with another dozen people, and bolted the door. The van drove off but as it pulled up at a stop sign a short way up the road, I ran after it and unbolted the door. The detainees leapt out and disappeared. So too did I, fearing that the police would grab me for helping prisoners escape.

Making use of Black Sash material, I sought an interview with Dr Piet Koornhof, whose doctorate I had admired at Oxford and who was one of the ministers responsible for the pass laws. No response to my request. So I telexed the draft of my article to him in Pretoria, with a warning that we would be publishing within the next few days, and that if he wanted to get the government's views into the *FM*, this was his last chance. Hardly had the telex been transmitted than my phone rang, with Koornhof on the line: 'Hell, man, I had to cancel all my appointments to read your blerry article and that Black Sash book.'

It didn't help. The government stepped up enforcement. The president of the Black Sash, Joyce Harris, later told me that the organisation's advice offices 'present an endlessly repeating kaleidoscope of broken families; of husbands begging for the comforting presence of their wives and children; of endorsements out of the urban areas to homelands which are often totally unfamiliar to those being sent there; of evictions from houses; of often fruitless endeavours to obtain permits – work permits, housing permits, living permits; of desperate struggles to acquire the basic rights of family life and the freedom to seek and accept employment'.[6]

Removal to one or other of the homelands was another aspect of the overall policy of limiting the numbers of Africans in the common area. Whereas pass inspections were directed at individuals, the removal policy was directed at entire communities. In the first place, as many Africans as possible would be moved from the common area to one or other of the homelands. Secondly, the homelands would then become constitutionally separate states from the rest of South Africa. Their 'citizens' would thereupon cease to be South African citizens. Both forced removals and the policy of stripping people of their South African citizenship received plenty of coverage in the *FM*. We did everything we could to unmask this wicked absurdity.

My first article on forced removals followed a visit to the Charles Johnson Memorial Hospital at Nqutu, some 80 kilometres from Dundee in what is now KwaZulu-Natal. After Robert Birley had delivered a lecture on a return visit to Wits in August 1970, he and Elinor were looking for somebody to drive them around the country. Back home from Oxford during the long vacation, I volunteered. The Wits SRC hired a car for us and off we set. One place where we stopped was Charles Johnson, a mission hospital established and run by two other quite remarkable people, Anthony and Maggie Barker. One of the other guests that night was Alpheus Zulu, the first African Anglican priest to be made a bishop. The Barkers were facing a crisis: the colour-blind institution they had created had been ordered to segregate its staff dining room and other quarters. Although the Barkers had been in South Africa since 1945, this was the last straw and they wanted to return to England rather than comply. Bishop Zulu and the Birleys urged them to stay, and Anthony Barker commented that God must have sent him the bishop that night to tell him what to do. They stayed.

The hospital was full of malnourished babies, which was what took me back there three years later for the *FM*. I wrote a cover story on mass removals. My article painted a picture of the conditions in which resettled people, having lost their previous sources of income, now lived in what later became known as 'dumping grounds'. And of course many babies ended up in cots at Charles Johnson. Malnutrition there was not just a misfortune or a tragedy: it was the predictable result of the forced removals policy.

On the cover of the *FM* we put a colour photograph by David Goldblatt of one of the children with wide staring eyes, distended tummy, and rib-cage clearly visible. The article – entitled 'The wasted people' – was designed to shock, and it did.[7] My title was a deliberate echo of *The Discarded People*, Father Cosmas Desmond's pioneering book on forced removals published some 10 years earlier. He, of course, had been banned.

The *FM* was printed overnight on Wednesdays and copies were delivered to us in time for our weekly editorial meeting on Thursday mornings. We took these with us as we trooped into George Palmer's office in case there was anything he wanted to discuss. On this particular Thursday, most of my colleagues turned their copies over so that they could look at the Fleur du Cap advertisement on the back rather than the baby on the front. A couple of readers wrote in to complain: why didn't we tell the world that South Africa was the only African state with a free press and an independent judiciary, there would be racial and tribal warfare if the whites were overthrown, and so on.

But there also came a letter from Dr Piet Riekert, economic adviser

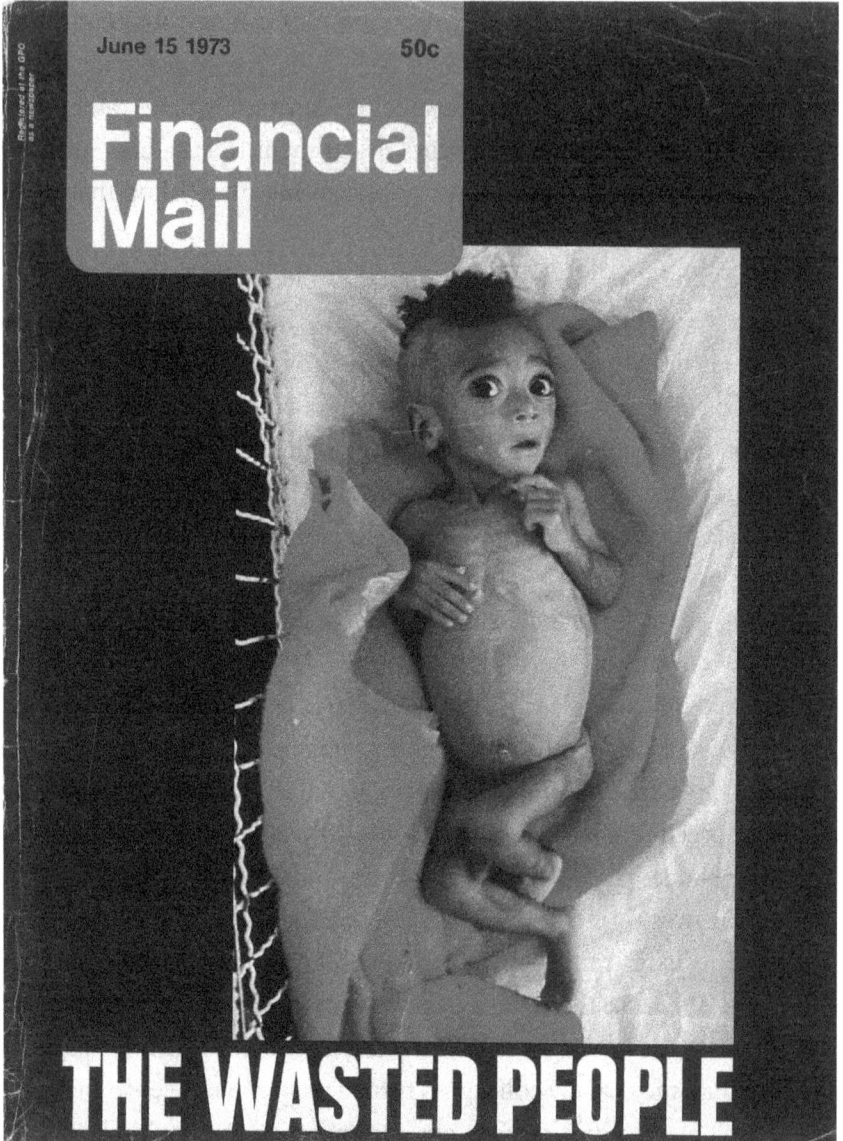

The Financial Mail's *cover, 15 June 1973: we did all we could to unmask both the absurdity and the wickedness of forced removals.*

Photo courtesy *Financial Mail.*

to the prime minister. It said that in view of the *FM*'s 'wide national and international circulation' the cover picture was 'irresponsible and most unpatriotic' in stirring up emotions. 'I am sorry George,' he admonished Palmer, 'I do not like this approach at all.'[8] Palmer called me in and asked what I proposed. I said that if the government didn't believe us, we should take them to see for themselves. So Palmer, Hatton, and I went over to Pretoria to meet Riekert. He brought along Braam Raubenheimer, who, as deputy minister of Bantu development, was the man responsible for forced removals.

Unfortunately, despite lengthy negotiations nothing came of our proposal to take them around the country to show them the results of their handiwork. Raubenheimer's officials unilaterally imposed restrictions on the joint investigating team we were setting up. These would have handicapped its operations. So we just pressed ahead with further exposés of forced removals. Riekert might have had the ear of – or been the voice of – John Vorster, but that was not going to stop us.

Looking back on these events, I realise just how brave Palmer was. Articles of this kind must have offended not only the government but most people in business as well. I wrote them, but the ultimate responsibility was his. However, it was clear that if you stood your ground the government sometimes backtracked. No doubt it got its way half of the time not by legislating but by bullying. The present government is much the same.

Eleven years after our meeting with John Vorster's economic adviser, I had the opportunity after joining the Institute to bring the government's forced removals policy to the attention of another prime minister, Margaret Thatcher. British diplomats asked me if there were any issues that Mrs Thatcher should raise when she met Mr PW Botha at Chequers in June 1984. Hammer him on forced removals, we said, and she did. As Robin Renwick, later British ambassador in South Africa, subsequently wrote, the South African state president got a 'forthright lecture' on the subject.[9]

A year after the Charles Johnson article I wrote another story on removals.[10] This was about 'The nowhere city'. The plan was to move 48 000 Africans from the Albany district (in which Grahamstown is situated) 45 kilometres away to a place called Committees Drift on the Ciskei side of the Great Fish River in the Eastern Cape. Here, according to Dr Piet Koornhof, at the time deputy Bantu administration minister, the government planned not only an industrial area but the 'finest black city in Africa'. Plans were at an advanced stage, so much so that 'many Bantu have expressed their appreciation to the government'. With Father Edmonstone, a local Jesuit priest, as my guide, I went to Committees Drift to take a look. There we found 'a dirt road, four goats, a barbed wire fence, and a police station on the right bank of the river (since evacuated in the floods)'. We put a photograph of this bleakness on the cover.

Among the people to be removed were the inhabitants of Fingo Village in Grahamstown. This was one of the few African townships where people actually still owned their property. Some of them showed me their carefully preserved title deeds signed by the governor of the Cape, Sir George Grey, 'In the name of Her Majesty Victoria'. They explained how officials were now trying to trick them into surrendering these ancient freehold documents to be replaced by modern but temporary occupation permits. Steve Biko, who had been banned and banished to the Eastern Cape, took me to visit various other dumping grounds, including some – one called 'Welcomewood', for example – whose existence Minister Raubenheimer denied.

The article on Committees Drift also brought a letter from a reader, this time one praising us: 'When a national journal of the calibre of the *FM*, whose chief concern is with business and finance, can at the same time show an example of so much concern with justice and decency as appears from your leader on The Nowhere City, it must surely be one of the most hopeful signs for the future of this unhappy land to appear in recent times.'[11]

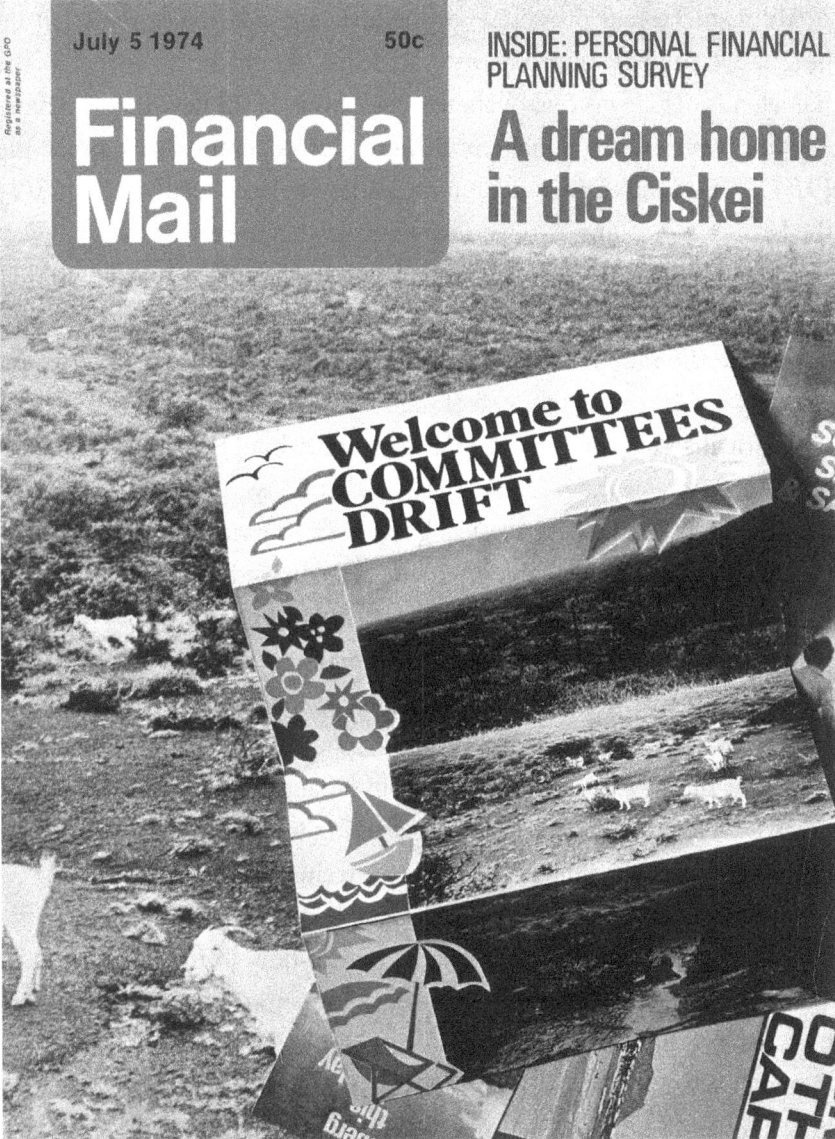

'The nowhere city': Financial Mail, 5 July 1974. *Piet Koornhof promised to build the 'finest black city in Africa' on this site in the Ciskei.*

Photo courtesy *Financial Mail.*

Although he had promised to liberalise the pass laws, Punt Janson had also said that 'unproductive' Africans should be removed to the homelands. This was one of the key functions of 22 new Bantu Affairs Administration Boards that were coming into operation as I joined the *FM*. Covering the entire common area, they replaced local authorities as the bodies controlling African townships in that area.

Right from the start we suspected that the boards would be used to step up deportations to the homelands. Kallie van der Merwe, chairman of the board on the East Rand, told me in his office in the HF Verwoerd Building in Germiston that one of their aims was that economically inactive Africans would in time disappear from 'white' South Africa. Some 300 000 Africans under his board's jurisdiction were likely to be moved to homelands, where better housing and social services, as well as political rights, would be available to them.[12] He showed me a map. Africans from the townships under his jurisdiction would be shifted to Ekangala, a new township in the KwaNdebele homeland some 80 kilometres away to the north-east near Bronkhorstspruit, a small farming town on the railway between Pretoria and Maputo. They would then commute to their jobs on the East Rand every day in Japanese-style bullet trains. All this was told to me by an engineer speaking with a straight face. Some of the removals happened. The Japanese trains didn't.

Not to be outdone, the Cape Midlands board said 'we must curb the flow to the white areas and create a counter-flow to the homelands ... We have room for productive elements, but not for superfluous people who are parasitic on us and especially on their own friends and relations. Such people we will, where possible, repatriate to their own homelands.'[13]

'Repatriate' was pregnant with meaning. It implied that Africans in the Western Cape were not in their own country but in a foreign one. Use the term often enough, get everyone else to use it, and eventually they have implicitly bought into the notion that Africans were no more entitled to be in the Western Cape than were real foreigners. Removal of citizenship was indeed to become the apogee of grand apartheid. But 'repatriation' also implied that the people to be repatriated to their own homelands had somehow originally come from there. In many cases this was not true. They had been born in Johannesburg or Cape Town or any of the other towns in the common area. They were as much South Africans by birth as was any white person. Yet official policy regarded them as superfluous parasites.

The Western Cape's repatriation programme for 'parasitic' human beings was the most notorious. The *FM* and I made sure of that. The Black Sash and the Institute shared premises in Cape Town. Noël Robb, who was involved in both organisations, drove me to Crossroads and other shack settlements on the sand dunes of the Cape Flats across the N2 motorway as it passed DF Malan Airport. David Russell, a local Anglican priest who later became bishop of Grahamstown, also took me to visit people living in shacks. They described how officials were trying to get rid of them. Sometimes the shacks were torn down. At other times, at a place called Werkgenot, they were set alight as their owners fled in terror. Some shacks were raided when men were at work during the day; their families were then put on trains to the Transkei and Ciskei homelands, whence they had supposedly come. Grassy Park, Modderdam, Kraaifontein – the pattern was the same. Blind people, epileptics, infants suffering from gastroenteritis – it made no difference. Many of those attacked fled into the bushes. I wrote all this up for the *Sunday Times* in London, which headlined the story 'Into the shanties comes government by bulldozer'.[14] On one occasion some or other minister was accused in Parliament of bulldozing shacks, and protested that they hadn't bulldozed them, but used a front-end loader.

I went to see the chairman of the Cape Peninsula Bantu Affairs Administration Board, a retired police commissioner called Brigadier van der Westhuizen. Families living lawfully in the area would be provided with housing, he told me, but the removal of 'illegal' people would definitely go on. If the people at Crossroads were allowed to stay, others would come in and there would be more squatter camps.

The *FM* conceded that many of the shack dwellers might be 'illegal'. But the real offender was the law itself. Women whom I'd interviewed in their shacks 'seemed quietly determined to stay with their husbands'. And indeed many of those put on trains to the Transkei and Ciskei had got off at the first station and made their way back to Cape Town.[15]

Van der Westhuizen was proved correct. More and more people did flock to Cape Town. Vast shack settlements are still there. They moved to the city because it offered better prospects than the impoverished homelands. But the *FM* was also proved correct. We predicted that what the government decided to do about Crossroads – and the other Cape Town squatter camps – would be a signpost to South Africa's future. So it turned out. In 1979 Crossroads was in fact reprieved.[16] On a visit some years later, described in chapter 8 of this memoir, I discovered that the raids and demolitions were coming to an end and some of the shack dwellers were being allowed to stay put. The government had capitulated in the face of their determination, partly, I suspect, because of the terrible publicity it got for itself with the help of the *FM* in articles written by our Cape editor, John Stewart, and by me.

In the meantime ethnic cleansing elsewhere went on apace. Where the putative homeland was not too far away, Africans relocated there from townships in the common area would commute daily or weekly to work in the common area.[17] They were designated as 'frontier commuters'.

I went to interview Ferdie Hartzenberg, senior deputy minister at the Department of Co-operation and Development. 'Co-operation and Development' was the new name for what had previously been 'Plural Relations', and prior to that 'Bantu Administration and Development', and prior to that 'Native Affairs'. As the policies got worse, so the government gave the responsible department more innocuous names. Bantu Administration and Development had never been a good choice, because we naturally abbreviated it to BAD, so that the minister became the BAD minister and all his officials BAD officials. No wonder they changed the name. The government had also set up a Bureau for State Security. This everyone abbreviated to BOSS.

Dr Hartzenberg – who later became leader of the Conservative Party – explained the logic to me. First priority was that Africans should live and work in their homelands. Where there were too few homeland jobs, they should commute daily from the homelands to jobs in the common area. Where distances for a daily commute were too great, they would be accommodated in hostels in the common area as migrant workers. The government, he was keen for me to realise, adhered to internationally accepted standards in applying the commuter policy. Under these rules workers could be expected to travel one and a half hours to and one and a half hours from work each day. With present roads and transport in South Africa, this meant 70 km. However, better roads and faster trains could lengthen the distance without extending the time. He had visited France, where people were commuting daily between Paris and Lyon by fast train in less than one and a half hours. What he did not mention was that his government planned to force settled communities to become long-distance commuters.

Eight more Sowetos would be needed by the year 2000, and the best place to build them would be in the homelands. This would help achieve the government's objective of having 72 per cent of all Africans living in the homelands by that year (against only 47 per cent in 1970).[18] Frans du Randt, chief commissioner for the Witwatersrand, told me that a daily commute between Johannesburg and Bophuthatswana would involve no more than two hours' travelling time.[19]

'Grand apartheid', as it was sometimes called, was thus a mixture of fantasy and cruelty. Although between two and three million forced removals took place, so did 17.12 million arrests under the pass laws between 1916 and 1981, according to official statistics. Africans, as I pointed out many years later in my book on *South Africa's Silent Revolution*, were simply voting against these laws with their feet.[20]

How was it possible that so many people failed to comply with the pass laws, despite all the raids, arrests, fines, and prison sentences? I put this question to Sheena Duncan, who headed the Black Sash advice offices. The suffering, she said, was worth it: illegal employment was the only way to feed one's children. There were so few jobs in the homelands that people with starving children had no means of survival except illegal employment in so-called white areas. Convicted people would simply go back to work when they were released, and wait for the next time. Dr Riekert confirmed this: illegal employment was a big problem. And Dr Koornhof had the solution. Hit the employers as well as the workers. The maximum fine of R100 was not a sufficient deterrent, so anyone employing an African in a prescribed area without permission would in future have to pay R500.

Employers were now joining the ranks of people prosecuted under the pass laws. One had been convicted for taking on 26 unregistered workers when he couldn't find registered people with the necessary skills. Officials told me that admission-of-guilt fines would no longer be accepted from employers with unregistered workers on their payrolls. The Johannesburg magistrates' courts were now hearing 80–90 prosecutions each week.[21]

These developments were part of a radical overhaul proposed by Dr Riekert six years after our meeting with him.[22] Africans who possessed Section 10 privileges would be given even more. They would be able to change their jobs at will. If approved housing was available their families could join them. They could apply for sub-economic housing. They could also buy a house on a 99-year lease. Some of the restrictions on black businessmen would be lifted. Riekert cited research showing that about 1 million men and 500 000 women possessed Section 10 rights. All of these people would be a lot better off. But everyone else would be worse off. As our headline put it, they would face 'laagers round the towns'.[23] The African population would thus be divided into 'insiders' and 'outsiders'. Thanks in part to the heavier fines for illegal employment, the latter would be almost entirely shut out of the urban labour market.

But Riekert's masterly plan for more sophisticated implementation of influx control – a kind of 'neo-apartheid' – turned out to be an emperor without clothes. As we shall see, the system was abandoned only seven years later when PW Botha repealed the pass laws on the grounds that they had become unworkable.

What also doomed the Riekert plan was that the new class of 'insiders' would have no political rights. They would not even have South African citizenship. The process of turning all Africans into foreigners – denationalising them – had been launched in 1970. By the time Riekert published his report it was well under way. Africans were not only being physically removed from the common area to the maximum extent practicable. Every last one of them, whether in the common area or a homeland, was also to be removed from the population register. Statistically, they would cease to exist. Crazy. But the National Party had come to recognise that it could no longer deny Africans the franchise on racial grounds. Dr Verwoerd had been one of the first to recognise that brazen discrimination was unethical.[24] But if all Africans could be turned into foreigners, well, that would be a different story. What country gave foreigners the vote?

This was a diabolical policy. But it was also the last throw of the apartheid dice. Having themselves renounced crude racial discrimination, the Nationalists could not go back there. What would now happen if it was impossible to turn all Africans into foreigners? I made sure that the *FM* reported every twist and turn of the attempts to implement this policy – the horror that overtook people as they realised its cruel implications, and the absurd contradictions it threw up. Given who was reading our analysis, we helped destroy the credibility of the supposedly more ethical policy among the Nationalist intelligentsia.

In terms of the Bantu Homelands Citizenship Act of 1970 all Africans in the country were not only South African citizens but would also become citizens of one or another of the 10 homelands to which they sup-posedly belonged by ethnic origin. This applied irrespective of whether they'd ever been to the homeland in question or had any desire to be linked with it. In due course each homeland would become a constitu-tionally separate and sovereign, independent state. Its supposed citizens would then lose their South African citizenship. Though the latter was an inferior form of citizenship to the South African citizenship enjoyed by whites, it was better than being a foreigner. And most Africans took the view that South Africa as a whole was the homeland of everyone.

On his sixtieth birthday in 1975 Prime Minister Vorster had declared, 'As far as we are concerned, all black people are citizens of one or another homeland. Citizens of homelands who live and work in this country are still citizens of their countries.' Deputy Minister Raubenheimer weighed in that the government saw all Africans in the common area as guest workers. Jimmy Kruger – the man who wanted to stop locking up pass offenders – said all South Africans, black and white, should 'learn to love' separate development 'warts and all'. The *FM* pointed out that half the Zulus did not live in their nominal homeland, and that only about 2 per cent of the supposed citizens of the QwaQwa homeland actually lived there.[25]

But the government started pressurising Africans into taking out citi-zenship of one or another homeland. They were offered 30-year leases over their houses in Soweto and elsewhere if they took out homeland citizenship. Minister Michiel Botha said Africans who identified them-selves with their own black nation would be more welcome in the white area than those who denied it. They would get more privileges, includ-ing preference in jobs, housing, having dependants with them, freedom of movement, hospitalisation, transport, schools, sport, etc. My mind boggled at a policy which granted privileges to people born and bred in a country only if they were willing to make themselves foreigners. And I quoted Desmond Tutu, whom I'd been to interview shortly after his appointment as dean of Johannesburg: 'Dear white South Africans, we want you to have a stake in South Africa and remain here so that we can go forward together in a united South Africa, not one that is balkanised into unviable bits of things that are the figment of somebody's imagination.'[26]

But the government was not to be deterred. The Transkei became a separate state in 1976. Thereupon all Xhosa-speaking South Africans lost their South African citizenship and became citizens of the Transkei instead. I described some of the resulting alarm and panic. A Xhosa Soweto resident who went to get a travel document for his wife found a stamp in it declaring her a prohibited immigrant. Another Soweto woman who applied for a passport was told to get one from the Transkei. People who applied for pass-books were being told to get Transkei travel documents instead. A man who went to register as a work seeker found a huge 'T' stamped across his pass and he was told he would lose his urban residence qualifications if he didn't get a Transkei document.[27]

One of those deported to the Transkei – probably the first to suffer this fate – was Pindile Mfeti, a kinsman of Thabo Mbeki, whom he apparently used to meet in Swaziland from time to time.[28] He had worked in the archives department at the Institute before joining the Industrial Aid Society, the training organisation for black trade unions on which I'd reported. He was repeatedly taken into detention, roughed up, and released after a few days. He made periodic trips to Botswana, I suspected to meet banned organisations, but he never volunteered any information about these trips and I never questioned him. In 1976 he was detained for 366 days without trial. He would frequently lose consciousness after various kinds of torture and assault, waking up several days later only for the whole process to start again. According to a memoir by his great friend Colin Smuts,

He said the whole interrogation would sometimes gain a momentum of its own and they would go crazy, like wild animals, pounding you, not caring whether they killed you or not. We concluded that those were the circumstances which killed Biko. He said it was surprising more people weren't killed under interrogation.[29]

After his release Pindile was banned, confined to the magisterial district of Germiston, and put under 12-hour house arrest. I arranged for him to see a doctor with a view to suing the security police for damage to his eardrums arising from assault. However, we were advised that it would be very difficult to pin anything on the police. Pindile found it impossible to take up job offers because the security police intimidated prospective employers. I knew Tony Bloom of Premier Milling because he had worked at my father's law firm, so I went to him for help. He arranged a job for Pindile in Johannesburg, but the security police refused Pindile permission to vary his banning order to travel to work there.[30] Bloom then gave him a job in Germiston, but the banning order was again amended, this time confining him to Alberton, so that he couldn't travel to Germiston to take up the job.[31] Helen Suzman tried to get Jimmy Kruger to vary the order, but Kruger wrote to her that Pindile had been engaged in 'subversive activities', was a Transkei citizen, and was therefore being deported.[32] Needless to say, he had never been put on trial for these 'subversive' activities.

One day in September 1978 I got a panic-stricken phone call from Pindile's family in Katlehong. Police had arrived at their house, loaded up his possessions, and shipped him to Butterworth in the Transkei, and his family with him. We exchanged letters from time to time and I tried to help him in various ways as he served his articles with a local law firm and studied via the University of South Africa. He was eventually allowed to make short visits to Johannesburg, and he, Colin, and I would party the night away.

Unbeknown to me, because I had no say in selections, Pindile later got a bursary from the Institute and a place at Wits. But the government would not give him a study permit for South Africa. He then got a place at the University of the Transkei. But the Canadian government, which was financing his bursary, refused to pay for it there because it did not 'recognise' the Transkei. This was an absurd position for them to take because it implicitly meant treating the Transkei as a separate country rather than as part of South Africa. But they would not change their mind, even though I once took advantage of a trip to the US to make a detour to Ottawa to try to persuade them to do so. In the end, Pindile got a place at the University of Natal in Durban and finance from the Dutch government to study law there. He enrolled in 1985. In May 1987, however, he disappeared without trace after ringing his wife Ncediwe to tell her he was on his way to a tailor to have some alterations done to a pair of jeans.[33] All the attempts that I and others made to find out what had happened to him proved fruitless.

The *FM* called upon the international community not to recognise the Transkei or any other homeland 'which plunges into the treacherous waters of independence'. Thereby, we said, the process of fragmenting South Africa could be halted. One day the Transkei could return like a prodigal son. We called for support for Chief Mangosuthu Buthelezi, chief minister of the KwaZulu homeland, 'in his refusal to be party to dispossessing black South Africans of their South African citizenship'.[34]

Vorster said he expected all homelands except KwaZulu to take independence within five years. The other supposed Xhosa homeland, the Ciskei, was among those that did. My own domestic servant, Laetitia Ngqiba, who was a Xhosa, now found herself a foreigner in the land of her birth. This meant that we had to go to Germiston to the office of the consul-general of the Ciskei to get her a work permit for South Africa.

In the end, however, only four of the 10 homelands opted for independence. Others could no doubt have eventually been bullied into it. However, since the 5.4 million Zulus in the country outnumbered the 4.5 million whites, there was little point in pursuing the policy if KwaZulu remained part of South Africa. And in 1986 PW Botha's government admitted that the policy of deflecting African political rights into the homelands had failed. However, having let the genie of political rights for Africans out of the bottle, the Nationalists could not now put it back. The only solution was to start talking about the only viable alternative – franchise rights in the common area. A cabinet committee was set up in 1983 to do this. By strategically using his position as KwaZulu chief minister to prevent the homelands policy from coming to fruition, Buthelezi played a key role in destroying it – but not before more absurdities played themselves out.

Among the victims were African businessmen and women. They were barred from trading in the central business districts of the cities, but even within Soweto and other black townships they were subject to numerous restrictions.[35] Now, however, some of the restrictions were going to be relaxed. Africans could thus form partnerships, prohibited until now. But there was the usual catch: if traders wanted to continue their operations they would have to become homeland citizens and if a company was formed each and every shareholder had to become a homeland citizen.[36] Here was yet another example of how a liberalising reform could create a new absurdity.

The same applied to the reintroduction of home ownership in the form of long-term leases. Building societies were willing to lend money to Africans on the same basis as to whites. But the BAD department wrote them a letter pointing out that all township property belonged to the relevant Bantu Affairs Administration Board, and that Africans could buy only the right of occupation. I went off to talk to the building societies, after which I reported one of them as saying, 'So-called ownership only by right of occupancy is pure bullshit. The European in South Africa is fighting for survival. Unless we do something we'll find ourselves in serious trouble.'[37]

This remark was made only a few months after the explosion in Soweto on 16 June 1976 when police opened fire on schoolchildren marching in protest against being forced to study through the medium of Afrikaans. The shooting was the immediate cause of the explosion, but we pointed out that grievances went much further. We put a photograph of Soweto in flames on the front cover, along with a quote from the minister of foreign affairs, Dr Hilgard Muller, speaking in Bonn a week later: 'South Africa is unwilling to make any drastic changes to the broad concept of separate development at a time when this policy is coming to fruition.' I'd written a tough leader, but Palmer put an even tougher introduction on top of it. Again quoting Muller's words, he wrote: 'The fruits of the policy of apartheid are frustration, injustice, and hatred. Among its latest consequences are arson, rioting, and slaughter. If it is continued, the end result may well be revolution. It is a policy which is rejected by the broad mass of the African people. Yet they are being subjected to it with a remorseless insensitivity that can only invite disaster.'[38]

On the night of the explosion Jackie Bosman and I and two other friends jumped into my car to go and see what was happening. We circumnavigated Soweto, but every entrance that we knew was blocked by armoured vehicles. Eventually we found our way in through the adjoining 'coloured' township of Eldorado Park. Soon discretion got the better part of us, mainly because we thought we'd be arrested, and we left.

By the end of the year there had been demonstrations in at least 160 black communities all over the country, and between 5 000 and 6 000 people had been arrested. About 400 were thought to have been detained without trial.[39] When Steve Biko was killed by the police in September 1977, I told the acting editor of the *FM* this was an event of great significance. He disagreed and I went home in despair. But he then rang me and said, 'OK. Do a cover story.' When I wrote this I pointed to the sad truth that Biko's name would become a household word among whites in South Africa only because of his death – which soon led to the imposition of a mandatory arms embargo against South Africa by the United Nations. We called for the government to enter into political negotiations with black leaders, including those banned and detained.[40]

A month later, in October 1977, the minister of justice, Jimmy Kruger, banned the leading Soweto newspaper, *The World*, and its Sunday edition, *Weekend World*, along with the Black People's Convention, which

Biko had founded, and various other Black Consciousness organisations. The Christian Institute and Beyers Naudé were also banned. Graham Hatton and I went over to see Dr Koornhof in Pretoria. We asked him why Beyers Naudé was among those banned. His reply: 'We decided to ban a whole lot of blacks and we banned him because we didn't want to appear to be racist.' *The World* and *Weekend World* later appeared as *Post* and *Sunday Post* but in 1981 they were forced to close by threat of banning.[41]

At the end of November 1977 Vorster won a smashing victory in a general election. In September 1978 he was replaced as prime minister by PW Botha. In mid-1979 it was clear that 'holy war' had broken out among Nationalists. Some thought you could make limited adjustments in policy without undermining the power structure of white supremacy.[42] Others, especially Dr Andries Treurnicht, took the view that apartheid had to be all or nothing. You could not keep the core of white supremacy intact if you started liberalising around the edges. Even superficial changes had unintended built-in consequences which would make them fundamental in the longer term. Sit next to a black to watch a rugby match at Loftus Versveld, and he would end up marrying your daughter and chucking you out of your own parliament.[43]

Wimpie de Klerk, editor of *Die Transvaler* and brother of the man who later became South Africa's last white president, said there was bitter dissent among Afrikaners over certain things. However, there was no dissent over such things as protection of group interests, and say over their own affairs, such as residential areas, schools, facilities, services and institutions. Nor was there any fighting over rejection of a unitary state and political integration.[44]

Not much more than a decade later, however, Afrikaners under his brother's leadership gave up most of this. All the intellectual and political energy they had spent trying to avoid doing so came to naught. In the end what the Afrikaners got during the constitutional negotiations that led to the handover of power to the African National Congress in

1994 was a unitary state with no special group protection for minorities. If ever there was a political leap in the dark, this was it. And, ironically, they had to put their trust in a bill of rights, the rule of law, the separation of powers, and some of the other liberal institutions they had for so long disdained.

CHAPTER 7

Soweto, apartheid, and business

Sympathetic to the militant students and highly critical of the government, the *Financial Mail*'s coverage of the Soweto disturbances soon had me back on various campuses addressing mass meetings. The first was one at UCT on the steps of Jameson Hall, where the other speaker was the Cardinal Archbishop of Cape Town, Owen McCann.

I reminded the audience that Afrikaners had had to fight for their language against people such as Lord Milner. However, Afrikaans had come to symbolise apartheid. And it was against apartheid that the pupils had revolted, rather than Afrikaans itself. The press had exaggerated the extent to which destruction in Soweto and elsewhere had been carried out by so-called tsotsis. There had been logic in the selection of targets: white property, symbols of white authority, and black collaborators with white authority. There had even been debates: should the public library in Dube be burnt as 'white man's property' or saved as a 'place of learning'? Some of the government liquor outlets had been looted by people who wanted drink, but pupils had poured the liquor into the street and shouted, 'Less liquor, more education. We want more schools, not beerhalls.'[1]

Soweto pupils had elected a students' representative council to speak for them. Would the government talk to them or would it ban and detain them as it had banned and detained so many others? Prime Minister

Vorster had arm-twisted his Rhodesian counterpart, Ian Smith, into releasing and talking to black leaders. It was time to practise in South Africa what was preached to Rhodesia. Our government should start talking to black trade unions and the Black Consciousness organisations. It was also time 'to lift all banning orders and release detainees and those men just a few miles from this campus on Robben Island'. I remember looking in the direction of Robben Island as I said this.[2]

The speech formed the basis of a couple of academic papers and articles in both South Africa and Germany[3] and then grew into the book *Soweto: Black Revolt, White Reaction*, which Ravan Press published in 1978. The print order was 700, but the book rapidly sold out and eventually ran into five impressions. It was also published in London by Pluto Press under the title *South Africa: The Method in the Madness*.[4]

I wrote it two fingers at a time in my flat on my Hermes Baby typewriter at night and at the weekends. The book had been inside me since Oxford. All the reading I'd done on how black lives were controlled now helped me understand why Soweto blew up. So did all the work I'd done for the *FM* on influx control and the administration of Soweto and other townships. This background information I supplemented with a 700-page diary, mostly handwritten, recording every incident as reported in as many newspapers as I could get hold of. The doctorate that never got written ended up as a book that made it onto bestseller lists.[5] Many years later a prominent academic who'd been a student at the time told me that my book had encouraged radical white students to oppose apartheid.

I had obtained some of the leaflets distributed in Soweto. The Soweto SRC urged parents and workers to participate in boycotts and stayaways, although some of its leaflets ended by threatening that 'your sons and daughters shall be on the watch out for sellouts and traitors'. There were also anonymous leaflets with instructions on how to make petrol bombs and even crossbows. One called for attacks on whites and on government property and employees. This was denounced by the SRC as seeking to expose parents and workers to bloodshed. I noted on my copy that a 23-year-old man had received a five-year jail sentence under the Terrorism Act for showing it to an employee at the OK Bazaars in Eloff Street and urging him to study it.[6]

One leaflet called for 'massive protests, actions, and demonstrations' in the name of the ANC. A woman received a three-year sentence for photocopying it on an office machine.[7] A second leaflet purporting to come from the ANC said, 'The war is on, so let us take it to the whites right into town. Kill them if you can, burn their buildings, let the trains and their vehicles go up in flames.'[8]

From Dar es Salaam came a message to all units of the ANC in South Africa from that organisation's secretary general, Alfred Nzo. It claimed that the 'vanguard force and the life-blood of our revolution – the black working class – has already flexed its mighty muscle during the current uprising'.[9] This was largely nonsense. Although workers had participated in one or two three-day stayaways organised not by trade unions but by the SRC, the main 'muscle' that had been flexed was murderous retaliatory attacks by migrant workers in hostels, who had themselves been violently attacked for not participating in stayaways of which they had been largely ignorant.[10] These attacks were forerunners of those launched against ANC members by Inkatha supporters 10 years later.

The most interesting paragraph in Nzo's leaflet read as follows: 'Our revolutionary council, consistent with the mood and general expectations of the revolutionary masses inside our country, has been urged to advance its plans and subordinate every bit of its activities to the urgent question of the launching of armed struggle in our country.' This implicitly confirmed that the ANC had had little to do with the revolt. Another ANC document said 'present-day youth lack a sound political direction and leadership'. They should discard their 'go-it-alone' policy and 'seek revolutionary leadership in the ANC'. Above all, they should 'transform revolutionary theory into revolutionary practice by joining Umkhonto we Sizwe'.[11]

I was worried that my manuscript might be seized by the security police, so lodged copies beyond their reach with Bill Vose at the British embassy. As the deadline approached I went on a six-week trip to the US at the invitation of its government. But the book was not yet finished. So I told the organisers of my visit I would have to take a week out of the trip to write the last chapter. Where, I asked, is the remotest place in America for me to do this? Bozeman in Montana, they said. Bozeman, however, was inaccessible because of an airline strike. The next remotest place was Billings, Montana. So there I flew with my notes and holed up in a hotel room with a heavy-duty typewriter that had been hired for me. Billings was two thirds of the way between Chicago and Seattle, and from my window I could see the daily Northwest Orient flights landing and taking off from an airport on a plateau above the town – a kind of mini Table Mountain. Across the road from my hotel were the General Custer Motor Hotel and the Hungry Bear Restaurant, usually filled with cowboys in big hats and tall boots.

For relaxation I hired a huge Chrysler and took drives along the Yellowstone River. I'd never driven on the right-hand side of the road before, so this sparsely populated farming state was a safe place to practise. My next port of call was to be San Francisco, which I'd asked the organisers to put on my programme because I had always wanted to see the Golden Gate Bridge. I picked up a hire car at the airport there with a map of the city on the seat beside me and somehow managed to navigate my way through the traffic to find the bridge and then drive across it. I parked the car at the far end and then walked back over the bridge. It fully lived up to my expectations and I wrote back to Pierre that if Michelangelo were to design a suspension bridge, it would look like this. From San Francisco I posted the final chapter of the completed book back to Ravan Press, with a copy to friends in London. The manuscript got safely to the printers, but the first set of printing plates mysteriously disappeared and had to be replaced.[12]

One of the people I visited in San Francisco was William B (Bill) Gould, dean of the Stanford Law School. He was an African-American who had visited South Africa a couple of times. I had invited him out for dinner and he was light-skinned enough to get in anywhere. But he insisted he would not eat in any restaurant from which black South Africans were excluded. That left us a choice of only one or two in Hillbrow. Professor Gould subsequently became chairman of the National Labour Relations Board in the US.

One of the first reactions to my Soweto book when it was published in 1978 was a private letter from a black journalist whom I'd worked with and who subsequently became an editor. He wrote, 'You score a handsome seven out of a possible ten. But one thing you have proved is that blacks are sleeping on the job. Reporters, authors, etc. Why couldn't they write and tell us the June 1976 story? Why must always whites "tell" the story of my people?' He was perhaps being less than fair to some of his colleagues. As I said in the preface, 'My greatest debt is to fellow-journalists, reporters and photographers alike, on various newspapers. Often at great personal risk or cost, they told the story of what happened in Soweto. Some of them saw their newspapers closed down, others are still in detention as this book goes to the printers. They brought honour to their profession. Without them, this book could not have been written.'

The preface also acknowledged Peter Randall, who was my editor but who had been banned and therefore supposedly could not perform that job because involvement in a publication was a breach of his banning order. Needless to say, we consulted periodically over numerous bottles of wine at his home in Valley Road, Westcliff, Johannesburg.

When the book came out there were a couple of negative comments. The British weekly *Time Out* said its 'limitations lie chiefly in its being written from the outside by a white liberal'.[13] The ANC journal *Sechaba* took me to task for failing to relate the revolt in Soweto to 'the history of struggle'. Its reviewer seemed irritated that I'd given more credit for the spirit of revolt to Black Consciousness than to the ANC and its trade union and other allies.[14] This was true, and rightly so. But the Black Consciousness movement had reached its zenith. Crippled by Biko's death in September 1977 and the bannings of *The World* newspaper and 17 Black Consciousness organisations a month later,[15] it was overwhelmed by the ANC in the 1980s as that organisation reinvigorated itself.

Sechaba and *Time Out* apart, press and journal reviews were generally complimentary. When the book came out in London, Ian Davidson wrote in the *Financial Times* that my purpose was to 'describe in relentless detail the policy of apartheid as it is applied in practice. The effect is devastating. Kane-Berman is not perhaps another John Maynard Keynes, but his book reminds me most powerfully of *The Economic Consequences of the Peace.*'[16]

RW (Bill) Johnson wrote in *New Society*, a journal published in London: 'Apartheid is not just a crazy set of laws which makes its victims go mad with anger every once in a while. It is an immense administrative system attuned with considerable logic, sophistication, and finesse to the fulfilment of a complex variety of goals and interests. Kane-Berman documents its contemporary operation and rationale with a large body of historical and statistical information reinforced and lightened by continuous on-the-spot rapportage. He is a clear and critical guide through the maze, unfailingly conscious both of apartheid's impact on the daily lives of the blacks and of what is fundamental and what only incidental to its deeper rationale.'[17]

Oscar Wollheim, an Institute stalwart in Cape Town, wrote that there would 'no longer be any excuse for saying, "But I never knew all this".'[18] Gita Dyzenhaus, Transvaal regional chairman of the Black Sash, wrote to say the book 'should be made compulsory reading for all white South Africans, especially for those in office'.[19] Tony Kleu wrote in *The Guardian* that I'd 'illustrated the Afrikaner's incredible complacency', the most striking example of which was the statement by Manie Mulder, chairman of the West Rand Administration Board, a month before

Soweto exploded, to the effect that 'the broad masses of Soweto are perfectly content, perfectly happy'. Black-white relationships, he added, 'were as healthy as can be'. Was there any danger of a blow-up in the township? 'None whatever,' Mulder had declared.[20]

Writing in the *Christian Science Monitor*, June Goodwin said I had exposed the myth 'built up by the press that the Afrikaner was going to change and turn away from apartheid'.[21] The book had indeed suggested that 'June 1976, like Sharpeville 16 years before, was another turning point where South Africa did not turn'. John Vorster's defiant attitude after his election victory in November 1977 seemed to rule out any fundamental change.

Twelve years after I wrote this, however, South Africa did turn, decisively. FW de Klerk, the man who executed the turn, had never been regarded as one of the more pragmatic, or *verligte*, Nationalists. In fact, apartheid was already beginning to unravel. We had reported some of the early signs of this unravelling in the *FM*. We had also noted how the far Right was predicting that if you tampered with apartheid even slightly, you would put the whole edifice in jeopardy. After I joined the Institute in 1983 as its CEO the disintegration of the system gathered momentum, a process I described in *South Africa's Silent Revolution*, published in 1990. Of course, what delivered the *coup de grâce* to apartheid was another process of disintegration, that of Soviet communism, which culminated in the collapse of the Berlin Wall in 1989. This created the opportunity that De Klerk seized a few months later when he released Nelson Mandela and other prisoners, and lifted the bans on the ANC and other organisations. When I had called for this on the steps of Jameson Hall 14 years previously it had seemed fanciful.

In fact, in the end, the ANC was the main beneficiary of what happened in Soweto. Although there had been signs of renewed underground activity prior to the township revolt, there had also been considerable disillusionment among the youth about the exiled ANC and PAC. The revolt, I argued, had been mainly inspired by the spirit of Black

Consciousness that Steve Biko had introduced into South Africa via the South African Students' Organisation, its schoolboy counterpart the South African Students' Movement, and the Black People's Convention. However, when pupils fled the townships in the face of intimidation and attack by the police they often ended up in military training camps abroad. This was because the ANC alone had the international connections and resources to receive them.[22]

The Soweto book finally got me into court before Mr Justice Gert Coetzee. The West Rand Administration Board had insured all its fixed property in Soweto with Santam. It now sought to recover from Santam R7 million in damage caused in the upheavals. Santam repudiated the claim on the grounds that the upheavals were a planned uprising – *volksopstand en volksoproer* – which was not covered by the policy. The board countered that the upheavals were only a civil commotion – *oproer en burgerlike beroering* – and that the policy therefore did cover them. On the strength of the book, Johann Kriegler, who was acting for the board and who later became a judge of the Constitutional Court, called me as an expert witness in May 1981.

I had argued in the book, and I repeated in court, that the violence erupted when the police opened fire on an essentially peaceful march. The extent of the furious reaction to the shootings was explained by resentment and frustration. But the day might have ended peacefully had the police not opened fire. In other words, my argument was that the violence was a spontaneous revolt against the apartheid system rather than a planned uprising or insurrection designed to overthrow it. This was why I had used the term 'revolt' right from the start, although 'uprising' was more widely used.

It would have been fascinating to hear how Judge Coetzee would decide whether the upheavals constituted a revolt or an uprising. However, the matter was settled out of court in March 1982, Santam paying the board's costs and R1.75 million in settlement of its damages claim.[23]

During the trial a former chief director of the board, JC de Villiers, read from a confidential document he had drawn up for submission to a commission of enquiry into the disturbances by Judge Piet Cillié.[24] In his testimony before Coetzee, De Villiers said that the Department of Bantu Administration and Development, under whose authority the board fell, had made 'a massive contribution to the build-up over years of an "anti-climate" in which the spark of the education medium was transformed into such destruction'. Ministerial control exercised through the department had created 'an administrative body concerned with Bantu administration which cannot be easily matched for its clumsiness ... I do not think it is possible to design a more clumsy system without becoming ridiculous.'[25] The document was a rare insight into what a top official felt about his ministerial superiors.

There were also several amusing moments during the trial. On 12 May 1981 a witness by the name of Patrick Zuma testified that people rejected the whole system of Bantu education.

'Rejected it as inferior?' – 'Yes.'

'Inferior especially to white education?' – 'Yes.'

At this point the judge intervened to comment drily, 'It is very difficult to be inferior to white education, but they succeeded.'[26]

On another occasion a witness was giving evidence in Zulu. Counsel's questions in English were translated into Zulu and the witness's replies in Zulu then translated back into English. But the witness was getting impatient as counsel tried to put words into his mouth. Eventually, when one such question was asked in English he did not wait for it to be translated, but immediately answered in a posh English accent, 'Upon that assumption, mi'lord, learned counsel's inference is correct.' The courtroom collapsed with laughter.

In the meantime I'd written another book, *Apartheid and Business – An Analysis of the Rapidly Evolving Challenges Facing Companies with Investments in South Africa.*[27] It was commissioned by Business International Corporation (BI), an American organisation that published newsletters on various parts of the world along with more detailed research reports. I got paid for it but my name did not appear anywhere on it, as BI, like the *FM*, did not by-line its reports. My instructions were that my target market was the putative top official at global headquarters to whom the South African chief executive reported. Pressures against foreign companies in the country were mounting, and I was to help this top official understand all the risks and opportunities South Africa presented for his company. People in America and Europe thought Armageddon was around the corner: was this hysteria, or was there a basis for the fear? Was Soweto really such a time bomb? How were companies dealing with the government? How were they dealing with black unions?

Published in 1980 when economic growth was heading up to 7 per cent after an annual average of 3.5 per cent in the 1970s, and 'massive capital investment by mining companies was in the offing' in the wake of soaring gold prices, the book pointed out that the South African economy was the 'envy of the world'. New capital was flowing in despite international pressures for disinvestment. Although various countries had tried to impose tougher sanctions following the bannings of the Black Consciousness organisations and the death of Steve Biko in 1977, the US and its allies had successfully fought to limit the UN Security Council's resolution of that year to the embargo on arms sales. Moreover, the revolt in Soweto and elsewhere a few years previously had not presented a serious challenge to the state and had been put down without the army having to be mobilised. The government had also started to relax some of the bureaucratic controls over the black labour market. Policy confining black people to unskilled jobs was being slowly abandoned. Black workers had been granted trade union rights. Prime Minister PW Botha was telling white South Africa that the military alone could not guarantee its survival and that they would have to 'adapt or die'.

However, these encouraging signs did not mean that the conduct of business in the 1980s would be easy. Exactly the reverse. The Rhodesian impasse was close to settlement, so South Africa would be the focus of the world spotlight. Apartheid was likely to remain a bitterly controversial issue in the world until it was finally eliminated, I concluded.

The book was based not only on research but also on interviews with Harry Oppenheimer and 18 heads of the South African subsidiaries of foreign companies, many of them household names. Most of them spoke to me openly even though their names would appear in the book. All of them identified skills and training as big problems. Few were convinced that the government was doing much to solve the problem of shortages of artisans and professionals. As for government promises of change, Tony Bloom, chairman of Premier Milling, said that it had been mainly a grandstand performance and that many businessmen seemed to have been hypnotised by the government.

I went on to describe the Riekert proposals to divide the black population up into 'insiders' and 'outsiders' as a form of 'neo-apartheid'. This was part of the government's strategy of building up a stable black middle class. I asked Oppenheimer about this, and he replied:

'I've never thought that building a middle class would slow down the demand for political power. Quite the contrary – it would speed it up.'[28]

The consensus among the executives I spoke to was that the police and army were tough and efficient enough to contain any revolutionary threats. As Syd Newman, chairman of Lonrho, put it, 'Revolution? We have very draconian laws and security police roaming all over the country – though I would hate to think how many unemployed, hungry, frustrated youngsters wandering the streets of Soweto.'[29] Several believed that continuing violence was inevitable, both spontaneous civic violence of the kind that characterised 1976 and the planned insurgency that had subsequently emerged. Few expected outright revolution. My conclusion was that peaceful reconciliation had a slender chance, but that the possibility of overthrow of the government was as remote as the possibility that it could crush resistance: 'The most likely scenario is a more or less stable condition of violent equilibrium.'[30]

Though priced at 1 800 Swiss francs a copy, the 288-book had to be reprinted. I got paid $17 500 for writing *Apartheid and Business*. This was R13 670 in those days. Today the same dollar amount would be worth R235 000. Such is the impact of the depreciating rand.

I wrote regularly for BI, reporting mainly to Graham Hatton, who joined them when he left the *FM*. I also spoke at various conferences they organised. To encourage open discussion, these were all closed to the press. Some were small affairs with only a few dozen participants and only two or three speakers. Others were bigger.

BI also specialised in 'government roundtables' where they would get heads of government and half their cabinets to meet BI's corporate clients in closed meetings. They had held more than 70 of these over the preceding 25 years with people who included four American presidents, three British and three Australian prime ministers, Alexei Kosygin of the USSR, Fidel Castro, Emperor Haile Selassie of Ethiopia, and numerous other heads of state or government from around the world. Now it was South Africa's turn at a roundtable in Cape Town in March 1983. Eight cabinet ministers participated, along with the governor of the South African Reserve Bank. The conference also included a lunch in honour of the prime minister, PW Botha. I helped to prepare numerous questions to be directed at the various ministers, but I did not participate in the conference itself. This might have been because one of the government representatives had objected that I was 'subversive'.

Three years later another roundtable was held with the South African government at the Mount Nelson Hotel in Cape Town. This time I did participate. PW Botha, by now state president, invited us all to a cocktail party at Tuynhuys. Although he did not himself take part, seven or eight of his ministers did. One of these was FW de Klerk, who projected an image of pragmatism at odds with his hard-line *verkrampte* public image. I told my parents afterwards that he, rather than his brother Wimpie, who had a *verligte* image, was the De Klerk to watch.[31]

Initially, the only black South African leader in the BI meetings that I attended was Mangosuthu Buthelezi, but later Oliver Tambo, Thabo Mbeki, Frene Ginwala, and Mac Maharaj were among the participants in London. By this time I had joined the Institute.

In June 1985, Malcolm Rifkind, the British minister of state for African affairs, told a BI conference at the London Hilton that pressure for sanctions would mount unless South Africa changed rapidly. Chester Crocker, the American deputy assistant secretary of state for African affairs, said that if the US Congress passed additional punitive sanctions, he would recommend to President Reagan that they be vetoed.

The conference shifted to the Plaza Hotel in New York for a day after two days in London. Some of the participants flew overnight by Concorde, but most of us trundled behind in a Boeing 747. Gerrit Viljoen, minister of co-operation, development, and education, spoke in both London and New York. He listed some of the reforms already carried out, including repeal of the legislation forbidding marriage and/or sex across the colour line. The law forbidding racially mixed political parties was also being repealed. PW Botha had taken a considerable risk in offering amnesty to prisoners convicted of political and security offences, provided they renounced violence, an offer accepted by some of them, but rejected by Nelson Mandela.

I had helped to get both Buthelezi and Viljoen to these meetings. Although participants recognised that the ANC was making its presence felt more and more both in South Africa and abroad, many were fascinated as they witnessed the gentlemanly but dramatic debate between Buthelezi and Viljoen as they sought common ground. Viljoen admitted that his government had misjudged the resentment of blacks at being excluded. Buthelezi's warnings of violence had been quite correct. The government was now determined to hold negotiations, whatever the obstacles. It accepted that the homeland policy was inadequate and that

146

permanent black populations outside the homelands were a fact of life and should be granted political participation. A special cabinet committee had been set up to look into this. Blacks would no longer have to forfeit their South African citizenship. There had to be a balance between power-sharing and self-determination. Replied Buthelezi: 'I want to say to the minister that my people have a common destiny with him and his people.'

Asked to clarify what he meant by saying the government had left apartheid behind, Viljoen explained that it meant the end of exclusive white political domination, along with discrimination based on race or colour. However, the government was *not* going the way of one man, one vote.[32]

ANC representatives used some of these BI meetings in London to dismiss the government's reforms as strategies to retain control. Speaking in May 1987 at the Mayfair Intercontinental in London, Oliver Tambo said every move by PW Botha underlined the need to intensify armed and political struggle. South Africa was in a kind of war, and economies were often destroyed in war. 'Afterwards, you build, sometimes from scratch,' as had been the case with the Marshall Plan in Europe. There might be a great deal of destruction in the struggle against apartheid, and the ANC did not want to inherit a waste land, so it 'may have to rely on international business to help build again'.

Business was enmeshed in the state, Tambo added, and needed to change sides. In fact, he said, he was encouraged that business inside and outside South Africa had begun to rethink its position on 'our struggle', even though this so far involved only 'hedging bets', not changing sides.[33]

Graham Hatton bravely tackled Oliver Tambo on 'necklacing' – a method of execution in which a tyre is hung around the neck of the victim before he is doused with petrol and set alight. Tambo said the police had started burning people before the ANC did. 'The ANC disapproves of this but understands how it came about. We will try to dissuade people but the police have been doing it to smear the ANC. I hope it will someday be something of the past, but when it goes the regime will have lost a very powerful weapon against the ANC.'

The fact that I'd helped to get Viljoen to the BI conferences was not without irony: he had once been chairman of an organisation set up at the behest of the Afrikaner Broederbond in 1948 to counter the liberal influence of the Institute. This was the South African Bureau of Racial Affairs (Sabra), which Viljoen had served as chairman in the early 1970s, after which he became chairman of the Broederbond. Sabra was later taken over by the far Right, prominent among whom was Professor Carel Boshoff, son-in-law of Dr Verwoerd. Vehemently opposed to the NP's policy reforms, it devoted itself to 'Project Oranje', a homeland for whites on the Orange River. In 1988 I invited Professor Boshoff to talk at the Institute. Many black people came to hear him. I thought they would give him a rough time with questions, but they didn't. Afterwards some of them shook their heads and told me that they felt sorry for him.

In my book on Soweto I'd written up a speech Viljoen made to a Sabra conference in 1972 pointing to the possibility that black cities in the white area would grow to be larger than white, enabling urban African leadership to wield 'enormous bargaining power'.[34] Whites were thus faced with two choices. One was to share political power and thus abandon control over their own destiny irrevocably. The other was to physically resettle 'a very much larger percentage' of blacks in the homelands. 'Far more drastic measures' would be required to bring this about. Yet here Viljoen was in London and New York, only 13 years later, announcing if not the final abandonment of the homelands policy, then at least recognition of the permanence of Africans in the common area and their entitlement to retain their South African citizenship. In 1989 he was appointed minister of constitutional development, in which capacity he participated in the first talks between the De Klerk government and the ANC.[35]

Despite the retreat from apartheid, pressure for sanctions against South Africa intensified. At the invitation of two congressional subcommittees, I went to testify against sanctions in Washington DC in March 1988. I had only seven minutes to speak, but the statement I handed in was later published under the title *The Erosion of Apartheid*. Stephen Mulholland, former editor of the *FM* and subsequently chief executive of Times Media Limited, successor to South African Associated Newspapers, was the man who arranged this.

Citing research we had been doing at the Institute over the past few years, I told the congressional committee that 'objective forces such as population growth, economic growth, skilled labour shortages, and urbanisation have created the conditions for necessary policy change'. When the surplus of white skilled labour dried up in about 1970, the government faced the choice of allowing the economy to stagnate or permitting black people to be trained. It chose the latter, and this shift from 'hard-line ideology to cautious pragmatism was the turning point'. The government had not intended that its pragmatic changes would lead to trade union or home-ownership rights, but as more and more blacks climbed the occupational ladder they became stronger in exerting demands for these rights. Attempts to destroy unions by bannings had failed. Moreover, when a handful of American companies started signing recognition agreements with unions, this presented the government with a *fait accompli*, and eventually unions were given statutory rights. Black people had voted against the pass laws with their feet by moving to town regardless. This had eventually rendered the pass laws unworkable, with the result that they were repealed in 1986.

All of this demonstrated that black people were capable of acting on their own to change their situation. They created *de facto* situations on the ground which necessitated changes in the law. The authorities didn't particularly want to change, but their will to resist was declining. The risk of sanctions was that they would slow down the pace at which the balance of economic power was shifting in favour of black people.[36]

Many years later various American and other multinationals were sued in American courts under a statute enacted in 1789 for collaborating

149

with apartheid. I was consulted by some of the companies. In a paper delivered in Zurich in 2003 I argued that in earlier years business had been 'content to play along with apartheid'.[37] It had, however, become more critical as 'apartheid got in the way of doing business'. Some companies had helped South Africa build up a major arms manufacturing and exporting industry. However, 'even the arms industry required the training of black workers to higher and higher levels of skill'. Local and foreign companies had 'participated in the dynamics of industrialisation and urbanisation that in the end made apartheid unworkable'. The economy had not sustained the apartheid state, but undermined it, a process in which business had been directly involved. Working with lawyers in New York for some of the defendant companies, I drew up an affidavit, but in the end it was never used. The case dragged on until 2014, when it was finally thrown out by the American courts on the grounds that it did not belong in those courts.[38]

Most of these speaking trips took me abroad only for a few days. But sometimes Pierre and I were able to tag a holiday on at the end. One trip to New York had me determined to drive across the Verrazano Narrows Bridge spanning the entrance to New York harbour. I thought it would be as magical as the Golden Gate. Not so! You couldn't see over the high sides of the bridge, and the traffic was going so fast there was no chance of finding a place to slow down for a better look. We then spent the rest of that Sunday afternoon in a traffic jam as the motorways through Brooklyn had all been reduced to a single lane so that road repairs could be carried out. Some years later, however, we got up before sunrise one morning in November on board the *Queen Mary 2* to watch as the ship sailed under the bridge to dock in New York.

London was, however, the favourite port of call, and we always stayed at the Oxford and Cambridge Club, even though this required jacket and tie in bars, dining rooms, lounges, and the library. Situated on Pall Mall a block away from St James's Palace, it was the ideal location. The club overlooked the Mall leading from Trafalgar Square and

Admiralty Arch to Buckingham Palace. From some of the bedrooms you would have a Mary Poppins view of London: Big Ben illuminated at night along with Westminster Abbey and the tops of the heavy Victorian buildings of Whitehall. If you leant far enough out of the window you could sometimes see whether or not the Royal Standard was flying over Buckingham Palace, so you would know if the Queen was at home. The main club library overlooked Marlborough House, once a royal residence. Some of the library's sash windows had been painted white to protect royal privacy, making the library rather dark. The club therefore wrote to Queen Mary, widow of King George V, then in residence at Marlborough House, asking if some of the paint could be removed. 'Remove it all,' she wrote back. 'I've always wanted to see what gentlemen do in their clubs.'

The club's location gave quick access to the square in front of Buckingham Palace one Sunday to watch a fly-past commemorating the sixtieth anniversary of the Battle of Britain. It lasted four hours, starting with the latest supersonic aircraft and ending with a Spitfire and then a Hurricane. The aircraft took off from airfields all over Britain and some even in Europe and then flew in a straight line down from St Paul's Cathedral in the City and over the Mall towards the palace, where the Queen and her family were watching. Just as the huge crowd in front of the palace and along the Mall was cheering as the last aircraft dipped in salute and then veered off into the blue, four Canada geese flew in their wake straight over the palace balcony almost as if they'd been part of the fly-past. The crowd cheered even louder.

Some years later we happened to be in London at the time of Princess Diana's funeral. Members were watching on television in a club lounge. The cortège paused in front of the palace to acknowledge the Queen, who was standing on a small grandstand on the pavement, and then proceeded down the Mall before stopping in front of St James's Palace. There were waiting Prince Charles, his and Diana's two sons, and the Duke of Edinburgh to join the procession. I suddenly realised that this was happening right outside the club, so I went up to the top floor and climbed out of one of the dormer windows onto the roof to get a better view than I could on television. Half a dozen automatic rifles were immediately pointed at me: 'Step back inside, if you please, sir.' I did so in double-quick time. I hadn't reckoned with the sharpshooters on the roofs of all the buildings along the route to deal with any day-of-the-jackal assassination attempts.

There were three tube stations within five minutes' walk, but most of the places we visited were themselves within walking distance: the theatres of the West End, the National Gallery, the Royal Academy, and of course Hatchard's and other bookshops in Piccadilly. We got to know that part of London as well as any part of Johannesburg. Mostly we did this on foot. You could walk across St James's Park and past the back door of Number 10 Downing Street and the underground cabinet war rooms to Westminster, across the river to the Royal Festival Hall or the National Theatre, or in the other direction through Mayfair up to Oxford Street and then back down Regent Street. During one walk across the park we suddenly heard a large military band strike up a beautifully orchestrated version of 'Sarie Marais' as they marched up the Mall. On another occasion, one Remembrance Day, a parade of elderly men wearing bowler hats and medals and sporting umbrellas as if they were rifles came by, their fallen comrades no doubt uppermost in their minds.

Despite its immense attractions, we did not spend all our time in London when in the UK. Some of our holidays we spent driving around visiting 'stately homes' and the gardens surrounding them. Many of these are open to the public, as is Buckingham Palace, because the tenants need the income from visitors. The grandest houses we visited were Castle Howard in Yorkshire, where parts of the television series *Brideshead Revisited* had just been made; Blenheim Palace near Oxford, where Winston Churchill was born and where the exterior parts of Kenneth Branagh's film of *Hamlet* were made; Hatfield House, where you can still see the oak under which Elizabeth I was informed of her accession to the throne; Chatsworth in Derbyshire, seat of the dukes of Devonshire; Highclere Castle near Newbury, later fictionalised as Downton Abbey; and Holyrood Palace near Edinburgh, a royal residence full of rather threadbare carpets. Some of these houses are hung with great art treasures. Most have beautiful English gardens. Some, such as Chatsworth, are working farms. The finest garden we saw was probably Bodnant in Wales with its spectacular plantings of rhododendrons and azaleas – rivalled perhaps only by the intertwined jacarandas and bougainvillaeas in Johannesburg in October and November each year.

We also visited French châteaux and the gardens surrounding them along the Loire. In my view they are much less attractive than the English ones, mainly because they are much more formal. There are great plantings and gravel pathways, but in some nary a tree under which you can sit to read a book. It struck me that the English gardens were for relaxation as well as to impress, whereas many of the French ones were mainly for show. But for me the most exciting thing about our trip along the Loire was the river itself. As a South African attuned to crossing one dry river bed after another in the Kruger Park and elsewhere, I couldn't believe as we drove along the Loire that a river could actually have so much water in it. We drove along roads as close to the river as we could, and I got out often to look at it. On another trip, when we visited Peter the Great's palace at Peterhof outside St Petersburg, I was almost shocked at the vast quantities of water cascading out of gilded fountains into the Gulf of Finland.

Having seen gardens in Britain, France, and St Petersburg with their abundant water, I appreciate all the more the heroic efforts of both my grandmother and my mother, who established wonderful gardens despite seldom having enough water. Pierre established a magnificent garden in our home in Auckland Park, where we lived for 28 years. Winter or summer, I spent every possible moment in that garden. One of the glorious things about the dry Johannesburg winter is that you can usually sit outside in the sun. Whenever I took Institute editorial work home to do in the garden, my productivity doubled.

South Africa has some beautiful gardens, many of them in private homes behind high walls. But in the last couple of years we have visited gardens in Elgin and Grabouw in the Western Cape when they've been open to visitors for a couple of weekends in November, entrance fees being given to local charities. Most of these gardens are on wine or fruit farms, and some have magnificent plantings of roses and other flowers. North of the little town of Bedford in the Eastern Cape are also some magnificent gardens which we visited. Some were at the end of a long dirt road an hour's drive from the town. In the township adjoining Bedford there were also a few gardens on show. It was moving to see the pride that some of these very poor householders took in their little gardens as they showed us around.

CHAPTER 8

Dreams and nightmares

The *Financial Mail* had for a time been 50 per cent owned by the *Financial Times* (*FT*) of London. Senior journalists on that paper such as JDF Jones and Bridget Bloom were frequent visitors to Johannesburg. Some of our staff also acted as stringers – correspondents – for the *FT*. Graham Hatton did most of the politics and economics, but sometimes he turned over politics and labour matters to me. I wrote both for the main paper and for its worldwide syndication service, as well as for various other foreign papers. I often used a telex service run by a man called 'Fingers' van der Merwe to file copy abroad. Fingers was a legend in the world of foreign correspondents. He ran offices in Johannesburg, Cape Town, and London and rented rooms to stringers who fed his operation. If you were out in a remote part of South Africa or Mozambique and you needed to get your story to Sydney or Düsseldorf or New York, you could ring him collect or reverse-charges anytime at his office or on his farm. He would start transmitting a telex as you spoke and the story would be fully printed out at the other end only a few seconds after you put down the phone.

So when I resigned from the *FM*, along with Bernard Simon, its main economics writer, it was to Fingers we went the very next day. He gave us an office and a telephone next to all the foreign correspondents in his News Services centre in Johannesburg. We went out and bought a couple of heavy-duty typewriters, second-hand desks, and old filing cabinets, and we were in business the day after. The *FT* was next door to us, with *Newsweek,* the *Washington Post, The Times,* the *Daily Telegraph,* the Associated Press news agency, various American television networks, and others just along the passage on the seventh floor of Union Centre on the corner of Simmonds and Pritchard Streets (now Bank City). Most of the foreign papers had sent out their own staff as their correspondents, but some used local stringers as well. This was in the days before e-mail communication, so the telex was the magnet that kept us all together.

Thus began my four years of self-employment. I had no employees and no bosses – only clients at the other end of the telex, most of them thousands of miles away. You got paid by the word so you had to produce. If you went on holiday or spent the afternoon at lunch in The Guildhall or at some other watering hole you earned nothing. And of course you had to seek out clients, as well as rely on word of mouth.

Mine included *The Guardian,* the *Sunday Times,* and the BBC in London, with occasional forays onto the pages of *The Times,* the *FT, The Economist,* and *The Observer* magazine – for some of which I'd been writing while still at the *FM.* Among my other British outlets were magazines called *South* and *8 Days,* along with the *New Statesman,* where Christopher Hitchens had responded enthusiastically to my offer to write for them. In Amsterdam was *de Volkskrant,* in Stockholm *Dagens Nyheter* and *Dagens Industri,* and in Düsseldorf *Handelsblatt* – for all of which you had to get your material in early, in time for it to be translated. In Dublin was the *Irish Times,* in Toronto the *Financial Post,* and in Atlanta *The Atlanta Constitution,* with occasional articles in the *New York Times* and *Business Week* and such specialist publications as *ILO Information,* published by the International Labour Organisation in Geneva. I was also the stringer for *The Australian* and the *Australian Financial Review.* Radio France International and the *Indian Ocean Newsletter,* published in Paris, were among other occasional clients, as was Radio Eireann in Dublin. I had mainly written on politics and labour for the *FM*, but now I had to branch out into economics and business as well. I wrote regularly for the *International Coal Report* published by the *FT*. In addition, I covered Botswana, Lesotho, and Swaziland for a London-based magazine called *Africa Economic Digest*. Local outlets included the *Sunday Express, Finance Week* and *Frontline*, the monthly journal founded and edited by Denis Beckett.

I was also once commissioned to help put together a special supplement on South Africa for the *International Herald Tribune*. The man who came out from its head office in Paris to see me was an Indian. I took him to Hillbrow, where he was amazed that he could walk on the pavement. He had come to South Africa under the impression that only whites could do this.

Quite a lot of what I wrote in *The Guardian* in particular was reprinted in other papers, including the *Washington Post*, the *New York Times*, the *Los Angeles Times*, the *Philadelphia Inquirer*, and the *Morning News* in Wilmington (Delaware). *Dagens Nyheter* articles were also sometimes reprinted in other Scandinavian papers.

All of this gave me platforms in many parts of the English-speaking world and even beyond. In addition, I wrote regularly for Business International, where Graham Hatton was now working. This included an update to *Apartheid and Business*, as well as contributions to their various newsletters. BI was later taken over by the Economist Intelligence Unit.

Most papers printed articles as I sent them, although *The Economist* invariably rewrote them, sometimes distorting the meaning. The *Investors' Chronicle* in London once doctored an article to turn 150 fatalities in conflict on the mines into a number of 'injuries'.[1] I thought this disgraceful and told them I presumed the reason they had done it was to ensure that my article did not contradict South African government advertisements in that issue of the magazine. The *New Statesman* once spiked an article I wrote about shack settlements on the dunes on the Cape Flats for political reasons. More of this below. The most exacting paper was *Business Week* in New York. In 1980 they commissioned a long article on black trade unions. Their response to what I sent was 18 questions to help recast the article for an American audience. To this I telexed a 10-foot reply. They then incorporated all my answers into the original article, and telexed it back to me for approval.[2] Thus did we avoid the distortions that sub-editors and/or headline writers can introduce into journalists' copy.

Johann and Marie Spies ran Fingers's operation in Johannesburg. If they had to stay late to file your stories in time, they always did so. I still miss that part of the Johannesburg city centre. You could walk to most places you needed to go to. The mining houses, along with bank and other corporate headquarters, were only a few blocks from us, and several black unions had their offices nearby. Every morning I used to go out to my bank to check whether payments had come in, and then walk over the Library Gardens square to do my posting at the beautiful old Rissik Street Post Office, now derelict.

International phone calls were still quite rare. If I needed to talk to one of my papers I would ring the international exchange in Cape Town, give the number I wanted, and ask them to make a collect call. They got to know my voice, so that I would no sooner say, 'Please get me a call to …' than they would interrupt with 'Good morning, Mr Kane-Berman, is it the *Irish Times* you'll be wanting today, or will it be *Volkskrant*?'

It was four years of hard work and great fun. With some papers you simply filed a story and if they used it they paid you. Others you would phone or telex with a suggestion which they would accept or reject. Or they would order something from you. Mainly at my own expense, I made a few trips to London, Amsterdam, Stockholm, Düsseldorf, and Dublin to see or seek out clients.

I made enough money in these four years to be able to put down a deposit on a house in Berea in 1981 and move out of the flat I'd occupied, initially for R30 a month, in Westminster Mansions next to the

Yeoville water tower. I was awakened after my first night in the house, sleeping on a mattress on the floor, by a woman with a cup of tea on a tray. Her name was Laetitia Ngqiba and she lived in a room in the back yard. I had never thought of employing a live-in servant, but Laetitia told me that she came with the house. She stayed in my employ for 26 years until her death in 2007. Across the road from the house was a park. When my parents came to visit, my father remembered that he used to walk across that park every morning in the late 1920s from his parents' house in Louis Botha Avenue to Tudhope Avenue to catch the tram to town where he was serving his articles. I made lunch for my parents. The following day my father pointedly presented me with two silver butter-knives as a housewarming present.

PW Botha was as dominating a figure in white politics in the 1980s as John Vorster had been in the 1970s. Vorster having presided over partial economic liberalisation, Botha now faced the challenge of political liberalisation which his predecessor had forsworn. He started off with much promise, declaring, 'This country does not only have whites, but blacks, coloureds, and Indians as well and I will take their interests into account as long as I am prime minister.'[3] He even suggested that some new constitutional arrangements might have to be devised for Africans in the common area.[4]

Recognising that such sentiments sounded heretical to most of his followers, I sent off articles around the world giving Botha full credit for being brave enough to express them. I told *de Volkskrant* that an opinion poll showed that 57 per cent of the people in Soweto thought he was leading the country well.[5] Economic prospects were also bright, as gold in 1980 averaged an unheard-of $613 an ounce, the rand was worth $1.28, and the economy grew at 6.6 per cent. By the end of the decade, however, Botha's own party had forced him from office.

Although many people loathed him – and still do – Botha to me sometimes seemed a rather tragic figure. In 1986 he opened the way to talks with Nelson Mandela, but he was also responsible for inflicting the disaster of the tricameral Parliament upon the country. In this he was encouraged by most of the business community, who largely ignored the almost universal opposition to it among blacks in general, and Africans in particular. It was in any event too late for pragmatic political reform. By the end of the 1980s the NP had lost the initiative to the ANC, whose 'people's war' was by then well under way. No amount of liberalising reform could have blunted the ANC's propaganda and revolutionary thrust, which by then had the support of much of the rest of the world.

Botha, on the other hand, could no longer rely even on his own party. The NP had painted itself into a corner by adopting policies from which it was now trying to retreat. When a heckler at a by-election meeting wanted to know why the government was 'doing so much for the blacks' by giving them better housing and not deporting them to the homelands, Botha retorted, 'My friend, you even need a black to change your nappy.' But the heckler had a point: he was, after all, merely asking why the NP was no longer carrying out its forced removals policy. 'Carefully nurtured on a diet of pure apartheid for the last 30 years,' I wrote, 'Afrikaner nationalists are now deeply confused by what they suspect is a change of direction by the government they have loyally and uncritically supported for so long.'[6] The same government, in their eyes, was now committing treason against white workers.

'Botha slays sacred cows to prevent a bloodbath' was the headline on a story I wrote in *The Australian* on Botha's first year as prime minister after replacing the disgraced John Vorster in September 1978.[7] He'd come close to heresy by declaring that his God was also the God of black people. Although interracial sex and marriage were illegal, he would consider legalising them. The country's security legislation would be reviewed, black organisations would be invited to discuss a new constitution, and the homelands would get more land. Whereas Vorster had said in the midst of the Soweto upheavals that there was no crisis in the country, Botha was now warning that the prejudice and hatred of white extremists could cause a 'bloodbath before breakfast'. One of his

ministers had said that recent events in Iran (leading to the overthrow
of the Shah in 1979) had shown it was stupid to rely only on the police
and the army for security.

Much of the prime minister's talk of change predated Robert Mugabe's
victory in the election in Zimbabwe at the beginning of March 1980
– an event which delighted most blacks in South Africa but shocked
most whites.[8] Some of the latter chose this moment to whip up a row
about the participation of coloured schoolboys in a hitherto whites-
only rugby tournament. Andries Treurnicht, Transvaal leader of the NP
and a member of Botha's Cabinet, wanted to know why the coloured
schoolboys could not play rugby by themselves. Botha retorted that it
was high time people realised the time for treating coloured people as
lepers was at an end. While soldiers of all races were standing shoulder
to shoulder against the Marxist onslaught on the country's borders,
politicians should stop playing political circuses behind their backs.
Adolf Hitler had also boasted that he could stand alone against the
world, only to fail.[9]

Botha's speeches were sometimes like a breath of fresh air, I thought.
Nor could his changes easily be dismissed as cosmetic. Even the budget
had begun to reflect a shift in priorities. Defence spending would rise
by 46 per cent, but black education in the common area would get 55
per cent more money, and black adult education 180 per cent more –
at a time when total government spending would rise by only 14 per
cent. Gerrit Viljoen, minister of national education, said the government was planning to end free schooling for whites, which I suggested
might free funds for diversion to black education.[10] Botha's government
also announced the end of tax discrimination against Africans. We had
exposed this in the *FM* back in 1973. Until then the heavier taxes on
Africans were a form of apartheid of which few people were aware,
and some even refused to believe. But Africans had had to start paying income tax at a lower threshold than applied to white, coloured,
and Indian taxpayers. Unlike these others, they received no rebates for

families either.[11] Now the finance minister, Owen Horwood, announced that the higher taxes on Africans would end in 1984.[12]

Botha appeared to think his relaxations in policy would meet the expectations of the country's black majority, while maintaining overall white control. However, I commented, 'the adaptations of which he talks will have to be much greater than he ever dreamed of if he is to turn South Africa away from the bloodbath he fears'.[13]

Part of Botha's problem was that apartheid was not simply a set of policies which could be repealed, an ugly aspect of an otherwise normal society, but a total way of life with a momentum of its own. And so it was that a year which had started with promises of some sort of political rights for urban Africans ended with draft legislation to remove their statutory urban residence rights altogether. The architect of this was the tireless Piet Koornhof, who invoked the names of Abraham Lincoln and William Wilberforce when he published a bill to replace statutory rights with rights defined in regulations and therefore entirely dependent on his discretion.[14]

Absurdly, almost unbelievably, pragmatic liberalisation of industrial relations was accompanied by the toughest influx-control proposals since the imposition of passes on African women in 1952. Both Koornhof and Botha had begun to assert that whites had the right to protect themselves against 'swamping' by blacks as demographers forecast an influx of between 10 and 20 million people into the cities over the next 20 years.[15]

Destruction of shacks on the sand dunes adjoining the formal black townships on the Cape Flats in order to drive supposedly illegal people out of the Cape Peninsula had been going on for several years, as described in chapter 6 of this memoir. Where there had been sufficient resistance and adverse publicity, Koornhof had sometimes backed down and even built houses for people previously living in shacks.[16] Some of the people who had built shacks on the dunes at Crossroads – just across the motorway from the Cape Town airport – had benefited. But these concessions seemed to encourage others to resist removal, among them a settlement of families whose shelters, often made of black plastic garbage bags on a framework of poles hewn from nearby bushes, adjoined the Nyanga township. Many of these shackdwellers had casual employment as chars or gardeners in Cape Town suburbs. Even in these jobs they could earn more than in their supposed homelands of the Transkei and the Ciskei. Many of the women on the dunes had moved there because they could no longer endure separation from their husbands.[17]

Koornhof declared that the government had given them two years' notice of its intention to evict them from their temporary accommodation and send them to the homelands. They'd been offered meal and train tickets, but had stayed illegally in the city as part of a campaign to wreck influx control. The 'squatters' were 'forcing the Government to act against them in the middle of winter', but it would 'not be blackmailed by such a campaign'.[18]

Visiting American congressmen wept after witnessing the conditions of black families whose shelters adjoining Nyanga had been demolished after police with dogs had moved in on them. One of them, Howard Wolpe, a leading campaigner for sanctions against South Africa, said, 'We saw the degradation of humans in the exercise of police power that was beyond belief.' Another congressman said he and his wife had stood in the hail and rain among 400 women and children whose shacks had been torn down, but could themselves stand it for only 30 minutes. The Cape had been hit by a violent storm which stopped pilots from boarding ships in the harbour. A white businessman who gave shelter to some of the families said he saw his action as akin to the sheltering of Jews in Nazi Germany.[19]

A thousand people were deported to the Transkei under police escort. Some immediately started the trek back to Cape Town, prompting the police to set up roadblocks to stop them.

Those who got through feared setting the whole process of demolition and deportation in motion once again, so some took refuge in

St George's Cathedral. A white woman came in and urinated on the altar, screaming 'Go back to the Transkei'.[20] The government said that as soon as funds became available, it would erect 5 000 kilometres of fences around the homelands to keep unauthorised Africans out of the common area.[21] The foreign minister, Pik Botha, said that the deported people were not South Africans, but 'like Mexicans in the US'.[22]

Koornhof was getting desperate. Maximum penalties for employing illegal Africans were to be increased again. In 1979 he had put them up from R100 to R500. Now they were to go up to R5 000 – equivalent as I told the readers of the *New York Times* and *The Guardian* to $4 350 and £2 500 respectively.[23] Anyone accommodating an unauthorised African overnight – whether in a white suburb or a black township – would be liable to R500 or six months' imprisonment, plus R20 for each night the offence continued. As usual, some of the proposals were dressed up as a liberal reform in that Africans with urban residence rights would be classified as 'permanent'. However, there was a catch. They could lose this status if Koornhof's officials did not regard them as having 'approved accommodation' – in practice difficult since the authorities admitted that 35 000 families in Soweto alone needed housing,[24] the government having imposed a freeze in 1968 on the construction of new black housing outside the homelands. Explaining the niceties of this system to the readers of foreign newspapers was not easy. But I was given plenty of space to do so.

As a former sports minister, Koornhof had been the architect of limited desegregation measures to stave off an intensified international boycott. Few people understood the complexities of his attempts simultaneously to relax and maintain apartheid, causing him to remark that every time he explained his sports policy people thought he was joking, and every time he told a joke people thought he was talking about his sports policy. Such self-deprecation helped him acquire a liberal image. The limited relaxations of certain aspects of the pass laws that flowed from the Riekert commission fostered this image. But people such as

Nic Olivier, a former Broederbond member and law professor at the University of Stellenbosch who was now an opposition MP and whom I consulted regularly, clinically dissected the new laws he was planning.[25] There was indeed so much criticism and so much adverse publicity that the proposed legislation was eventually shelved.

And the government started to make more concessions, especially on the Cape Flats, where its behaviour was subject to close scrutiny by the press, the Institute, the Black Sash, other non-governmental organisations, and opposition MPs. Once or twice when I had appointments to visit MPs, I found their offices empty because they had rushed out to Crossroads or some other shack settlement in an attempt to stop police raids.

But now an unofficial ceasefire seemed to have come into operation between the government and the shackdwellers on the dunes. A few thousand sites were made available on which people could erect their own houses, the government providing rudimentary services. Ken Andrew, an opposition MP, suggested that this might be a 'massive reversal' of policy. He was right. Some of the shackdwellers were even declared to be legal. Nobody could be sure how long the ceasefire would last because the 'demolition parties and their machinery and dogs could pounce out of the night at any time, as they have done in the past'. However, 'it is certain that in this place and in this respect at least, apartheid is collapsing as a result of its own contradictions and passive resistance by its victims. It can no longer be enforced on the dunes without brute force on a scale that the South African government, except when it goes crazy, seems to shrink from.'[26]

I wrote this after being taken on a tour of some of the dune settlements by Melford Yamile, one of the local leaders. He had survived after the police had fired a bullet right through him during one of their raids. Many of the people who'd been bussed off to the Transkei after the raids on Nyanga were now back on the dunes, 'living in pup tents and large black plastic dome-like shelters subdivided inside into dozens of tiny compartments as each family struggles for a bit of privacy'. Amidst the maze of shelters was a clinic run by Regina Ntongana, who had lost two infants after being deported to a part of the Transkei where she said water was as scarce as work. 'Here at least, if your child is sick, you can go to a clinic,' she said.

The victory of the shackdwellers on the Cape Flats against the merciless campaign the apartheid machine had waged against them was hugely significant. I wrote an article for the *New Statesman* suggesting that they had won the 'battle of the dunes'. Some of the films in the *Star Wars* series were then on circuit, so I headlined my article 'Dune Wars'. When it failed to appear I rang to ask why. They told me the government came out of my article in too favourable a light. This, they sniffed, did not accord with the view of it that 'we have here in London'. As we shall see in chapter 10, not many people were willing to recognise that the South African government was capable of doing anything decent. Their suspicions were justified. But they had the consequence that the courageous achievements of ordinary black people in defeating or defying apartheid laws were downplayed or ignored. Only later, when I was running the Institute, did I come to appreciate that these achievements did not suit those with revolutionary agendas.

Elsewhere, ethnic cleansing continued. One of the places I visited was Driefontein, a village about 200 miles east of Johannesburg. It contained 300 individual landowners who grew maize, sugar, beans, potatoes, and pumpkins. They also reared cattle, goats, and fowls. When the rains were good they sold their surplus output in nearby towns such as Wakkerstroom. Some of the landowners leased out part of their land to tenants with whom they practised sharecropping. They had dug wells and boreholes and built houses, shops, schools, and churches. This successful and happy farming community was now under sentence of death because it had been declared a 'black spot', and its 5 000 members were to be removed. I described the threat facing them in long articles in the *Rand Daily Mail*, the *New Statesman*, the *New York Times*, and the London *Sunday Times*.[27] Driefontein gave the lie to the myth that blacks could not farm. Nor were there any signs of the malnutrition often found in the concentrated settlement camps set up for people forced out of 'white' areas.

Driefontein's leader was a gentle and infinitely courteous man called Saul Mkhize. He could not for the life of him understand why the government wished to destroy his community. Nor why Dr Koornhof spurned his approaches over more than a year to stop the removal. I teamed up with Josie Adler of the Black Sash and Geoff Budlender of the Legal Resources Centre to try to help Saul to get the minister to change his mind. Instead I found myself speaking at Saul's memorial service in St Mary's Cathedral after he'd been shot dead by a white constable he was trying to protect from an angry crowd.[28]

Five years after the attacks on the Nyanga people, and three years after Saul Mkhize's death, PW Botha's government abolished influx control in its entirety. By this stage I was running the Institute. Along with the recognition of black trade union rights, this was the most important reform in South Africa since the Second World War. What these two reforms had in common was that they had been forced upon the government by ordinary black people.

'In a quiet way,' as I wrote in *The Guardian*, the people who kept on returning to Cape Town despite all the risks, had been engaged in 'passive resistance – something South Africa has not seen for a long time'.[29] It was this that ultimately broke the back of influx control. But there were other factors as well. The courts struck down key aspects of the pass laws in the Komani and Rikhoto cases.[30] Business, which had supported some of Koornhof's supposed liberalisation measures, started to voice criticism. The Urban Foundation, a business research and lobby group set up in the wake of the Soweto upheavals under the leadership of Jan Steyn, a former judge, urged the abolition of influx control. So did WJP Carr, a former manager of Soweto: the people involved were 'the indigenous population of this country and it's unnecessary to legislate so ferociously against them as if they were our deadly enemies'.[31] And officials responsible for enforcement of shack demolitions and deportations began to acknowledge publicly that attempts to keep Africans out of the Western Cape were a failure. It was even announced that a new black township called Khayelitsha was to be built on the Cape Flats. Although this was 25 miles outside Cape Town, the announcement signified a reversal of the previous policy of freezing housing construction for Africans in the Cape Peninsula.[32]

It was no accident that Pik Botha had described Africans deported from the Western Cape as similar to Mexicans in the US, or that they had been deported under aliens legislation. As pointed out in earlier chapters of this memoir, the NP's ultimate aim was to turn all Africans into foreigners. The coloured and Indian minorities could then be brought into Parliament, which the whites by virtue of their superior numbers would dominate. PW Botha's plans for the two minorities precipitated the second split in the NP in 13 years.

As we saw in chapter 2, the first split, over the incorporation of Maoris in All Black rugby teams touring South Africa, had resulted in the formation of the Herstigte Nasionale Party in 1969. Now, in March 1982, Botha's NP expelled Andries Treurnicht and 15 other MPs who rebelled against his plans for limited power-sharing with the coloured and Indian minorities.[33] The rebels, who then launched the Conservative Party at a meeting in the Skilpadsaal in Pretoria, saw this as the thin end of a wedge that would lead to total integration.[34] Among their number was Bessie Scholtz, a mother of 11, who called upon whites to have bigger families.[35] A year after Treurnicht had been forced out of the Cabinet, Carel Boshoff resigned as chairman of the Broederbond and was replaced by Professor JP de Lange, a leading *verligte* educationist and rector of Rand Afrikaans University.[36]

Treurnicht – who had himself once been chairman of the Broederbond – and his supporters were Johnny-come-latelys. The HNP had been arguing about thin-end-of-the-wedge risks for years. In a general election campaign the previous year, one of the leading HNP men, Gert Beetge, had stated, 'Apartheid is like a spider's web. When the government tries to take away one of its strands, it endangers the whole structure.'[37] PW Botha's policy, in HNP eyes, was one of giving up, giving in, and giving way to blacks.[38] 'We are a nation of granite,' said the HNP, 'but we have leaders with feet of clay.' In making concessions to blacks in some fields, the government was setting 'the law of rising expectations in motion, and increasing the danger of confrontation arising from the gap between reality and heightened expectations'.[39] General Hendrik van den Bergh, a former head of BOSS, said people who believed that material comforts alone would temper black political aspirations were living in a fool's paradise. The government was creating rising expectations among urban blacks, and it was precisely when a government relaxed oppressive rule that people took up arms against it.[40]

The Right were not idiots. In fact, they had a clearer understanding of policy than did the mainstream NP. The NP thought they could have everything both ways. The Right knew this was impossible. As Professor Carel Boshoff, who had become chairman of the Broederbond in 1980, said, 'economic integration in a system of separate political sovereignties' was a 'false doctrine'.[41] In this, of course, he was eventually proved entirely correct. But the Right had no solution either. I once attended a house meeting addressed by Clive Derby-Lewis, a leading member of the Conservative Party later imprisoned for his role in the assassination of Chris Hani in 1993. He was complaining about uncontrolled influx of blacks into the common area. I pointed out to him that Koornhof and others were moving heaven and earth to stop this, but couldn't. What made him think he could succeed where Koornhof had failed? He had no answer. Even Treurnicht, before he led the rebellion against political rights for the coloured and Indian minorities, had sometimes sounded like PW Botha. Addressing a meeting in the mining town of Carletonville near Johannesburg he had once said, 'You can't just swear the black people away. Is there a man here

169

who can stand up and say he has never had a black servant in his house?'[42]

The election brought out the NP's ambivalence on race. Although Botha had toned down his liberal rhetoric in the face of the HNP onslaught, he was still going around – even to areas where the HNP had strong support – preaching the message that neither the economy nor the country's defence effort could do without the contribution of blacks.[43] Half the workers in arms factories were black, because there weren't enough whites to do the work. 'Do you want them to be loyal and not commit sabotage?' The defence minister, Magnus Malan, said that the black component fighting in the border war had risen from 20 per cent to 28 per cent; it was disgraceful for the HNP to claim that integration was being used in the armed forces to soften up whites for general integration.[44] Other ministers went around boasting that the government was spending 12 times as much on white schoolchildren as on black. They also boasted that white social pensions were three times those of blacks. Nor was a cent of white tax revenue spent on blacks. And if the HNP really thought blacks were so well off, it should change places with them.[45]

The election would demonstrate the 'great paradox' of South African policy. During the campaign the NP would appeal to white racist instincts to rally its supporters. After the election, those very same white supporters would be expected to endorse the limited adjustments in racial policy that Botha wanted to make.[46]

It was not long before the foreign minister, Pik Botha, was apologising to the Malawian ambassador in Pretoria after the Hoërskool Waterkloof had refused to allow its rugby team to play against a Christian Brothers College team of which the ambassador's 18-year-old son was a member. There were eight children of black diplomats in white government schools, but they could not join in sport unless certain conditions had been met. The ambassador said his son's treatment proved that some South African parents were teaching their children racial discrimination at an early age. 'I am all the more surprised that it happened in Waterkloof, where all those enlightened Afrikaners are said to live,' he commented.[47]

Yet despite what happened on the playing fields of Waterkloof, apartheid in education was beginning to unravel. Roman Catholic schools in the Transvaal had for several years been admitting blacks without seeking permission, and the authorities were turning a blind eye rather than carrying out their earlier threat to withdraw the registration of schools that admitted blacks and thereby force them to close.[48]

As for higher education, the government in 1983 established the first university for Africans outside the homelands. This was a breach of its own influx control policy, which previously required that Africans wanting a post-primary education had to go to a high school or university in a homeland. But Cas Crouse, rector of the new university, said there was 'an enormous need to bring tertiary education to the heart of the big black cities'. So Vista University opened campuses in Soweto and three other African townships in the common area.[49] I thought this an important enough liberalisation of policy to later invite Professor Elwyn Jenkins, director of the Vista campus in Mamelodi township outside Pretoria, to address a meeting at the Institute, of whose board he later became chairman.

The government also began to retreat from the apartheid it had imposed on the open universities in 1959. White universities would now be permitted to admit blacks on a quota system. But the universities said that even if the quotas allowed 80 per cent of their students to be black, they would still be 'totally abhorrent and unacceptable'.[50]

Half-hearted though the NP's retreat from apartheid was, the HNP was able to push up its share of the vote from 3.3 per cent in 1977 to 14.1 per cent in April 1981, although it still failed to gain a seat in Parliament.[51] But PW Botha was losing to the left as well, for the liberal Progressive Federal Party under Frederik van Zyl Slabbert gained eight parliamentary seats to bring its total up to 26.[52] On the Treurnicht rebellion against attempts to restore some sort of 'half-baked' political rights to coloured people, I could not resist recalling in the *Irish Times* how PW Botha's NP had used bicycle chains in the 1950s to try to break up meetings protesting against the removal of coloured voters from the common roll. My father had witnessed some of this. 'That they should now be gouging one another's eyes out because of the "coloured" people is only fit and proper,' I wrote.[53]

As Botha was preparing to introduce his power-sharing plan, the ANC was intensifying the insurgency campaign it had re-launched after the Soweto upheavals in 1976. According to the government, 48 people had been killed by insurgents in 220 incidents since 1976.[54] In February 1983 some 86 blacks were injured when a bomb exploded in a building in Bloemfontein where they were queuing up for passes.[55] In May 1983 a car bomb exploded in a street outside a building in Pretoria whose tenants included the headquarters of the South African Air Force. Nineteen people were killed and more than 200 injured in this, the ANC's most lethal attack yet.[56]

A day or two after the bomb, the air force attacked seven targets in Maputo, killing five people. The government said the ANC was using Mozambique as a base for infiltration into South Africa.[57] This was the third military strike by South Africa into a neighbouring state, including a raid on Maseru, capital of Lesotho, on 9 December 1982, in which 42 people had been killed.[58] A leaked report from the American Central Intelligence Agency suggested that youngsters who joined the ANC in the wake of the Soweto upheavals were becoming more powerful in the organisation's military wing and were pressing for the abandonment of the earlier policy of avoiding civilian casualties.[59] The tough police action after the Soweto upheavals had caused several thousand black youngsters to flee into exile and give the ANC 'a new lease of life'.[60] This is exactly what I had predicted in my book on Soweto.[61]

Moreover, following the bannings of its organisations and of sympathetic newspapers, the Black Consciousness movement was in disarray, while there was growing support among the black intelligentsia and white intellectuals for the ANC.[62] Whatever the South African government's military might and its economic leverage against its neighbours might be, 'there is not a single black political or labour leader of any consequence who finds its policies remotely acceptable'.[63]

Rising tension within the country and the region meant that pressures for tougher economic measures against South Africa were intensifying. But there was no shortage of foreign suppliers and contractors for Eskom, which was planning to triple or even quadruple the country's generating capacity by the end of the century.[64] Sasol was increasing its oil-from-coal output. Moreover, only five years after the Security Council had imposed the arms embargo against South Africa in November 1977, the country was launching an arms export drive. Armscor, the state-owned weapons manufacturing and procuring company, had even put one of its prize products on show at an arms fair in Athens. This was the G6, a six-wheeled self-propelled armoured vehicle on which was mounted the G5, a 155-millimetre heavy artillery piece which previously had had to be towed by another vehicle, limiting its mobility. Necessity had been the mother of the invention of the mobile G6 when the South African Defence Force found itself outgunned by Cuban-manned Russian artillery in Angola in 1975.[65]

Although it was an open secret, South Africa's invasion of Angola could not be reported in local newspapers because of restrictions in the Defence Act. The defence force knew these were farcical because every other newspaper in the world could report it; when I rang for comment their press liaison man would sometimes greet me with 'Hello Mr Kane-Berman, how nice to hear from you, what lies can I tell you on behalf of the defence force today?' Armscor, naturally, was only too happy to show off the G6 and other products and took me on a tour of some of its 15 factories in Pretoria, which I wrote up for *The Guardian* under the headline 'South Africa launches world-beater arms exports'.

Underneath all this South Africa continued as normal. More than 3 000 police took part in a pass raid in Hillbrow, Yeoville, and Berea.[66]

A banning order was served on a leading Soweto educationist, Fanyana Mazibuko, who was trying to offer schoolchildren better maths tuition than was available in most black schools. He was thought to be around number 165 on the list of banned people.[67] Among journalists detained were Thami Mazwai, news editor of *Sowetan*, the major black daily paper in the country, and Zwelakhe Sisulu, president of the Media Workers' Association of South Africa. Khotso Seatlholo, one of the presidents of the Soweto students' representative council, who had fled the country but had now returned, was arrested. The Afrikaans Sunday paper *Rapport*, however, endorsed the comment of an MP who had said that the country's problems could not be solved by filling Robben Island with prisoners.[68] Another banning order was served on Beyers Naudé.[69]

Finally, Richard Attenborough fell foul both of apartheid laws and South African liberation politics. He proposed visiting the country for the opening of his film *Gandhi* in 1983. But although theatres had been desegregated, cinemas (apart from drive-ins) had not. The government was willing to open charity premieres to people of all races, but one of the charities hosting a premiere in an Indian suburb in Johannesburg said Gandhi's 'whole struggle was against permits and for us to accept a permit would be the height of insult to his memory'. Some of the organisations hosting illegal but racially mixed charity opening nights told Attenborough not to come because to do so would be to break the international cultural boycott of South Africa. I telephoned Mrs Ela Ramgobin, granddaughter of Gandhi, who said Attenborough would not be welcome. Her husband, Mewa Ramgobin, whom I'd known in Nusas, was entering his fourth five-year banning order. Attenborough cancelled his trip.[70]

To stave off the 'total Marxist onslaught' that had been launched against the country, the government had adopted what it called a 'total strategy'. This policy was so full of contradictions as to suggest that it lacked 'total conviction at the top', resulting in 'total confusion below' and 'total rejection opposite'.[71] But now there was a straw in the wind.

The trickiest question for the NP had always been how to accommodate the political aspirations of Africans in the common area, given that they heavily outnumbered whites. Botha suggested in 1982 that it was 'increasingly urgent' to satisfy these 'political aspirations'. FW de Klerk, one of his senior ministers, said the future of urban Africans was the subject of 'intense' debate within the party. One of the ideas being discussed was that such Africans would be given seats in homeland legislatures, which would then have 'extraterritorial jurisdiction' over their 'citizens' in the common area. But *Beeld*, the Afrikaans morning newspaper in Johannesburg, commented that Africans would not be satisfied with such a plan, and that some of the homelands refused to take 'independence'.

By the end of 1981 four of the 10 homelands were independent, and Koornhof said he expected another four to follow them. This would leave only KwaZulu and Kangwane as part of South Africa, mused Koornhof, in a sign that the government now recognised there was nothing it could do to overcome the refusal of those two to take independence. Their total citizenship of 6.25 million, Koornhof went on, was fewer than the 7.8 million white, coloured, and Indian citizens in the country.

What could his musings possibly mean? That Africans who retained their South African citizenship could now be safely incorporated in the same institutions as the three minorities because the three minorities would outnumber them?[72] I discussed Koornhof's remarks with Mangosuthu Buthelezi. He was not willing to speculate, but I knew he would never accept any kind of special deal for KwaZulu or himself, or do anything behind the back of Nelson Mandela. So whatever Koornhof's musings might have meant, they were a non-starter. But they were an indication that more and more Nationalists were coming to recognise that their dream of a South Africa without any African citizens was now unattainable. This amounted to tacit acknowledgement of the end of Dr Verwoerd's 'grand apartheid' scheme.

Many years later I was reminded of how passionate I must have felt about the monstrous design to strip Africans of their South African citizenship. It came in a letter from Rudolf Gruber, a member of the Institute's Council resident in Berlin. Previously resident in Bonn, he had represented the South Africa Foundation in Germany until that organisation was eventually wound up. Funded by business, the foundation sought among other things to argue against economic sanctions. Like other foundation representatives, Dr Gruber made periodic visits to South Africa to update himself on developments within the country. In his letter, Dr Gruber recalled that we'd first met in 1976, when he'd sought from me an assessment of the independence of the Transkei, about which I'd written in the *Financial Mail* and whose independence celebrations he had recently attended. He recalled our meeting at the Mariston Hotel in Johannesburg: 'You delivered a hatchet job on the whole sorry exercise, and made an indelible impression on me. Never had I heard anything like it for depth of knowledge, stringency in argument, and brilliance of phrasing and expression. If there had been a short-hand record of what you said, it could have gone straight into print without any corrections or improvements of any kind. It was a veritable tour de force.'[73]

Rudolf Gruber is one of the most remarkable men I've ever met. He is so alert, so well informed, and so engaging that it's easy to forget that he is blind. On one occasion he and I spoke together at a conference on South Africa in Hamburg. For almost an hour he recited reams of statistics on all aspects of the country. I recognised most of them because they were in the most recent edition of the Institute's *Survey*, which I had edited. But they were all in his head.

CHAPTER 9

Survival

Survival had to be topmost priority when I took over as director (later renamed chief executive) of the South African Institute of Race Relations on 8 September 1983. We had suffered three years of heavy losses, and the honorary treasurer, Harold Bernstein, had reported that our liquid position was 'dangerously low'.[1] At my very first board meeting our chairman, Ernie Wentzel, warned we could face legal action for carrying on the affairs of a bankrupt organisation. The five-year pledges from business that had been an important source of income had run out, so we had had to mortgage Auden House, our famous property at 68 de Korte Street, Braamfontein, to the bank as security for an overdraft.

Had I known how serious the organisation's financial position was, I might never have applied for the job. I had no management training, little managerial experience, and I didn't know how to read a balance sheet. Nor was I aware of the extent to which the Institute had lost its way. But I knew I could not preside over the closure of an organisation which had celebrated its fiftieth birthday only a few years earlier. This was no ordinary pressure group or think-tank. As Ellen Hellmann had written in an essay marking the Institute's half-century, it was 'the first national multiracial organisation specifically established to promote interracial goodwill and conduct investigations bearing upon race relations'.[2] Dr Hellmann, a social anthropologist who had long played a dominating role in the Institute, died the year before my appointment, and this unique asset was now in my hands.

When the Institute came into being in 1929, the Union of South Africa had been in existence for nearly two decades. Apart from the fact that the Union Constitution entrenched white supremacy, key features of apartheid such as the Land Acts and the industrial colour bar were already on the Statute Book, with more in the pipeline. The Boer War had ended 27 years earlier, but most whites still believed that better 'race relations' meant improving the relationship between Afrikaners and English-speaking South Africans. Blacks didn't matter. As Alfred Hoernlé wrote, whites favouring a 'more humane' approach to them were regarded as 'heretics', 'traitors', 'kaffirboeties', or 'most scathing of all – liberals'.[3] In the Cape there was some mixing between black and white. Elsewhere, outside the workplace, where economic interdependence was a fact of life, contact was limited. According to Hellmann, 'The predominant characteristic of the white group, secure in its hegemony and cushioned in its relative isolation, was its unawareness of the conditions under which other groups lived.'

However, starting in 1921, a man called JD Rheinallt Jones had established a number of interracial 'joint councils' to promote goodwill between people of all races. They were attacked by white conservatives, who saw them as a threat to segregationist ideology, and by militant blacks and whites, who rejected their conciliatory approach. The council movement nevertheless grew and on 9 May 1929, with American money from the Phelps-Stokes Fund and the Carnegie Corporation, the Institute was established to promote their work. In all, 80 joint councils were established in the ensuing years, although by 1978 there were only two left, the Institute having taken over most of their work.

The Institute, which was registered in 1937 as a non-profit company under Section 21 of the Companies Act, began without ready-made policy or a programme of action. Its beliefs were not set out until 1952 in a booklet entitled *Go Forward in Faith*. This said the organisation's approach 'has been permeated by the principles of Christian living and the values basic to Western civilisation'. These included belief in the value of the individual human being, in fundamental rights, and in equal opportunities. Territorial apartheid was 'completely impracticable', but 'economic integration' did not mean residential integration or miscege-nation – the latter being an emotional issue that bothered whites more than blacks.

To the 'frequently posed' question 'Do you want your sister to marry a black man?', the booklet said the answer was 'Does my sister want to marry a black man?'

Democracy had 'seldom, if ever, been applied in a multiracial society with peoples of varying cultures and different stages of development'. The Institute nevertheless committed itself to common citizenship. 'In the long run' the representation of Africans in the central legislature should be no less than that of 'Europeans'. For the future, the booklet said:

> The only credo that one can cling to is to abjure self-interest and politics of expediency, to stand firm on principle and go forward in faith, believing that to do so is the only way to serve finally what is right and just, believing too that the use of the right means is itself creative and that by unjust means no justifiable end can ever be attained.[4]

The next policy document came out 20 years later under the title *The Road Ahead*. Drawing on the Institute's own investigations, it said that all blacks in the common area were exposed to 'gross political, economic, and social discrimination'. There were 'many signs of deep resentment and growing antagonism not only to the regime but to the white people as a totality'. The point of no return had not yet been reached, but there could be no long-term stability for South Africa without transition to a system in which political power was shared by all races in the com-mon area. There were 'grave difficulties' in doing this in a multiracial society with differing cultural backgrounds and levels of education, not to mention 'marked numerical disparities between the various population groups', but these could be overcome.

The call for political rights in the common area excluded people in the homelands. This made *The Road Ahead* controversial within the Institute itself. But the document was highly critical of influx control and other key apartheid measures, along with detention without trial and other erosions of the rule of law. It called for trade union rights for Africans, the end of enforced segregation in sport and elsewhere, and the progressive elimination of racial discrimination. Since whites controlled all the power, the onus was on them to change their attitudes.[5]

As these documents show, the Institute's position on political rights was gradualist. It was also prescient in warning of the difficulties of sharing power in a multicultural and multiethnic society. Even so, it was putting forward a view of South Africa fundamentally at odds with the policies implemented by successive governments. There had been a flicker of hope after the Second World War, when the Smuts government indicated that it would adopt liberalising proposals put forward by the Fagan Commission, some of them emanating from the Institute. But Smuts was defeated in the general election of 1948 which brought the National Party to power.

Most Institute members were English-speaking whites, but prominent liberal Africans and Afrikaners were also elected to its presidency and other positions, among them Professor ZK Matthews, Dr EG Malherbe, and Professor DDT Jabavu. Prominent liberal intellectuals such as Alfred Hoernlé helped mould early Institute thinking. Numerous prominent South African liberals were among its office bearers and members.

In the earlier years, the Institute, which was always free of alignment to any political party, enjoyed easy access to the government. After 1948 this changed. In 1951 the organisation sought a meeting with the new minister of native affairs, Dr HF Verwoerd, to present proposals to ease racial tensions. He was not prepared to meet a racially mixed delegation.

Nor was the Institute prepared to split its delegation into two. So the meeting never took place. Later the Institute was subjected to a hostile commission of enquiry. Some of its staff were banned, others taken into detention without trial. A few publications were also banned.

There was, however, always much more to the Institute than its courageous advocacy of a common society and the beacon it held aloft throughout the long dark night of apartheid. The organisation was also known for two other things. One was its fact-finding. The other was the projects it launched to deal with particular problems or meet particular needs. As we shall see, when I took over I strengthened the fact-finding work but shed all but one of the projects.

From the start the Institute proclaimed its belief in 'the pursuit of truth as a value in itself'. It further believed that 'the systematic seeking out of facts [about] the quality of life of disadvantaged groups in South Africa would increase public awareness and promote interracial understanding, without which there could be no peaceful future' for the country.[6] Fact-finding is what made the organisation famous. Down the years the Institute published around 1 000 reports on almost every aspect of South African society, from the cost of living in Soweto to studies of censorship laws to monographs on farm labour to guides on how to run voluntary societies. It hosted countless speakers and numerous conferences, and then published transcripts of what was said. All of this was aimed at public education. The Institute was known to be willing to speak the truth without fear or favour, but also for ensuring that when it spoke it did so only after its research had uncovered the facts.

I pulled the front covers off copies of all our publications, framed them, and hung them in our offices wherever there was space. The best known was the *Survey of Race Relations*, published annually since after the Second World War, in which its most famous writer, Muriel Horrell, served as an officer with the South African Air Force in Egypt – although as a woman she was not entitled to fly combat despite being a qualified pilot.[7] The *Survey* gathered into a single volume statistical information on all aspects of the apartheid system, along with analyses of all the relevant legislation. It soon established for itself an international reputation for objectivity and accuracy. The Library of Congress in Washington DC was only one of many around the world that subscribed to it. In 1989 I was shown a full set of *Surveys* in the Institute for African Studies of the USSR Academy of Sciences in Moscow. When Nelson Mandela was writing his memoirs after his release he discovered that some of his own copies were missing so he contacted us for replacements. We circularised all our members in the hunt for the missing copies, which we passed on to him. Muriel Horrell had by then retired after compiling 27 *Surveys,* but when she died in 1994, I described her as 'the queen of a million footnotes'.[8] This was the celebrated publication for which I was now responsible.

I was also responsible for the Institute's numerous special projects. These included a youth programme, a national feeding scheme called Operation Hunger, an oral history project, shops in six cities providing outlets for rural handicrafts, a project to bring domestic servants and their employers together to enable the latter to understand more about the needs of the former, a project to teach literacy to migrant workers living in hostels, and a bursary programme. Some of these were run by dedicated and remarkable people. Some were better funded than others. Some were running out of money.

Rex Welsh, general secretary of the Rhodes Scholarships in South Africa, wrote to me that the Institute was lucky to have me. The first piece of practical advice I got was from Arnold Kane, my father's younger brother, a chartered accountant under whom some of my Wits contemporaries had served their articles. He told me never to rely on auditors to pick up fraud or theft. 'It's your job to put systems in place to make sure they cannot happen.' The second piece of practical advice was from my father: 'To reduce the risk that incoming cheques will be stolen, make sure that two members of your staff always open all the post together.'

I was only the fifth chief executive in more than 50 years. That the Institute had even survived was itself an achievement, for it had all along been preaching to whites a message few of them wished to hear. The Right had always been hostile to liberalism, but now liberals were under renewed attack from the Left. Following the upheavals in Soweto and elsewhere in 1976, a new mood of militancy was abroad among black youth. Insurrectionary activity organised by the ANC was on the increase. Portuguese rule in Angola and Mozambique had collapsed after a coup in Lisbon in 1974. Robert Mugabe was in power in Zimbabwe. And PW Botha's government was about to launch its new tricameral Parliament. What kind of role could there be in this polarising atmosphere for an organisation committed to using research and ideas to bring about reconciliation and change? How could we play such a role anyway if we were running out of money?

Even before I took up my new job, I had joined an Institute delegation to see the Anglo American Chairman's Fund, headed by Michael O'Dowd. He gave us emergency bridging finance on condition that we got matching sums from elsewhere, which we did. He also told us we had become a 'holding company of worthy causes' and had better decide what exactly it was we wanted to do. This was one of the best pieces of advice we ever received. Another port of call was Jan Steyn, executive director of the Urban Foundation, following which a management consultant called Frank Cauldwell came to see me.

At Frank's behest we established a strategic planning committee to take the organisation apart and put it together again. Three key decisions were speedily made. The first was to restore research to pride of place as our major activity. The second was to hive off all but one of our projects or decentralise responsibility for them to our regional offices. The third was to revitalise membership as a key source of income.

Putting research back on top was a case of going back to basics. Our projects were either set up as separate trusts, or decentralised to our regional offices. Ken Owen later wrote in *Business Day* that I had done a 'quite brilliant job of focusing the work of the Institute on questions of reform rather than on the old do-gooding charity stuff'.[9] I would not have dismissed any of our projects as 'do-gooding', but divesting the Institute of them made me extremely unpopular in some of our regional offices, visits to which I sometimes dreaded. One shop we were running claimed it was making a profit, except that it omitted the salaries of its staff from its costs – which I discovered the Institute was paying out of other funds. The same shop discovered some small-scale internal theft, and then tried to make sure I never found out about this.

The only special project we retained at national level was our bursary programme. This grew from strength to strength. In the last 30 years the Institute has awarded bursaries worth R230 million to some 3 695 students, most of them black.[10] Nelson Mandela was one of our beneficiaries in 1947. Shortly after his release from prison in 1990, he rang me at the Town House, the hotel where I was staying in Cape Town. I was out, so he left a message. This had the hotel staff all agog as they basked in my momentary celebrity status as the recipient of his call. When I rang him back, Mandela explained that he needed a bursary for the child of a domestic servant. I said I would send him the application forms, but that I had no say in the selection of our students as this was in the hands of an independent committee which would not welcome any attempt by me to influence its decisions. I don't suppose too many people have turned Mandela down. I certainly felt guilty enough to write to him a few days later explaining how the Institute's bursary selection process worked.

Divesting ourselves of our projects was a political as well as a financial decision. Instead of tackling problems by charitable work, however valuable that might be, we saw our role as dealing with policy. This meant analysing its impact, as the Institute had always done, but also putting forward liberal alternatives and making sure the government and everyone else knew about them. The shift was critical. Instead of trying to alleviate its impact, we were out to change policy. This was not only more difficult but also more controversial. It was also more exciting to be engaging in the battle of ideas than to be running charitable projects.

Equally critically, we intended to reassert our independence. The Institute, as Neil Jacobsohn, a senior journalist on *Business Day*, wrote some years later, had drifted into 'protest politics'. Cas St Leger of the *Sunday Times* said that we 'had become firmly associated in many minds with the far Left'. My president, Lawrence Schlemmer, my chairman, Ernie Wentzel, and key members of our governing bodies were determined to change this. And they had picked me for the job. I had to prevent the Institute from sliding further away to the Left as so many other liberal institutions had done, along with sections of the press and much of academia. But there was more to it. As Ernie in particular recognised, revolutionary violence was not only on the increase, but many liberals were turning a blind eye to it. Somebody had to stop this happening at the Institute. That too was part of my job, although it wasn't until I was in the hot seat that I realised just how fierce opposition from the Left could be. As Jacobsohn wrote, the Left was 'unwilling to loosen its grip' and it was not 'until near bankruptcy focused minds' that I had been able to take action.[11]

It took some time to establish my authority. Some of our research staff supported the United Democratic Front (UDF), which was closely aligned with the ANC, if not a front for it. I knew from my own supporters among the staff that some of their colleagues had tried to block my appointment. Some of the black staff alerted me to the fact that some of the white staff were trying to whip up opposition on the basis that I was a 'racist'. Some of the members of our Council – the body responsible for policy and for nominating the Board – were also in the UDF camp. But this was a battle for the soul of the Institute and I had to win it. If we slid away, liberalism in South Africa would have been dealt a crippling blow. We had no choice but to face down all our opponents, and we did. We were one of the few anti-apartheid organisations that never joined the UDF. Rumblings continued for some years, and even on one occasion escalated into public revolt among some of our research staff against our work on political violence. This happened on the eve of a speaking trip I was making to Europe, and I was tempted to cancel the trip. I decided, however, that this might be read as panic so I went ahead with it. But I left instructions that the rebels' critique should be refuted point by point, which it was. In the end, opposition drifted away or petered out as we ensured that we got our facts right and refused to backtrack.

Many liberals applauded our decision to resist the slideaway, but some sections of the broad anti-apartheid family were outraged and accused us of moving to the Right. The accusations intensified as we began criticising anti-apartheid organisations for stoking violence in black townships. Even greater outrage greeted us when we pointed out that most of the victims of the violent struggle against apartheid were not whites but ordinary black individuals trying to go about their daily business – men to work, women to the shops, children to school. Liberals, we were told, were not supposed to talk about any of this. They were supposed to cover it up. When I spoke about Ernie's warnings at his funeral service in St Mary's Cathedral in April 1986, the Black Sash's magazine omitted that section of my eulogy.[12] More about this type of cover-up below.

In the meantime, unpopular though it was in some quarters, our strategic plan worked, though it took us nearly three years to turn our accumulated deficit into a surplus[13] and eliminate our overdraft.[14] We launched a new category of corporate membership to supplement individual and institutional memberships. Instead of asking a handful of business leaders to go out and obtain pledges on our behalf, we went out ourselves and sold memberships to the private sector on the basis of research and other services we would supply. Our new membership manager, Jenneke Kardol (later Stekhoven), did a brilliant job getting our corporate membership drive going. In later years the stylish and dedicated Sue Gordon went out and sold corporate memberships until she retired at the age of 78. Sue seemed to have more energy than many people half her age.

Nor did we neglect other sources of funding. Core support from key donors and funds for particular research projects are as important as membership income. Our long-standing supporters include not only the Anglo American Chairman's Fund, but also the Oppenheimer Memorial Trust. The Friedrich Naumann Foundation, headquartered in Potsdam and associated with the Free Democratic Party, Europe's leading classically liberal party, is also a key supporter of long standing. The International Republican Institute and the National Endowment for Democracy in Washington DC came on board in 1994 for 20 years. Elisabeth Bradley gave us several magnificent donations. Harry Barker, who had once written to me that my father was 'a courageous man apart from being such a good lawyer',[15] left us a nice share portfolio. Dick Gawith – the businessman who coined the slogan 'Nobody makes better tea than you and Five Roses' – gave us funds for a study on black economic empowerment (BEE). The Donaldson Trust sponsored some of our publications in tribute to Marjorie Britten, who had served the Institute and some of its bursary trusts over many years. To my regret, I never put her name forward for the honorary life membership which was her due. I should have done the same on her retirement for Jill Wentzel for her bravery in writing *The Liberal Slideaway* (see chapter 11).

On fund-raising, I was never able to relax, ever. Many donors in Western Europe and the US – whether government, churches, foundations, or even business groups – wouldn't even consider you without an endorsement from the ANC, which by then had won recognition in many parts of the world as the sole authentic representative of black South Africans. We declined to seek any such endorsement. On one occasion we were invited by the European Community (forerunner of the European Union) to submit a budget for bursaries for black students to Brussels. We did so, only then to be told to channel it via an ANC-aligned trust in Johannesburg. This we also refused to do.[16] Anti-apartheid groups within South Africa told foreign donors to steer clear of us because of our refusal to join the UDF.[17] A contract to administer a large bursary programme for USAID was delayed for a year by ANC-aligned church organisations trying to block it. In the end we signed contracts to administer bursaries for USAID to the value of almost $30 million. But the difficulties we faced were an early warning of the ANC's determination to assert political hegemony.

I also scored a couple of own goals. About a year after I took over I visited Stockholm, where some of our money had previously come from.[18] As I arrived, the results of an opinion survey by Lawrence Schlemmer were published. They showed that three quarters of blacks were opposed to economic sanctions against South Africa. This was not what the Swedes, loyal and generous supporters of the ANC, wished to hear. So one of the Swedish ministries asked me if I knew this Professor Schlemmer. Yes, said I, he's the president of my Institute. Well, they wanted to know, how reliable is his opinion research? Probably the best in the country, I replied. Well, they persisted, perhaps all those blacks who oppose sanctions don't really understand all the issues at stake. Funny you should say that, I replied, our government uses exactly that reason for not giving blacks the vote.

The words were out before I could stop myself, and it was goodbye to Swedish funding for 30 years, until they gave us a small donation for a project in 2014.

Fund-raising for the Institute, now the responsibility of Frans Cronje, my successor, remains as tough as ever. Most corporate social investment programmes focus on charitable rather than policy work. Most local corporates and donors are more terrified of the ANC than they ever were of the NP, especially in the 1980s as the NP's moral authority waned. Only a handful of local corporates are now willing to finance policy work for fear that it might antagonise the ANC. But building a school, for example, carries no risk and can easily be totted up as a success, with photographs to prove it. It is also still very difficult for the Institute to get foreign funding for research or policy work that isn't of the most politically correct and anodyne kind. All the more credit therefore to the American, Belgian, Danish, Irish, and Australian embassies for the support they gave us, although never for longer than a few years. However, unlike organisations which had to close when their foreign funding dried up, we were able to keep going because we had local funding as well. The spread of funding reduced our vulnerability if any particular source dried up. It also enabled us to remain independent of political influence.

I ran the Institute for the last seven years of the apartheid era, and almost the first quarter century of the post-apartheid era. Throughout that time I was editor-in-chief of the *Survey* (whose name I changed to *South Africa Survey*). This sometimes felt like being on a treadmill. No sooner had one year's *Survey* been sent off to the printers than we were busy planning the next. Lying on the beach one day at Mykonos, I rebelled at the thought that when I got back to work the following week there would be a pile of chapters awaiting my edit. When I told the head of research on my return that the *Survey* would now be her responsibility in its entirety, she was horrified and bullied me into changing my mind. The main result was that over some 30 years I edited almost 22 000 pages of the *Survey*. The complete set back to 1946 runs to some 34 000 pages and stretches nearly seven feet on my bookshelf. Paging through the *Survey*, a visitor to my office once asked how many years it took us to produce. When I replied that we did it every year, his jaw just dropped.

Anthony Robinson, one-time *FT* correspondent in Johannesburg, wrote that the *Survey* 'shines an unblinking light on the country's all-pervasive apartheid system'.[19] One academic at Wits said the *Survey* had been 'innately radical and subversive in tearing apartheid and its logic apart'. Indeed, whenever whites today claim that they never knew about all the horrors of apartheid, I retort that it was all there in our *Survey*, as well as in the press and even in *Hansard*, thanks to speeches and questions asked in Parliament. Throughout the apartheid era, South Africa remained an open society. This helped to undermine apartheid.

Despite restrictions on what the press could say on such matters as oil supplies, arms, and troop movements, and despite bans of individual journalists and newspapers, the whole apartheid story was told in great and damning detail in the country at the time. Liberal institutions played the leading role in this, demonstrating the power of the printed and spoken word. No amount of government propaganda inside or outside South Africa was able to hide the truth we systematically exposed to the light of day, helping to shame the NP into changing course. This means that the *Survey* is the story of the rise and fall of the apartheid system, told in South Africa by South Africans. It is also the story of the first two decades of rule by the ANC.

Obtaining all the statistical data was not always easy – although it once brought unexpected recognition. When four of the homelands became constitutionally separate states, as we have seen, the government excluded their people from official population figures on the grounds that they were no longer South African citizens. I was having none of this attempt to make millions of people disappear, and made sure we got the figures from other sources. In 2006 I was pleasantly surprised to be invited to a conference at Rhodes University in Grahamstown to receive an award from the International Society for Quality-of-Life Studies for having retained these people in all our population data 'during this dark period'.[20]

We were constantly on the lookout for new information, for example on the state of the South African family. To this day I remember a visit as a journalist to a spanking new hostel at Sasolburg in the Orange Free State where I was almost reduced to tears at the sight of a beautifully embroidered pillow case on one of the migrant worker's beds: 'Goodbye my darling, I'll miss you.' Knowing how destructive of family life the influx control and migratory labour systems had been, I was anxious to find out whether stable families were now the norm. The results of our investigation were horrifying. 'Nine million kids with no dads' was the headline on the front page of the *Sowetan* newspaper on 5 April 2011 over a report on some of our research.[21]

Our work on the family generated enormous interest not only in newspapers circulating mainly among blacks but also on radio phone-in programmes. One of many alarming – nay, tragic – figures is that more than half of African children grow up in households where the father is absent, although alive.[22] Combing through this and other disturbing data on family life, I'm reminded how privileged I was to grow up in a happy and stable family who were all together in a comfortable home. I also suspect that the absence of family life for so many of our people lies at the heart of so many of the country's problems, among them crime and poor education.

Both in the *Survey* and in a monthly update to it called *Fast Facts*, which we launched in 1991, we monitored progress in dealing with the backlogs the new government inherited in 1994. In fact, we'd started doing this much earlier, when the NP government committed itself to reducing them. When Ian McRae, chief executive of Eskom, began talking about 'electricity for all' in 1987, I visited him at Megawatt Park to learn more. He had a huge photograph in his office showing power lines going into shacks. I was intrigued that this could be done, and we reproduced the photograph on the cover of the 1989/90 *Survey*.

We were the first independent organisation to provide data showing improvements year by year in access to housing, water, electricity, and the like. I highlighted this in my annual 'South African Mirror' Powerpoint slideshows for Institute members.

Mr Zuma's government loves what it calls 'a good story to tell', especially when part of the story is told by us. We in turn are delighted when government departments order copies of the *Survey* and make use of these to tell the good story. The result, to our amusement, has been accusations from the official opposition that we are making propaganda for the ANC. The Democratic Alliance on one occasion even demanded that we re-jig some of the figures in *Fast Facts* to show the Western Cape, which it rules, in a better light. However, giving the ANC credit for reducing socio-economic backlogs did not stop us from pointing out that its own policies were to blame for some of them.

Although the *Survey* was aimed at educating its readership, it also educated me about all social, economic, and political aspects of the country. I learnt not only by editing nearly 1 000 pages of detail each year, but also by keeping abreast of all major and many minor developments for possible inclusion in the *Survey* or *Fast Facts* or some of our other publications, as well as in material for speeches or newspaper articles. Designing the economics pages of the *Survey* and *Fast Facts* taught me more about economics than I'd learnt at Oxford. These pages are compiled by Tamara Dimant, a Latvian immigrant who spoke only rudimentary English when I hired her to work in our library in 1992. She and I both learnt on the job. She said 'you frightened me to death' but that she learnt a great deal at the 'university of John Kane-Berman'. She took to the *Quarterly Bulletin* of the South African Reserve Bank as a duck to water. Sarah Zwane also taught herself on the job. I inherited this treasure as a secretary when I joined the Institute, but she wanted to work in the research department, not for me. She graduated from electric typewriter to typesetting the *Survey's* carefully designed tables, and much else besides. To the immense sadness of everyone in the Institute, she died as this memoir was nearing completion.

As a newspaper junkie all my life, I started off every day at the Institute by reading all the Johannesburg dailies and marking clippings for the files on every aspect of South Africa I'd started keeping at the *Financial Mail*. A couple of hours every weekend was spent on the Sunday newspapers – although sometimes I resented having to do this and took them to work to look at the next day. Trips abroad did not interrupt the habit. The Oxford and Cambridge club took all the London dailies, and I started my day on every visit there by reading the lot. On arrival in any other city, the first thing I would always find out was where to buy the *Financial Times*, the *Wall Street Journal*, and the *International Herald Tribune*. From a hotel near the pyramids in Cairo, to a kiosk on Mykonos, to the vast railway station in Leipzig, I always somehow managed to locate at least some of these papers. There is very little South African news in any of them these days, but there is bound to be something of relevance – such as how Germany might be reforming labour law, India relaxing curbs on foreign investment, the UK encouraging more private education, China reacting to the growth of Christianity, or Sweden reforming the welfare state. And in any event, I need my daily fix of newspapers – not just news, but also editorials, opinion pages, book reviews, and, with a bit of luck, comic strips. News meant newspapers and newsprint, not television, which I never watch.

If this daily newspaper fix sounds like an obsession, perhaps it is. And it has served me well, both as a journalist and at the Institute. But my reading goes beyond newspapers and beyond South Africa. When I was still at school, an aunt asked me whether I had any hobbies. My uncle Marcus, my father's elder brother, firmly replied that reading was my hobby. And he was right. It has been all my life.

Most of what I've read has been biography, autobiography, the two world wars, Nazi Germany, Russia, and economics. I've read at least one biography or autobiography of just about every British monarch since Richard III and every prime minister since Sir Robert Peel. I must have read 30 or 40 books on or by Churchill, including books on his admirals, spies, and generals. On Margaret Thatcher I've probably read 15 or 20 books. But I've also read biographies or memoirs of numerous British politicians who never made it to 10 Downing Street. One of them was on Sir Stafford Cripps, whom Churchill inevitably rechristened Sir Stifford Crapps. Tony Blair, who did make it to the top, never interested me, but I read books by and about his great enemy, Gordon Brown.

I've also read several dozen other books on the Second World War, among them many inherited from my father, including biographies of Alexander, Auchinleck, and Wavell, under all of whom he served during his time in the Western Desert and Italy.

A dozen or so books on Ronald Reagan, and perhaps half that number on John F Kennedy, top my reading list on American presidents, with

Lincoln, Jefferson, Franklin D Roosevelt, Truman, Johnson, and Nixon lower down. I admired Reagan for ignoring the advice of all the experts when he made his great speech in Berlin calling on Mikhail Gorbachev to 'tear down this wall'. While at Oxford, I read most of the standard books on the American political system, but also *The Autobiography of Malcolm X*, along with many of the other polemics by such writers as James Baldwin, Bobby Seale, Stokely Carmichael and Eldridge Cleaver. I also read Frantz Fanon, Julius Nyerere, and Kwame Nkrumah, plus Solzhenitsyn, Camus, Kafka, Koestler, and even Jean-Paul Sartre.

More recently I've devoured books by Thomas Sowell of the Hoover Institute at Stanford University on both economics and cultural matters. Apart from Sowell, I've recently read Adam Smith and Friedrich Hayek, along with commentaries on Marx and Keynes. I've also recently read a couple of dozen books on globalisation and the great financial crisis of 2008, along with 10 or 12 on the great global warming scare and several on what's wrong with the European Union.

My reading on the Second World War goes far beyond Churchill and his leading commanders. Books on strategy, on the decisions on each side that won and lost the war, and about some of the unsung engineers and other heroes in the back rooms are also on my shelf, along with accounts of the campaigns in Burma, North Africa, Italy, the Pacific, and elsewhere. Nor did I forget the critical naval war in the Atlantic and around the South African coast, or the participation in the war by so many African countries. Basutoland (now Lesotho), for example, raised money to kit out a squadron of Spitfires for the Royal Air Force. That country also provided muleteers to supply ammunition to Allied troops on the Italian mountains and evacuate casualties. When people talk about Britain 'standing alone' against Hitler, they forget that Britain might have been alone in Europe but that all her former and present colonies across the Empire and Commonwealth fought with her.

People often say that 'military intelligence' is a contradiction in terms, but books on how intelligence was used during the war show this to be nonsense. So does any decent account of the D-Day landings in June 1944, one of the greatest logistical exercises in history. Sometimes if I can't sleep at night, I try to re-construct the war through its main battles and other turning points. In August 2016 I went to talk about the war at a retirement village in Weltevreden Park, and was moved when several of the audience got up afterwards and recalled their personal experiences, from anxiety over a husband reported missing after the fall of Tobruk, to wartime rationing in the UK, to blackouts in some of South Africa's coastal cities to make ships in harbour less visible to enemy submarines. One woman remembered having received a single apple from Canada when fruit was the rarest of treats in England: she put the wrapping away carefully and then smelt it from time to time to remind herself of the apple. Another of those present remembered hearing Neville Chamberlain's wireless broadcast on 3 September 1939 announcing that 'this country is now at war with Germany'.

On Nazi Germany itself I also read extensively, including biographies of the top Nazis by German as well as other writers. My reading also included studies on the machinery of mass murder, analyses of the German economy, and accounts of what happened to Germans after the war. One of the books I most recently read is an account of what ordinary Germans thought, did, and said during the war. It reinforced the conclusion I had long since reached, namely that they could not but have known what was happening to the Jews and others. However, they then reacted as ordinary people usually do – they turned a blind eye. The whole point about the ordinary Germans is that they were not evil, but ordinary.

Some of my reading focused on the great battles between Germany and Russia on the Eastern front. When it came to atrocities against peasants or Jews or anyone else, there was nothing to choose between Nazis and Communists. While running the Institute I had the opportunity to deliver one or two speeches and write several articles about the failures of Western intellectuals to tell the truth about the crimes of communism.

I always enjoyed the outrage Ronald Reagan provoked among such people when he described the Soviet Union as an 'evil empire'.

Doing so much reading while running the Institute meant guarding my weekends jealously. The Institute always closed between Christmas and New Year. Many of our friends went away, but this was my annual reading holiday – sitting in the garden with a book. On our Cunard voyages, Pierre and I spent most of the time reading. I would never leave myself at the mercy of a ship's library, even on the great *Queen Mary 2*, so always took enough books with me. On one trip I took a tattered old copy of David Thomson's *Europe Since Napoleon* which I'd found among my father's books. It had been on my reading list for years and now was my chance – sitting in a deck chair sheltering from both the sun and the wind. By the time we docked in Southampton the book was falling apart, so I reluctantly dumped it and made straight for Hatchard's when we got to London to buy a new copy.

Everywhere I went I carried a list compiled from reviews in various newspapers of the books I wanted. Change planes at Frankfurt or some other airport, and I would head straight for the bookshop with my list, seldom coming away disappointed. If they didn't have what was on my list, I'd usually find something else. And I never flew anywhere without taking enough reading material to cater for however long a flight might be delayed. In my car I keep copies of *Romeo and Juliet* and *The Merchant of Venice* in case I should get stuck somewhere without anything to read. These, however, are not my favourite Shakespeares – I have about a dozen copies of *Hamlet* or books about Hamlet in various parts of our house. Hamlet has intrigued me since I saw one of the famous St John's productions by Walter Andrewes while still a junior. I later badgered one of the masters into hiring Laurence Olivier's film, which described Hamlet as a man who 'couldn't make up his mind'. Decades later, after watching Kenneth Branagh's film, I came to the conclusion that Hamlet had a different problem: he couldn't stop talking.

CHAPTER 10

The silent revolution

If 1983 was a turning point in my life, it was a turning point for South Africa as well. Prime Minister PW Botha announced that a referendum would be held on 2 November among white voters to approve the new constitution establishing the tricameral Parliament. The Institute's board (then misleadingly called an executive committee) agreed that I should go around the country to brief our members.

This set the pattern for my time at the Institute, during which I made more than 700 speeches around the country and abroad analysing trends, making forecasts, and offering alternative policies where necessary. I did not want to be only a corporate bureaucrat, but to enjoy myself engaging in the battle of ideas using both the spoken and the written word as I had done at Wits, on the *Financial Mail*, and during my freelance years. Little did I realise at the time how intense the battle would become. Apart from speechmaking, I wrote many newspaper articles, among them a fortnightly column in *Business Day*. This ran from 2002 to 2015, when the paper terminated it after I'd written about 250 columns. After *Business Day* axed me, James Myburgh gave me a weekly column on *PoliticsWeb*, where I write whatever I like, which is a great privilege.

I wrote to inform, to expose, to excite, to provoke, and to amuse myself. I seldom went into print without showing drafts to at least two colleagues, as well as to Pierre. And I was fortunate to have Alfred Nkungu as my research assistant. 'Everyone else uses Google,' I said on one occasion, 'but I do not need to because I have Alfred.' I was also fortunate to have Susi Eusman, who ran my office with superb efficiency and ghost-wrote most of my formal Institute reports, leaving me to devote time to speeches and articles and also time to edit the *Survey*, *Fast Facts*, and other publications.

Many whites argued that the new constitution, by including the coloured and Indian minorities in Parliament, was a 'step in the right direction' and that Africans would be next. But this was not the plan for Africans, who would be hived off into a separate constitutional orbit via the homeland independence policy.[1] The tricameral Parliament was also a slap in the face to all Africans, not least those still committed to non-violent strategies.

George Palmer, who'd been my editor at the *FM*, came to my talk in Auden House. He told me that he'd arrived thinking the new constitution was a step in the right direction, but that after listening to me he agreed that it wasn't. Among business leaders, Harry Oppenheimer, Zach de Beer, and Tony Bloom were almost alone in publicly rejecting it. We invited Mangosuthu Buthelezi, the most prominent critic of the new constitution outside the ANC, to address a meeting as well. In a 76 per cent poll, just short of a two-thirds majority of whites voted for the new constitution.[2] Botha, who would now absorb the job of prime minister into his new post as executive state president, rightly claimed that the results had exceeded his 'wildest expectations'. But the tricameral constitution was destined to be one of the shortest-lived in history.

In September 1984, when the first elections for the tricameral Parliament were held less than a year after Botha's triumphant referendum, violence erupted. This appeared to be, and was in some part, spontaneous. But the ANC and its military wing, Umkhonto we Sizwe, plus the SACP, were also instigating conflict. Assisted by the newly formed United Democratic Front, they were doing so as part of their no-holds-barred 'people's war' strategy to make the country ungovernable. We knew this because we subscribed to the BBC monitoring service, which posted us transcripts of broadcasts by the banned ANC on Radio Freedom from Addis Ababa and elsewhere, in which Oliver Tambo, Thabo Mbeki, and others called for violent attacks on local councillors, policemen, homeland 'puppets', and so on. I also made use of trips abroad to read up back copies of ANC and SACP publications then banned in South Africa. Friends subscribed to these on my behalf, and I then studied them in the library of the Oxford and Cambridge Club in London.

The South African press, of course, could not quote banned organisations or banned people. The intention was to stop them spreading their message. One unintended consequence was that large sections of the population remained unaware of what some of these organisations were saying. As we shall see in the next chapter, this helped them to win the vital propaganda war against the government – an example of how counter-productive censorship can be.

As violence flared in South African townships and grabbed the local and global headlines, and as Botha declared states of emergency in the hopes of stopping it, something else was going on. This belligerent and supposedly intransigent government, whose retreat from social and economic apartheid had been under way since the 1970s, was now beginning to retreat from political apartheid too. I'd written about this during my freelance years, but now at the Institute we were able to investigate it more thoroughly. We thought everyone would cheer the retreat, but we soon found out that we were wrong to expect this.

On the basis of our research into trends in policy, legislation, and Nationalist thinking, I told the Chicago Council on Foreign Relations in June 1985 that the 'entire edifice' of apartheid was 'crumbling' – so much so that the NP 'has stopped believing in its own ideology'. The system was collapsing under the weight of its own contradictions, for it rested on the 'fundamental absurdity that one could make use of blacks as labour but deny their existence as people'. The new constitution had attempted to impose on South Africa a system of political segregation at the very moment when the momentum towards economic integration had become unstoppable. 'One or the other had to give, and it cannot be denied that economic integration is beginning to win the day.'[3]

Six months before this we had received a phone call from Kobus Jordaan, an official in the office of Dr Gerrit Viljoen, a senior member of the Cabinet. Could he come round and talk to us? He wanted to know what was behind the violent disturbances in black townships. Well, we asked, has your minister not appointed a commission of enquiry to get all the answers? Yes, indeed, came the reply, but my minister knows that the commission will tell him only what he wants to hear – whereas the Institute will tell him the truth. This was too good an opportunity to miss, so in a three-hour meeting I told him what I thought about his government's policies. Unbeknown to him I later received a copy of his 'strictly confidential' report, in which he had accurately recorded what I had said.

In February 1986 Kobus Jordaan contacted us again. This time the request was to give a briefing to a special Cabinet committee set up in 1983 under the minister of constitutional development and planning, Chris Heunis, to investigate the position of Africans outside the homelands. Another opportunity too good to miss, especially when the official told us that we could strengthen the pragmatists in the Cabinet against the hardliners. And of course it was ironical that the government was now soliciting our views 35 years after Dr Verwoerd had declined to hear them unless we split our delegation on racial lines.

So off we went to the HF Verwoerd Building across the road from Parliament. There we held forth before seven or eight ministers for a couple of hours. Pik Botha seemed the least receptive. One of the others was Louis le Grange, minister of law and order, whose policemen were busy trying to curb disturbances in Alexandra township. We told Le Grange that his men's behaviour, which we had publicly criticised in the past, often made things worse, not better. Kobus Jordaan telephoned me afterwards to say Mr le Grange had appreciated our frankness.

I drew an important lesson from this experience. The Institute had previously criticised the tricameral Parliament and the homelands policy in the most forthright terms. We had also called for the bans on the ANC and other organisations to be lifted.[4] None of this stopped the Cabinet committee from soliciting our views. Far from it. They had sought us out precisely because we had spoken out so strongly in public. Now the government wanted to hear more. In other words, if you want to be taken seriously, you must put forward a clear and honest alternative. None of the pussyfooting which has frequently characterised business dealings with the ANC ever since it came to power.

Our contacts with Nationalist ministers strengthened our research-based conviction that apartheid was on the way out. We had in fact established a policy research unit under my old *Financial Mail* colleague Steven Friedman to analyse the reform process and identify strategies for speeding it up.[5] In addition to Steve's brilliant analysis, we'd launched two quarterly publications to keep track of the government's commitments to political and socio-economic reform. Financed by American companies eager to accelerate change, these were entitled *Quarterly Countdown* and *Socio-economic Update*.

I also ghost-wrote a memorandum which the American Chamber of Commerce in South Africa (Amcham) presented to Heunis's special Cabinet committee. Not too sure how to pitch a paper on political reform for a business organisation to sign, I decided to write what I thought and let Amcham tone it down if they wished. To my pleasant surprise, it went to Heunis unaltered. We later published it without disclosing that I was the author.[6]

Heunis was under pressure to implement the proposals of the KwaZulu-Natal Indaba, a constitutional conference jointly convened by Inkatha and the Natal Provincial Administration, which was controlled by the New Republic Party, an offshoot of the old United Party.

They wanted an outsider as deputy chairman, so I commuted regularly to Durban to fulfil this role in the first multiracial constitutional conference in the country's history – nearly 80 years after the uni-racial national convention of 1908, which also met initially in Durban, had established the Union. In November 1986 the Indaba put forward a plan for majority rule in that province as part of a federal South Africa. Although the NP's representatives sat on the sidelines instead of joining the other 36 delegations, my experiences in the Indaba convinced me that negotiations could work for the country as a whole. I was also becoming more and more convinced, as I told *Time*, that whites in general were becoming more receptive to the idea of change.[7]

In 1987, I addressed a conference hosted by the American company Unisys at Saint-Paul-de-Vence on the French Riviera. This medieval town, not far from Nice, was an even more glamorous conference venue than the Plaza Hotel in New York, where I'd spoken a year or two before at a Business International conference. After the opening speeches we were taken to Monte Carlo and then for lunch at a restaurant overlooking the sparkling Mediterranean. I could immediately see what had attracted everyone from Winston Churchill to James Bond, and later the two 'dirty rotten scoundrels' in the marvellous film of that name. Utterly seduced, I could have stayed for weeks but had to rush back to South Africa straight after my own speech to fulfil another commitment.

The venue itself almost invited optimism. And I pointed out that although almost everyone thought South Africa was teetering on the brink of revolution, it was in fact teetering on the brink of negotiation. With the hated tricameral Parliament, and the futile policy of trying to cajole all the homelands into 'independence', the NP had walked up its last constitutional dead end. A country which had become steadily more integrated socially and economically could no longer be ruled by a segregated political structure in which only minorities were represented. The contradiction had become unsustainable. But a legitimate new political structure could come about only through constitutional negotiations with all black leaders.[8]

I knew from talking to Mangosuthu Buthelezi that the government was anxious to draw him into negotiations about some sort of 'internal' solution. However, he would not join any talks on constitutional matters unless Nelson Mandela and imprisoned PAC leaders were given the same opportunity. He had been making this clear to the government since as long ago as January 1975, when he first put the demand to John Vorster, and I knew it was something on which he would not budge. Perhaps partly encouraged by the success of the Indaba, the Cabinet decided in May 1989 that constitutional discussions with 'all parties' could now be initiated.[9] It later transpired that the government had been talking to Mandela since 1985 and negotiating with him since 1987.[10] In October 1989, at a conference in Germany, Oscar Dhlomo, one of Prince Buthelezi's colleagues involved in discussions with the government, told me that the assurance had been given that Mr Mandela would soon be released. I repeated this at a Business International lunch in London later that month, only to be told by the ANC representative present that I was making propaganda for the government.

My conviction that apartheid was irreversibly on the way out earned me dozens of speaking invitations, some of them no doubt because this was what people wanted to hear. I enjoyed these engagements immensely, partly because it was fun to challenge conventional wisdoms and partly because I was able to sound a genuinely optimistic note at a time when there was so much gloom around. Would that were the case today!

One of the meetings I addressed was in the Superbowl at Sun City, after which the British writer and journalist Paul Johnson asked for a copy of my speech to give to Margaret Thatcher. But some people were sceptical, even though we argued that apartheid was going not because the NP wished it, but because the NP could not stop it. In March 1988 we held a briefing at the Carlton Hotel for various newspaper editors. Johnny Johnson of *The Citizen* and Ken Owen of the *Sunday Times* agreed with our arguments. Rex Gibson of *The Star* ridiculed them.

I said that the government sought to cope with pressures for change by making concessions of a 'thus-far-and-no-further' nature in the hope that these limited concessions would reduce the pressure for further change. In fact, most concessions did exactly the opposite. The process was like that of peeling an onion:

> The onion represents apartheid, with so-called petty apartheid, such as the old prohibition on black consumption of hard liquor, on the outer layers, and the most important statute, the Population Registration Act, at the core. As you peel off each layer you expose the one underneath. Thus, if you repeal the pass laws you remove the layer protecting the Group Areas Act. This is because increased urbanisation resulting from the repeal of the pass laws in the context of the huge housing shortage in the black townships simply squeezes more people out of those townships into white suburbs. Eventually you will get to the core, the Population Registration Act, without which there can be no statutory apartheid, even in the political field' [and which was repealed in 1991].[11]

But there was a second string to my bow. The 'silent revolution', as I called it, was the work not of political parties or leaders, but of ordinary people. Black workers had joined trade unions despite the difficulties, millions had voted with their feet against the pass laws by moving to town regardless of the risk of arrest, the black minibus taxi industry had grabbed market share despite government attempts to drive it out of business, and black shebeen owners had been defying liquor laws for years. Grassroots civil disobedience had been taking place on a massive scale, and the government seemed powerless to stop it. Whites had also played a part: independent schools had started admitting black pupils even though this was illegal. And usually when blacks moved into white suburbia in defiance of the Group Areas Act their white neighbours adjusted to the new reality without complaint[12] – although one anonymous correspondent wrote in to tell me that when the Group Areas Act went he would 'go into action to finish what the dumb bastard Hitler bungled'.[13]

The formal relaxations of apartheid laws did not create any of this change. They rather gave *de jure* recognition to *de facto* change that had already happened on the ground thanks to the actions of ordinary people. Numerous black journalists, especially those espousing the Black Consciousness philosophy, applauded the Institute for pointing this out.[14] I always enjoyed doing so, especially being able to describe the victories of ordinary people against the might of the state. Nobody who witnessed this could fail to be moved by it.

But many liberals and people on the Left, including white journalists, were hostile to our arguments because we were opening up the possibility of successful reform forced upon the government by blacks who no longer fitted the paradigm of being little more than helpless victims. Had not the rise of the black union movement, the courage of the families on the Cape Flats, and the militancy of the students of Soweto shown this? Many people were nevertheless unwilling to contemplate the possibility that the NP government was anything other than wholly evil and reactionary and therefore incapable of implementing any reforms, even under pressure.

Obtaining press coverage for our arguments was a constant battle. As Jill Wentzel wrote: 'The silent revolution undermined the view that the only choice available to South Africa was between apartheid and violence. It showed that the country was capable of changing itself peacefully and that ordinary blacks had the power to effect that transformation. Throughout the 1970s and 1980s, however, local and foreign media reporting played down socio-economic change and persisted in portraying blacks as passive victims capable only of suffering under apartheid rather than playing a major role in destroying it.'[15]

In June 1990 we organised another conference at the Carlton Hotel where some of the people who had brought about change on the ground could tell their stories. The result was a booklet entitled *Beating Apartheid and Building the Future*.[16] The conference was dedicated to the memory of Granny Moyo, who had died a few years previously at the age of 101. She had hawked fruit and vegetables for 58 years, but had died shortly after one of her many encounters with the police when they tried to drive hawkers off the streets. One of the speakers at our conference was Lawrence Mavundla, president of the African Council of Hawkers and Informal Businesses. At a memorial service for her he had asked, 'How much money did she spend on fines for earning an honest living? How many days did she spend in jail? We honour her braveness for not giving up and for hawking until her last day on earth. Granny Moyo your spirit lives on and that's why we can sell freely today.'

One of the other speakers was Steyn Krige, former headmaster of Woodmead School north of Johannesburg. When the school opened in 1970 he tried, without success, to get permission to admit children of all races. The governing body then decided just to go ahead and admit them anyway. By 1978 some 60 per cent of the pupils came from the African, Indian, and coloured communities. 'The skies did not fall down,' said Krige. 'All that happened was that the young people quickly forgot all about the concept of race and simply got on with the serious business of living.' There was plenty of support for the school, but Sybrand van Niekerk, administrator of the Transvaal, said action would have to be taken against it for breaking the law. Krige suggested that instead he should just ignore Woodmead, in return for which the school would keep him fully informed but keep itself out of the press. So the government turned a blind eye. One cabinet minister told Steyn that what he was doing was great, although 'I must not be quoted on that'. This, I discovered, was Gerrit Viljoen, then minister of national education.

While Woodmead proved that racially mixed schooling could be successful in South Africa, my former St John's headmaster, Deane Yates, was proving it in Botswana at Maru a Pula, a school he founded in Gaborone. He and Krige then teamed up in 1981 to establish the New

Era Schools Trust (Nest) in South Africa. Said Yates: 'It is only by growing up together in their formative years that the boys and girls of the emerging South Africa will remove apartheid from their hearts.'[17] They asked me to join the board, among whose other members were Michael O'Dowd and two of the university vice-chancellors I'd known, 'Boz' Bozzoli and Richard Luyt. Also on the board was Brian Hawksworth, who later became honorary treasurer of the Institute. We drew up a 200-member 'hit list' of prominent people to whom we would go and sell the then still revolutionary idea of racially mixed schooling. I took Yates and Krige to see everyone I knew who I thought might support their initiative. One of our strongest supporters was Professor JP de Lange, rector of Rand Afrikaans University and then chairman of the Broederbond. We had to do everything discreetly to avoid press publicity that might have provoked a hostile reaction from the Right and a government clampdown. With private sector support, Nest opened three schools between 1987 and 1992.

My involvement with Nest inspired me to take up the issue of school desegregation whenever I could. Invited to talk to the Institute of Personnel Management in November 1985, I told them that a 10-year-old white child today who got his first job in commerce and industry 15 years hence at the age of 25 would be working in a very different economic environment to the one we were used to. His boss or his secretary could be black, yet he was growing up in a segregated environment, as were black children. How would they all work comfortably together in adult life if their schooling didn't prepare them for it? Although many people would oppose enforcing desegregation, the government could allow all private schools to segregate themselves if they wished to. It could also establish and subsidise non-racial government schools.[18] My speech earned a large and excited headline in a black newspaper: 'Put all our kids in one school!'[19]

I repeated these arguments at every opportunity, including when I set out a detailed strategy for speeding up the desegregation of education in my opening address to the 72nd annual conference of the Natal Teachers Society in Pietermaritzburg in July 1987.[20] 'The case for desegregation,' I told them, 'rests not on ideology but on common sense.'

I loved making speeches like this, loved it more when they got good publicity and so spread the word. I also liked to think that they were encouraging people to think of new possibilities. The leadership of organisations that invited me to talk would have known what I was likely to say, so presumably they wished their members to hear it and so strengthen liberalising tendencies.

In fact by the early 1990s school desegregation was gathering momentum – so much so that it overtook the Nest schools. White government schools were given the option of desegregating themselves. By May 1993, some 80 per cent of white government schools had elected to become 'model C' schools with control over their own admissions policy.[21] These schools, which took many of our potential pupils away and undermined our fund-raising efforts, were cheaper than Nest schools. But Yates and Krige had helped pave the way towards the end of apartheid education even before the change of government in 1994.[22] So here was another example of the crumbling of apartheid that I was so keen to tell everyone about.

All our arguments were later published in *South Africa's Silent Revolution*, which was written before FW de Klerk's momentous speech on 2 February 1990 but only came out afterwards. Thanks to my friend Rudolf Gruber in Germany, it was translated and republished there.[23]

The book made it onto bestseller lists. One of my former *Financial Mail* colleagues, ZB Molefe, now deputy editor of *City Press*, said it was a 'prophecy fulfilled'. While I was a journalist I'd written extensive articles about the silent revolution, he said, but, 'like all prophets, few people understood or took serious notice'. Now the silent revolution had become a reality whose success was snowballing. I'd also exploded 'the myth of black helplessness' which held that blacks could do nothing for themselves and that only violence, sanctions, or anti-apartheid politicians could dislodge apartheid.[24] Under the headline 'take a bow, simple folk', the Durban paper *Ilanga* said I'd 'chronicled the contribution made by vast numbers of ordinary South Africans in forcing the apartheid policy to its knees'. The book was a tribute to the 'innumerable South Africans who had fought and won private battles against oppression and the apartheid state'.[25]

Writing in *Leadership*, the glossy but stimulating and classy journal founded and edited by Hugh Murray, another one-time *FM* colleague, Clive Keegan paid tribute to the Institute for its 50 years of resolute advocacy of racial tolerance and liberal values. In showing how ordinary people had played a key role in the erosion of apartheid, I had 'reinvigorated the primacy of the individual above the state'.[26] This was an astute comment that explained much of the hostility to my arguments from people on the Left, with their belief in vanguard roles for certain parties. I suspect that another thing that bothered some on the Left was the possibility that if they did not control the process of change, the chance of imposing a communist system on the country might slip from their grasp. The last thing they wanted was a real democracy as opposed to a 'people's democracy'. Arguments about the past were thus also arguments about the future.

Jeremy Cronin, writing as a member of the central committee of the South African Communist Party, said he was mildly irritated that the blurb on the back cover had described me as South Africa's leading authority on apartheid. However, he said, 'Kane-Berman's latest book is not that bad'. I naturally added this to the list of comments on the back cover of the second edition. Cronin said that although I would 'disavow historical materialism', I was essentially agreeing that 'the masses – not individuals, not leadership collectives – make history'.[27] Quite right. Moreover, they had done so without the help of vanguard parties such as his own.

Some years later, as the 1994 election approached, I relied on the arguments in the book to have a bit of fun endorsing the ANC's argument that the NP was not entitled to claim that it had 'swept away the apartheid laws'. The NP claimed that South Africa had changed because the NP had changed. But the truth was the opposite. The NP abandoned apartheid not because it wanted to, but because it could no longer enforce it.[28]

Of course, the NP was not the only one to claim credit for what ordinary people had done. Writing in the *African Communist* in 1995, Ronnie Kasrils, member of the political bureau of the SACP and deputy minister of defence in the Mandela government, seemed to endorse my view that change came about 'primarily through the struggle of the masses'. That struggle, however, had been reinforced by Umkhonto we Sizwe, its underground structures, and the international anti-apartheid movement. It was necessary to 'guard against all attempts to subvert' this history.[29] This was much the same argument as the *African Communist* had used against my Soweto book, which had given the pupils of Soweto, rather than the ANC, the credit. Umkhonto, of course, played a key role in the insurrectionary violence of the 1980s. But it had nothing to do with the success of the silent revolution.

If 'the masses' had done pretty well without the help of parties claiming to be their vanguards, there were also fears that the NP's reform process, however clumsy, might work. The *African Communist* thus quoted Oliver Tambo and the ANC as having called as early as 1985 for an intensification of the fight lest the Botha government 'defuse the revolution'.[30] Frank Chikane, general secretary of the South African Council of Churches and later director general of the Presidency under Thabo Mbeki, had the same fear. He later said that by releasing Mandela, De Klerk wanted to regain legitimacy, divide the struggle, and weaken the sanctions campaign. This, Chikane said, could be 'dangerous'. He was of course right. Those were indeed among De Klerk's objectives. And they did present the ANC and its allies with a dilemma. As we shall see in the next chapter, they tackled it by demonising him in a brilliantly successful campaign of armed propaganda.

Some of those who ridiculed my story of the silent revolution did not even want to give it a hearing. My colleague Jill Wentzel challenged two senior journalists on *The Star* as to why the Institute got such limited coverage. She was told that instructions had come from 'the top' that the ANC should get maximum support as there was no other means of getting rid of the Nats.[31] When I wrote an article for that newspaper to commemorate the Institute's sixtieth birthday on 9 May 1989, the sub-editors carefully excised from it my statement that the emergency regulations had not eliminated all non-violent opposition to apartheid. The article was sent to all the other papers in the Argus group, which ran it without *The Star*'s sneaky little excision.

One man who did agree with our arguments was Boris Asoyan, a one-time KGB man, journalist, and diplomat. He had invited my then deputy, Theo Coggin, and myself to dinner when he was Soviet *chargé d'affaires* in Maseru. The vodka and caviar to which he treated us were flown in regularly by Aeroflot from the USSR via Mozambique. After dinner Boris looked at his watch and pointed out that there was a curfew in Maseru, so he had better drive us back to our hotel. I half hoped that we might be stopped. A news story that Theo – who later became one of the Institute's board chairmen under whom I served – and I had been arrested while driving around Maseru with the Soviet ambassador after curfew would no doubt have confused some of our left-wing critics.

Boris Asoyan said Mikhail Gorbachev's liberalising *glasnost* and *perestroika* policies were echoed by PW Botha's 'Pretoriastroika' policies. I had in fact given a few lectures on the topic 'Mr Gorbotha and the Reform Process' to half a dozen audiences, among them the Union of Jewish Women in Johannesburg[32] and a fund-raising lunch that Mike Rosholt hosted for us at Barlow Rand.[33] Both men were trying to bring about change in societies which had no choice but to change, but in which the very process of change carried high risks, not least to their own jobs.

The Russians had tried to make contact with the Institute in 1985.[34]

However, suspecting that this might be some sort of security police trap to nab me for furthering the aims of communism, I ignored the Russian letter. But the Soviets made contact with us again in 1988 via an academic at the University of Stellenbosch. They explained that they wanted to start talking to South African organisations that were independent of both the ANC and the government. I accepted an invitation to visit the USSR in November 1989.

I nearly didn't get there. Having been told to collect my visa at the Soviet embassy in London, I queued up in the street outside for more than six hours. Once inside, I was told no one had any knowledge of any visa for me. It was also closing time – on a Friday. Fortunately, I managed to get through that night by telephone to one of my hosts in Moscow. When I went back to the embassy the next day, a Saturday, and presented my telexed letter of invitation to the young consul on duty, he came out from behind the glass screen and asked me, 'How's the Institute?' You could have knocked me over with a feather. It turned out that he had once worked at the Soviet embassy in Lusaka, where he'd received all the Institute's publications. He had received a message overnight from Moscow and issued my visa there and then.[35] If this was one stroke of luck, another was that the embassy was open on the Saturday. This was only because it was to be closed on the first two days of the following week, which were public holidays commemorating the revolution in 1917.

By the time I got to Moscow the remnants of that revolution were imploding. I had the good fortune to be there when the Berlin wall collapsed. In a lecture I gave, I told the Russians that apartheid was also collapsing. My hosts were the Institute for African Studies of the USSR Academy of Sciences, headed by Anatoly Gromyko, son of Andrei Gromyko, long-serving Soviet foreign minister and later president.

The African Studies Institute told me they thought conditions for a settlement in South Africa were more favourable now than at any time previously. Gorbachev and the foreign ministry favoured non-military

With Anatoly Gromyko of the Institute for African Studies in Moscow,
November 1989, as the Berlin Wall collapsed.

solutions to regional issues. If the South African government moved correctly, the Soviets would not support any hardening by the ANC of its preconditions for negotiations.[36] Despite the Soviet Union's long years of support for the ANC, the SACP, Umkhonto, and 'armed struggle', these Russians at least seemed to favour negotiated solutions.

The African Studies Institute was unable to arrange a meeting I had requested with Simon Makana, the ANC's representative in the USSR. This was evidently because the ANC disapproved of efforts by the African Studies Institute to establish contacts with South Africans without reference to themselves. So I got Mr Makana's phone number, rang him up, and asked if I could visit. He laid on a little tea party for me in the scantily furnished office which served as his 'embassy'. He was one of a number of exiles I visited on trips abroad, starting with Johnny Makhathini, head of the ANC's international department, during a visit to Paris in 1975 when I went there to write a survey on France for the *Financial Mail*. He invited me to visit Algeria as his guest. I had no visa but he told me he could fix this. Assuming that the South African government would somehow find out about this visit, I thought it prudent to be open about it so told the South African ambassador in Paris I would be going to Algeria as the ANC's guest. Unfortunately, Mr Makhathini was then called away to a UN meeting in New York, so I never got to Algeria.

On other trips I arranged meetings with ANC representatives in New York and London, among them Frene Ginwala. Vella Pillay, SACP representative in London, was another person I had meetings with. He told me he'd gone into exile in the late 1940s to escape the restrictions of the Mixed Marriages Act. During a trip to Australia, I visited PAC representatives, whose office in Canberra was a large caravan emblazoned 'Pan-Africanist Congress of Azania Government in Exile'.

Apart from being in Moscow on the very day when the collapse of the Berlin Wall signalled the beginning of the end of the USSR, the highlights of my trip to Russia were visits to some of its art treasures and palaces. I also went to the Moscow circus, where one of the highlights was the famous dance of the cygnets from *Swan Lake* performed by four burly men dressed as ballerinas. Otherwise I found Moscow pretty bleak.

On one occasion I booked a taxi at my hotel to take me to dinner with Quentin and Mary Peel of the *Financial Times* who had been posted there after having spent some years in Johannesburg. The hotel concierge gave me a reference number and a receipt for my deposit. When the taxi failed to arrive and I got more and more agitated, she merely shrugged her shoulders and kept on saying 'It's a pity, it's a pity'. Fortunately, a car arrived to make a delivery at the hotel. While the driver went into the hotel, I hopped into the back of his car. This startled him when he returned, but I stilled his objections by flashing a few dollars at him and so persuading him to drive me to the *FT* office, where the news of how people were flooding out of East Berlin and other communist-controlled cities to freedom in the West was chattering in over the Reuters ticker.

On another occasion, my Russian guide, Ildus, asked me to go into a foreign currency shop to buy some flowers to give to his wife, the first time in years he had been able to do this. Flowers, he said, were unavailable in ordinary shops. Having bought some roubles on the black (that is, the free) market, I felt very wealthy but in the end gave them away when I left because I couldn't find much to buy, apart from a couple of Shostakovich symphonies on long-playing records. There was no chance to browse at the Melodya record shop, let alone put on earphones to test out the records. You asked for what you wanted and somebody went and found it.

During the same trip I took the overnight train to Leningrad, as it still was. My guide took me to see *Swan Lake* at the Kirov, the theatre named after a one-time party boss in the city who had been assassinated in 1934, providing the pretext for some of Stalin's purges and show trials. As we waited outside the theatre beforehand, we were accosted by local people offering to buy our tickets. Ildus told me people could spend their entire lives in Leningrad without ever being able to see a ballet. I invited him and my local guide, Eugene Boytzov, to dinner, but they said there were no decent restaurants in the city not booked out months in advance. We visited the Catherine Palace outside the city. It had been ruined by German artillery during the three-year siege of Leningrad during the 'great patriotic war', as the Russians called it, and was being rebuilt inch by inch by Finnish architects. 'What's wrong with Russian architects?' I asked Eugene. 'They're too busy building communism,' he replied. We also visited a cemetery containing the remains of 470 000 people who had died during the siege. My two companions were amazed when I told them, proudly, that South Africa had entered the war against Nazism almost two years before Hitler invaded Russia. I invited Eugene for a drink in my hotel, but he refused on the grounds that it was barred to ordinary Russians.

215

In March 2015 I used my experiences in Leningrad to illustrate the differences between communist and free-market systems to a new liberal students' group at the University of Pretoria. I told them how during my 1989 visit I had been unable to find very much to buy, not even vodka. 'Russian housewives used to walk around with what they called a "perhaps" bag in case they found something they needed to buy. They had a joke as well. A woman queues up for three hours to buy some bread and when she gets to the front of the queue she's told it's the wrong one: "This is the queue for the shop that has run out of meat. The queue for the shop that has no bread is the one across the street."

'In 2013 I went back to the same city, now called St Petersburg again. No queues, except at the art galleries. Shops full of goods of every kind and brand. Hawkers with little stalls on the wide pavements. As many takeaways and fast-food joints as in any South African city. That's what happens when the magic of the market takes over from the deadening hand of the bureaucrat'.[37]

CHAPTER 11

Turmoil in the townships

Barely had I returned to South Africa from my trip to Russia in November 1989 than FW de Klerk made his dramatic announcements on 2 February 1990. I visited several of his ministers in Cape Town that morning and the day before. They told me they knew the eyes of the world would be upon them when De Klerk opened Parliament, but they gave no hint of what he might say.[1]

With half the rest of the world, Pierre and I watched Nelson Mandela's release on television a week later. We also listened to his first speech, in which he called for an 'intensification of the struggle on all fronts'. Our hearts sank. This could only mean more violence. Even though Mandela subsequently spoke in a more conciliatory tone, violence intensified. The Institute's daily monitoring thereof enabled us to predict only a couple of months after his release that 1990 would be the most violent year in our modern history. So it turned out, with at least 3 770 deaths in political violence.[2] Perhaps I was naïve, but this was the last thing I expected when De Klerk took his great leap forward.

The Institute had begun monitoring township disturbances since the eruptions in September 1984.[3] By the end of February 1987 conflict within black communities had replaced security force action as the main cause of fatalities.[4] Our sources for what we reported included newspapers, the police, and various agencies monitoring violence. But we were also in touch with journalists, black as well as white, who told us how risky it was to write about some key aspects of township violence. If they went into print with articles that displeased activists in 'certain organisations' they would 'get a call', after which they feared physical attack.

In August 1990 we organised a seminar where some of these journalists could talk about these problems. We soon learnt that 'certain organisations' was usually code for the ANC and its allies. Our president, Stanley Mogoba, who chaired the seminar, said the audience had been shocked by what they'd heard. Helen Suzman, who was also there, said people in the townships who wanted to lead stable lives seemed to be 'totally intimidated and overcome'. But she was one of the exceptions among liberals. The journalists told us that white liberals and white journalists were reluctant to criticise black organisations for fear of having their own liberal credentials questioned. If you questioned strategies or their consequences, you were accused of being 'against the struggle'. We published the proceedings of the seminar under the title *Mau-Mauing the Media: New Censorship for the New South Africa*.[5]

In my book on Soweto I'd paid tribute to black journalists for telling the story of violence inflicted by the police in the townships despite the risks of banning and detention. Now it required equal courage to report on the intimidation used to enforce work stayaways along with consumer, rent, and school boycotts. But the story got out – thanks less to mainstream white newspapers, which chose to play it down, than to the black commercial press.[6] The Institute collated much of the material and published it: men stripped naked and flogged after sentence by a 'people's court' for ignoring a stayaway call; a man dying of an overdose after being forced to swallow tablets he had bought from a pharmacy in defiance of a consumer boycott; a woman forced to cut up her daughter's wedding dress after ignoring a boycott. We obtained enough reports to realise that stories such as these were the tips of an iceberg. And their victims were invariably ordinary people just going about their daily business.

218

There were four main elements in township violence. Confrontation between the police and activists was only one. The other three were sometimes lumped together as 'black-on-black' violence. This included conflict between rival black organisations; assassinations of black local councillors, police, and others seen as collaborators; and coercion to enforce boycotts and stayaways, which, as in Soweto in 1976, sometimes provoked a violent backlash.

Although under-reported, and the context often omitted, many of the events on the ground followed what the ANC was urging on Radio Freedom and no doubt also through various underground networks. In May 1985 Thabo Mbeki called for the enemy to be attacked on all fronts and for underground units to spread to every factory, mine, and farm, every school, and every village. Oliver Tambo called for the 'Pretoria puppets' in the homelands to be destroyed. A broadcast from Addis Ababa in September that same year called for the people's war 'to engulf the entire country'. A broadcast in December 1986 urged the 'masses' to use Molotov cocktails, spears, sticks, petrol bombs, and small arms seized from whites. The struggle should embrace rent strikes, bus boycotts, the overthrow of township councils, and the creation of people's courts. Youth – described as 'young lions' – were urged to bring education to a standstill. In September 1986 Chris Hani, secretary general of the SACP and former chief of staff of Umkhonto we Sizwe, praised them for clearing the townships of 'collaborators' and 'puppets'.

While this material was being broadcast, the ANC called for homeland governments to be overthrown to help render South Africa 'ungovernable'. Umkhonto was authorised to strike at 'soft' targets to intensify the people's war. In November 1986 Mangosuthu Buthelezi was portrayed as a counter-revolutionary 'snake' who needed to be 'hit on the head'. Joe Slovo, national chairman of the SACP, said that 'mass political struggle, coupled with an intensification of revolutionary violence, remains the imperative'. Alfred Nzo, then general secretary of the ANC, endorsed necklace executions. At a meeting in Lusaka in July 1989, the

ANC, the UDF, and Cosatu decided to promote an 'upsurge' of 'volcanic material'. The UDF, launched in 1983 with prominent clerics such as Desmond Tutu among its patrons, had all along assisted the ANC in helping to render black areas ungovernable.[7]

I raised some of these issues at a Business International conference in London in September 1990. One of the causes of the violence was indiscriminate shooting by the police. Another was that the ANC was stoking revolutionary violence. That organisation was also in conflict not only with the police, but with Azapo, Inkatha, and other parties as well. The minister of finance, Barend du Plessis, who was at the conference representing the government, did not deny my allegations about the police.

But Thabo Mbeki, presumably relying on the gathering's ignorance of everything he himself had broadcast on Radio Freedom, spent 10 minutes replying to me. He said that young people might have been 'running wild', but he denied that the ANC was orchestrating violence. He and I could not be talking about the same country or the same organisation. Anthony Sampson, who was one of the other speakers, agreed with him. But Bobby Godsell got up and said Mbeki had dismissed my remarks 'somewhat too lightly'. At the cocktail function after the conference I sensed that I was being given a wide berth, although a few people came over and told me that I had 'destroyed' Mbeki.[8] Two days later, I raised the question of violence at a conference in Switzerland. One of the other speakers was Marcel Golding, assistant general secretary of the National Union of Mineworkers. He complimented me on having addressed the question of revolutionary violence in public.[9]

Doing so was the great no-no. South Africa in the 1980s became less racially polarised but more ideologically polarised. On the one end of the spectrum was the NP government, grappling with clumsy reform. Although it ran a number of murderous covert operations against political activists, some authorised and some not, it was also trying, sometimes clumsily, to keep the peace in the townships. At the other end were the ANC and its allies, out to make the country ungovernable. If you weren't for the 'struggle' you were an apologist for the 'racist regime'. There was not much room here for any middle ground.

The conflict tore white liberals apart. They'd all opposed apartheid and the security legislation designed to prop it up. But now, as violence intensified, they were split three ways. Some simply cast all the blame on the government and refused even to consider that the ANC might be stoking it. Others thought that even if the ANC were stoking it, whites had no business to criticise what the oppressed were doing to end oppression. In any event, whatever violence might be perpetrated by the oppressed was as nothing compared to the 'structural violence' of the apartheid system.

But a minority, horrified by the mayhem in the townships, spoke out. The Institute was in the last camp, although some of our members were in one or other of the first two. So were many journalists, non-governmental organisations, academics, prominent clerics, and, as far as we could judge, most of the foreign embassies in Pretoria – not to mention the entire global anti-apartheid movement. Moreover, if you were in the third camp you could expect to be vilified by liberals in the first two. This is exactly what happened to me and to some of my colleagues, among them Lawrence Schlemmer, Anthea Jeffery, and Jill Wentzel.

All of this was written up by Jill in her book *The Liberal Slideaway*, published in 1995. She described not only some of the terror experienced by so many ordinary township people, but also how so many liberals turned a blind eye to it, not least in the Black Sash. She wrote, for example: 'As pupils in many parts of the country inflicted a reign of terror in many areas, liberals campaigned against the arrest of children. It was clearly part of their job to do so. Nevertheless, few cared to ask: "What do you do with a nine-year-old with a petrol bomb?"'[10]

Youths and even younger children were both victims and aggressors. The Sunday newspaper *City Press* blamed them for introducing the necklace and going on the rampage, stoning and burning houses belonging to rival activists. The ANC claimed that some 500 fully trained members of

Umkhonto were operational in South Africa, providing skills and guidance to young militants. But necklace victims included black schoolboys who wrote their matric exams in apparent defiance of school boycotts.[11]

Although the ANC began talks with the government in 1990 there was no let-up in the people's war. In August 1992 Harry Gwala, a prominent ANC and SACP leader in Natal, said mass action had to be intensified, with a view to making the country more ungovernable than it had been during the states of emergency declared by PW Botha in the 1980s. Ronnie Kasrils led a charge on Bhisho, capital of the Ciskei homeland, in September 1992 which resulted in 29 deaths at the hands of the Ciskei police. Following this, the secretary general of the ANC, Cyril Ramaphosa, declared that the organisation was determined to cleanse the country and would now go after Buthelezi and Lucas Mangope in Bophuthatswana.[12]

By the middle of 1993, more than 300 councillors had been intimidated into resigning, 953 policemen had been killed, and necklace executions of supposed collaborators and others had claimed more than 500 lives, virtually all of them black.[13] Many years later Azapo pointed out that not a single white person had died by necklacing.[14] Attacks on councillors and policemen often took place at their homes, where the victims included sleeping children. Some of the necklacings occurred as a result of sentences by 'people's courts'.

Although security forces, along with Inkatha, were involved in violence, Umkhonto was the primary perpetrator. A key reason for the intensification of the people's war was to eliminate all black opponents whom the ANC could not co-opt. Principal among these was Inkatha, which the ANC had tried but failed to co-opt at a meeting in London in October 1979.

The ANC, many of whose leaders were communists steeped in Marxist-Leninist ideology, saw itself as the only legitimate representative of blacks. But this pretension was a denial of one of the realities of politics in South Africa, which is that black political loyalties are diversified. The PAC broke away from the ANC in 1960. The Black People's Convention (BPC) was founded by Steve Biko in 1968. Inkatha Yenkululeko YeSizwe (later the Inkatha Freedom Party) was founded in 1975. And after the banning of the BPC in 1977, the Azanian People's Organisation (Azapo) was founded. I had long argued for the deregulation of black politics so that people could choose between these various organisations, which they couldn't do as long as some were banned and their leaders imprisoned.

Azapo, Inkatha, and the PAC had all accused the European Community (forerunner of the European Union) of providing funding only for projects within the ANC's camp. I said foreign governments should lay off supporting one political tendency at the cost of others. Instead of playing a party-political game in South Africa, they should help the country make a transition to a multiparty system.[15] Azapo, Inkatha, and the PAC were able to get on with one another despite their differences. However, they all complained of attacks by the ANC.

Our pleas for tolerance resulted in my receiving several speaking invitations from black organisations. One of these came from the Inyandza party led by Enos Mabuza, chief minister of the Kangwane homeland, in what is now Mpumalanga. Dr Mabuza – who later became a vice president of the Institute – was generally thought to be sympathetic to the ANC. When I asked why I'd been invited to talk at his party congress in Nelspruit,[16] the answer was that he liked what I was saying about tolerance.[17]

The people's war provoked a furious backlash, not least from Inkatha supporters, some of whom were clandestinely armed and trained by the South African Defence Force. One massacre followed another. Some of these were in rural areas, some in urban shack settlements, some in urban townships. Some were organised from hostels controlled by Inkatha. Some were organised attacks by the ANC on hostel residents. Sometimes the aggression came from one side, sometimes from the other. Some attacks were launched with the intention of provoking counter-attacks. At the same time, the 'people's war' unleashed mayhem and anarchy to an extent that the old 'armed struggle' never had. Disciplined violence was replaced by uncontrollable violence. Most of the victims seemed to be ordinary people who were simply in the wrong place at the wrong time.

The violence was often blamed on youths who were 'running wild', as Mbeki put it. But their behaviour had been encouraged by the ANC and the SACP. Oliver Tambo and Nelson Mandela both admitted that it was difficult to control youths after telling them to make the country ungovernable.[18] One journalist, Phil Molefe, said 'the black community was reaping the whirlwind of hailing ten-year-olds as "young lions"'. Another, Nomavenda Mathiane, said 'political organisations have created monsters they cannot control'. And Breyten Breytenbach told a French magazine that young township blacks in South Africa were like China's red guards during the 'cultural revolution'.[19]

Some middle-class whites, their own children safely at school or university, romanticised the 'young lions' in the townships who sought to shut down black education in the name of 'no education before liberation'. The killing of civilians by limpet mines in shopping centres in white areas generated massive and usually adverse publicity. But attacks on black councillors and policemen, or the use of coercion to enforce boycotts, attracted much less press attention, still less criticism. Sometimes attacks on black councillors were ignored altogether.[20] The people's war was waged almost undetected by the white community.[21] Even today, the great majority of whites remain ignorant of the havoc caused by the people's war or the terror that so many people experienced.

Among those who both witnessed and experienced township terror were the police. Nick Howarth, who headed a section of the police's East Rand riot unit not long after finishing school, later published an account of its work. His men faced an almost impossible job as members of the ANC and IFP butchered one another or innocent passers-by. The unit's Casspir armoured vehicles were themselves under incessant

224

attack from rocks, petrol bombs, hand grenades, sniper fire, and machine guns. Often the Casspirs would be piled high with bodies collected by the police, but local mortuaries were already overflowing so makeshift arrangements were made to dispose of the dead.

Sergeant Howarth wrote that the ANC wanted the police out of the townships in order to take control of them, but the riot units feared this would mean an even greater bloodbath there. By the end of 1993, 260 policemen had been killed countrywide. Several were necklaced. Throughout this time the ANC told the media the police were perpetrating violence. According to Howarth:

> The men in the riot units around South Africa in the late 80s and early 90s were branded as brutal and racist. They were not that. The number of lives they saved and the good they did far outweighed anything bad they might have done. They were just average young men who did a job that nobody else wanted. If it wasn't for them, South Africa might not have been able to change to a democracy. They played a vital role in keeping the peace against all odds against great adversity and the cost of many lives. To this day they have not received a shred of gratitude or recognition for what they did.[22]

Though the people's war caused mayhem in the townships, it could not overthrow the government. But it could be used as 'armed propaganda' to weaken De Klerk at the negotiating table. He had seized the initiative in February 1990 in an act of brave statesmanship that one rarely sees in politics here or elsewhere. He also played the local and foreign media brilliantly. This enabled him not only to seize the moral high ground, but also to catch the ANC on the back foot. He therefore had to be discredited. This was done by brilliant ANC propaganda which blamed him for orchestrating violence via a clandestine 'Third Force' consisting of the police, the defence force, Inkatha, vigilantes, and miscellaneous 'hit squads'.[23] The aim was supposedly to destabilise the ANC. The Third

Force was widely propagated by the ANC and its supporters, many of them in newsrooms around the country. It was also widely accepted as the gospel truth, one key consequence being to shift the balance in the negotiating process towards the ANC.

Given the NP's history, including the brutality which the Institute had chronicled in great detail down the years, the third-force theory had a superficial plausibility. De Klerk himself later described how difficult it had been to shut down 'unauthorised, illegal, and criminal activities' and how he felt it necessary to purge several top officers at the end of 1992.[24] But the theory failed to pay any attention to the ANC's own declared intentions to launch a people's war and make the country ungovernable. Moreover, if the state and Inkatha were plotting to orchestrate violence, why would they have killed hundreds of policemen and assassinated 335 Inkatha office-bearers and officials?[25]

The third-force theory, I argued, turned a blind eye to all these other aspects of violence. In fact, it consigned them to George Orwell's 'memory hole'. Many Western intellectuals had done the same with Stalin's crimes. Now sections of the liberal community, others opposed to apartheid, and parts of the media were doing it with the people's war in South Africa.[26] Down the South African memory hole were dropped not only all those assassinated policemen, black councillors, and Inkatha members, but also victims of necklace executions and thousands of ordinary people identified with neither one side nor the other but simply caught up in the people's war.

Objecting to the Institute's reports on these killings, one business apologist for the people's war, safe in a suburb of Sandton, wrote to me that they were 'immaterial'.[27] Some of the very same white liberals who had spoken up so strongly for the black victims of NP policies now turned a blind eye to the black victims of the ANC's campaign to render the country ungovernable and eliminate opposition.

Indeed, if you pointed to the killings of IFP members or suggested that some of the violence in which the IFP was involved might be in retaliation for attacks, you were invariably accused of being an apologist for Buthelezi. On one occasion, two British journalists reported to Helen Suzman that I was in his 'pocket', to which she replied that I was 'in nobody's pocket but raised issues no one else did and put the record straight'.

Helen was one of the exceptions, for Buthelezi was one of those people that many liberals, journalists, clerics, diplomats, and others loved to hate. No doubt some, excited by the romance of 'struggle' in far-away townships, took their cue from the UDF and the ANC. The former had made plain at its launch in 1983 that Buthelezi would not be welcome as a member. The latter had called him a 'snake' that had to be 'hit on the head'. Others believed that he had been co-opted into the homeland system. Yet Buthelezi had publicly vowed never to allow that system to come to fruition by accepting independence for KwaZulu. While others suspected that Buthelezi would do some sort of deal with the NP behind the backs of the ANC, I knew that he would not back down on his demand for the release of Mandela and other political prisoners as a precondition for national constitutional negotiations. Nor could he be enticed into any deals short of such negotiations. He was both too astute and too principled.

Moreover, I admired his determination, despite intransigence from the government and vilification from the Left, to find a non-violent way out of the dead end up which the NP was taking the country. This took more courage than was displayed by white fellow travellers and armchair revolutionaries who clapped their hands with glee as the people's war wrought mayhem in the townships.

Apart from all the Inkatha officials assassinated, one of those who paid a heavy price for working with Buthelezi on trying to find a non-violent path out of the dead end was Lawrence Schlemmer. He had received death threats from the hard Left and in 1986 his home and his university office were simultaneously firebombed. Both the home and the priceless library in his office were destroyed.[28]

Buthelezi's supporters were obviously perpetrating violence, both in KwaZulu and on the Reef. De Klerk indeed later wrote that some of the 200 members of the KwaZulu police clandestinely trained by the South African Defence Force as VIP protection units had become involved in 'murderous offensives' against the ANC.[29] However, those who made so much of this failed to take account of the thousands of Umkhonto units trained in the Soviet Union and elsewhere who were already in the country or returning to it – according to the government's intelligence services, some 13 000 of them. A great hue and cry went up about the 'traditional weapons' (spears, sticks, and knobkerries) that IFP members carried in public. But the far more lethal AK-47s which Umkhonto was bringing into the country were invariably overlooked.

My book quoted some of the belligerent language sometimes used by Buthelezi: for example, that non-violent strategies did not rule out 'an eye for an eye and a tooth for a tooth' if that choice were forced upon the IFP.[30] However, nobody, not the commission under Judge Richard Goldstone appointed by De Klerk to investigate violence, not Buthelezi's enemies in the media, produced convincing evidence that he was involved in the promotion of violence as a political strategy, unlike the ANC and its allies.

Not only had many liberals turned a blind eye to the ANC's strategies, various clerics had given their blessing to revolutionary violence on the grounds that it was a 'just war'. I backed this contention up with references to statements by the South African Council of Churches (SACC), and to the Kairos document signed by 150 clergy and theologians from 22 denominations in 1985.[31] Tens of thousands of leaflets in all the main South African languages were distributed calling for intensification of 'conflict and struggle'. Stone-throwing, arson, and the killing of collaborators should not be called violence, they said, but self-defence since only oppressors used violence. Youths were a particular target of this incendiary propaganda. I used an invitation to address the Sandton Rotary Club in February 1991 to say that 'black people in the townships are reaping the whirlwind that the churches have helped to sow'.[32]

What the Rotarians thought about this I do not remember. But the SACC expressed its disgust at my 'vicious and unwarranted attack'. Its general secretary, Frank Chikane, said I'd taken 'an ideological stand against the victims of apartheid'. The ANC Youth League said the church had advocated the use of organised violence employed by a disciplined liberation movement, but not the stabbing and necklacing of people.[33] Bruce Evans, Anglican bishop of Port Elizabeth, demanded an apology for my 'malevolent' statement.[34]

But Tom Stanage, Anglican bishop of Bloemfontein, who'd been at my Oxford college some years before me, telephoned to say he was 'proud' of me.[35] And Bill Burnett, former archbishop of Cape Town, wrote to encourage me 'in what you have to say about the Church's misuse of its authority in implicitly and explicitly encouraging violence'. He said he'd lost many good friends for his own criticism of the 'dangerous and false theology emanating from some of our bishops'. His letter ended: 'Keep right on.'[36]

I did just that. The British weekly *The Spectator* wrote an editorial endorsing my argument. It drew attention to the connections between liberation theology and Marxism, and to the 'notorious' Programme to Combat Racism launched by the World Council of Churches. It also discussed the funding that 'radicalised' church aid agencies in developed countries had put into armed liberation movements.[37]

My remarks were also endorsed by Rachel Tingle in a book published by the Christian Studies Centre in London.[38] The book added fuel to the flames. Two missionary divisions of the Methodist Church in London accused us of being in some sort of 'alliance' with the book and declined to renew their membership of the Institute.[39]

Although I never lost sight of the horrors of township violence, which is why I spoke out in the first place, I enjoyed the uproar I provoked among clerics trying to wash their hands of the consequences of their endorsement of violence. Leaks to me of discussions in various synods about what I'd said added to the enjoyment. Nothing that any of my critics said was able to refute my argument that liberation theology had helped to sow the whirlwind of violence in the townships.

I put all our work on coercion together in a book entitled *Political Violence in South Africa*, which we published in 1993. Writing in the weekly *Mail & Guardian*, David Beresford said I'd been 'less than charitable' in my understanding of the circumstances in which the ANC had launched its 'campaign to reduce the country to anarchy'.[40] He seemed to think that I should somehow be an apologist for this campaign.

A British reviewer, Anthony Daniels, wrote of how successfully the ANC and its camp followers had 'assiduously promoted the view that the oppressed can do no evil' and that it had taken 'great courage' on my part to challenge this. He said that I'd referred to 'stark realities which the Western media have consistently ignored, despite all the time and space they have devoted to South Africa'.[41]

Reviewing my book in *Business Day*, Alan Fine agreed that the people's war and the campaign to make the country ungovernable had been 'sorely neglected' in the debate on violence.[42] In *The Star*, Patrick Laurence noted that I'd not discounted the possibility of a third force given the NP's record of ruthless and Machiavellian manipulation. However, he agreed that insufficient attention had been paid to the ANC's revolutionary campaign to make the townships ungovernable as a major cause of violence.[43]

Fine and Laurence were both right. But it was extraordinary that so little media and public attention was paid to the strategy causing such mayhem in black communities. Without the Institute's efforts the people's war and its terrible impact might still lie buried. So would a key part of its purpose. Many years later Patrick Laurence thus wrote that the people's war had been 'directed against black citizens who dared to oppose the ANC as much as against the apartheid regime'.[44] To ignore this is to ignore the dark side of the organisation ruling South Africa today.

My book took the liberal intelligentsia to task for abandoning their traditional watchdog role, including that of standing up for the under-dog. In particular they had 'failed to speak up for ordinary people against the coercive strategies of revolutionaries'. Some liberals had condoned violence, but others had been reluctant to take the ANC's commitment to revolution seriously. Even though 'the pattern of actual violence cor-related closely with the type of violence called for by the ANC, some academic observers took the view that the "people's war" amounted to little more than rhetoric'.[45] Liberalism's finest hour this was not.

My book relied not only on my own work but also on that of five col-leagues, Anthea Jeffery, Jill Wentzel, Paul Pereira, Ellen Potter, and Alfred Nkungu. Apart from studying the press, police reports, documents pub-lished by various violence monitoring agencies, and transcripts of Radio Freedom, we interviewed ANC and Cosatu officials, along with police officers, academics, opposition politicians, and well-informed jour-nalists.[46] There were few aspects of violence that we did not carefully scrutinise and categorise.

Anthea and I addressed numerous meetings in various parts of the country. We also hosted a discussion at Auden House between Jacob Zuma, then deputy secretary general of the ANC, and Frank Mdlalose, Inkatha chairman. It was chaired by our president, Stanley Mogoba, a member (and later president) of the PAC who had once been impris-oned on Robben Island.[47] Afterwards I took them all to dinner at our local Braamfontein steakhouse, the Turn 'n Tender.

It was not until 2009 that the Institute was able to complete a com-prehensive study entitled *People's War: New Light on the Struggle for South Africa* by my colleague Anthea Jeffery.[48] This made use of docu-ments unknown to us when we started analysing township violence a quarter of a century earlier. It was clear that we had been right all along, not only about the causes of violence but also about how important it was for the ANC and its allies to portray it in a 'politically correct' light. As Raymond Suttner of the SACP had written, 'We need in particular to take more determined steps to win the propaganda war as to the meaning and cause of the violence. We need to step up this campaign until it reaches a point where massive pressure can be exerted on all peace-loving people to force the government to end the war.'[49] This was code for handing over power to the ANC, which effectively happened with the launch in December 1993 of a Transitional Executive Council which it was able to dominate in the period leading up to the election in April 1994.

Although the ANC accused both De Klerk and Buthelezi of having double agendas in that they were negotiating but also stoking violence, this was true not of them but of the ANC itself. The organisation itself stated that it could not win at the negotiating table what it had not won on the ground. It could not win any conflict with the government's security forces, but it could raise the political costs of deploying them by stoking violence through mass mobilisation and then casting all the blame for the resulting mayhem upon De Klerk and Buthelezi. The third-force allegations could then be used to demonise both De Klerk and Buthelezi and so weaken them in the constitutional negotiating process.

This was done with especially brilliant success when the ANC used a massacre on the night of 17 June 1992 in the Boipatong township near Sharpeville as a pretext to walk out of the Convention for a Democratic South Africa (Codesa), which was the forum for multiparty negotiations about a new constitution.

Prior to the massacre the ANC had been threatening to launch a pro-gramme of 'rolling mass action' designed to force the 'De Klerk regime from power' in an ANC version of the 'Leipzig option' that had toppled the East German regime three years earlier. The strategy was born of the ANC's frustration at its inability to get its way in Codesa, where it found itself in a minority on several key issues related to limitations on power.

The ANC had all along also wanted all the key decisions on the country's future to be made bilaterally by itself and the government. It further wanted the new constitution to be written not by a multiparty convention, but by an elected constituent assembly with sovereign authority; this, of course, it expected to dominate. The NP opposed this, arguing that the constitution should be the outcome of multiparty talks. But after walking out of Codesa using the government's alleged involvement in the Boipatong massacre as a pretext, the ANC was able to turn the multiparty talks into an essentially bilateral affair after concluding a 'record of understanding' with the government a few months later in September 1992. This meant that the multiparty talks were reduced to a rubber stamp. One key consequence was that the new constitution provided for a centralised system of government, despite the fact that most of the Codesa delegations had favoured federalism as a means of decentralising power and accommodating the country's political and ethnic diversity.

The massacre was as defining a moment in South African history as was the Sharpeville massacre in 1960. Initially the massacre appeared to be 'black-on-black' violence. 'As such, it was of little use to ANC spin doctors,' according to Rian Malan in an analysis written for the Institute and published in our journal *Frontiers*. However, the propagandists got to work, and by noon on the following day the ANC had put out a statement to the effect that the attackers were ferried into Boipatong and its neighbouring Joe Slovo shack settlement by police Casspirs, that the police had participated in the attack, and that army vehicles had also been used. 'We charge FW de Klerk with direct complicity in this slaughter,' said Cyril Ramaphosa. Ignoring the fact that Ramaphosa had already effectively stalemated Codesa, Mandela announced that he was pulling out of the talks on the grounds that he could no longer justify talking to 'a regime that is murdering black people'.

The ANC's well-nigh instant version of the massacre was accepted as gospel truth around the world, not least by the UN Security Council, which sprang into action with special hearings. Here at last was the final proof positive of the Third Force. De Klerk, who had been riding high in international esteem, was now caught with the smoking gun in his hand. But it was nonsense. There was never any doubt that the slaughter was perpetrated by Inkatha supporters, 17 of whom living in the KwaMadala hostel in Boipatong were subsequently convicted by Judge JMC Smit of the murder of 45 township residents (although he declined to impose the death sentence on the grounds that they had been the victims of earlier attacks by ANC supporters).

But nobody ever found any proof that the police were complicit in the massacre in any way. When Judge Richard Goldstone and a British policing expert drafted in by De Klerk declared that they could find no evidence of police involvement, this was brushed aside by the ANC and downplayed by the press. The court under Judge Smit which convicted the 17 hostel residents of murder heard testimony from 120 Boipatong residents from almost every house where death or serious injury occurred. They were more likely than anyone else to have seen the police ferrying the killers into the area and joining in the attack. None of them had. Evidence against the police also crumbled under cross-examination. So Judge Smit also dismissed allegations of police involvement. This too was largely ignored by the media and the ANC.

It was also ignored by the Truth Commission, which pronounced after a cursory investigation that the police had planned and helped to execute the massacre. Nor did anybody pay much attention to a ruling of the Truth Commission's amnesty committee under Judge Sandile Ngcobo in November 2000, more than eight years after the terrible events at Boipatong. After a far more thorough investigation than the commission itself had thought fit to conduct, the committee also dismissed the allegations of police involvement.

But the truth no longer mattered. The spin put upon Boipatong was game, set, and match to the ANC. As Malan wrote, '[It] was the beginning of the end for the National Party.' Two articles we published in *Frontiers* by him and by Anthea Jeffery are among the few accounts of what actually happened.[50] Joseph Goebbels would have appreciated the ANC's spectacular success in the propaganda war. He had regarded the 'intellectual

Rock-solid as Institute presidents: With Lawrence Schlemmer, Helen Suzman, and Hermann Giliomee at the Institute.

conduct of the war' as no less important than the shooting war.[51]

Although our writings on violence were subject to often extremely hostile scrutiny, no one was able to upset any of our findings. Moreover, were it not for our work, the people's war would have been airbrushed out of South African history. Professor Hermann Giliomee, a leading academic at the universities of Stellenbosch and Cape Town who served as both president and vice president of the Institute and wrote a major historical study entitled *The Afrikaners*, warned of 'Orwellian' thought control in the rewriting of history. The ANC, he said, was using the Truth Commission to produce what one truth commissioner, Richard Lyster, called a 'publicly sanctioned history' that 'can be taught in schools' to the exclusion of 'contradictory versions'.[52]

Nothing the Institute published while I was running it generated as much controversy as our work on political violence. We had a few board resignations. Ernie Wentzel's untimely death in 1986 was a huge blow to the Institute and to the entire liberal community. But Elwyn Jenkins, Charles Simkins, and Theo Coggin proved indomitable as board chairmen. Lawrence Schlemmer, Helen Suzman, Hermann Giliomee, Themba Sono, and Bill Wilson were also rock-solid as Institute presidents, as was Stanley Magoba, who was himself put under enormous pressure to repudiate us. Helen Suzman on one occasion wrote that we would not allow our research on violence to be subject to some sort of 'thought control'.[53] Told that a prominent academic at the University of Cape Town strongly disapproved of me and what I was saying about violence, she retorted, 'Well, he probably disapproves of me too, and I don't give a damn.'[54]

Kader Asmal, whom I had visited during my freelance days when he was in exile in Dublin and who was now minister of water affairs and forestry, objected to our 'stance over death squads/third force matters'. 'However well-intentioned in the cause of factual accuracy, [it] had the effect of aiding the forces of darkness.'[55] I wondered whether this meant he admitted we were telling the truth, but that we should rather not do so. Someone even fabricated a story for a communist magazine published in Germany to the effect that I was a member of the National Intelligence Service and the Institute a front organisation for it.[56]

But we also had lots of support. The chief justice, Mick Corbett, told me after listening to one of my lectures in Cape Town on political violence that he agreed with every word I said. Jan Steyn of the Urban Foundation, himself a former judge, praised our 'vigorously independent viewpoint'.[57] Others hailed our 'lucid, dispassionate, and brave analysis'. Mary Mathews praised our 'fiery courage' under attack.[58] Pat Flemmer wrote in from East London to say that she was a Black Sash member who found it 'disturbing that so few liberal whites feel able to criticise actions of blacks – even if wrong'.[59]

Ina Perlman also wrote in. We'd made her an honorary life member of the Institute in recognition of all the work she'd done there and at Operation Hunger. She now wrote to say that Ellen Hellmann, who had for many years ruled the Institute as chairman of its general purposes committee, had once said that she hoped that when the time came to be critical of the then oppressed, the Institute would have the integrity to meet that challenge. We had, Ina said, 'more than fulfilled her hope'.[60] She could not have paid us a greater compliment.

And so we entered the post-apartheid era. Some people told us that we had done our job and no longer had a role. Not so fast, we said. Is not the price of liberty, everywhere, always, eternal vigilance? Liberalisation could be tricky. 'It went wrong in France in 1789 and the French people landed up with a more tyrannical regime than that of Louis XVI. The same happened in Russia in 1917.' Revolutionaries had now come to power in South Africa. Some of them talked the language of liberalism, but others had a history of violent intolerance of opposition. The ANC and the NP had similar track records in dealing with dissent, whether in detention camps outside the country or detention cells inside it.[61] We needed to be on guard to ensure that there were no detours on the road to a free multiparty democracy. And we pointed out the irony in the fact that many countries had recently thrown communists out of government, while South Africa's first post-apartheid government would include quite a number.[62]

We identified some of the key challenges the country would face. One was unemployment. Another was dealing with material backlogs. Many groups would seize on continuing inequality to argue that apartheid was still in place and that South Africa therefore needed a command economy to deal with them, not a market economy.[63]

The Institute, I told a meeting hosted by Richards Bay Minerals in that town, 'fully expects to have to fight some of the old battles again – not against apartheid, but against an officious bureaucracy and an intrusive state'.[64] There were signs of executive interference to undermine the independence of public prosecutors.[65] The health minister seemed hostile to private health care and the new education minister to model C schools, even though these were a success story in desegregating education. Hostile public and official attitudes to illegal immigrants were disturbing. And it was not clear how strongly the ANC would clamp down on corruption. Crime and lawlessness were another problem.[66]

However, South Africa started the democratic era with huge advantages. These included critical newspapers, independent black trade unions, and thriving non-governmental organisations.[67] Another asset was the independence of the judiciary and of the legal profession, plus the willingness of lawyers to take on politically unpopular cases. Along with competing political parties, these were the working capital of a free society. Unlike in the former Soviet Union, they did not have to be created from scratch. And finally, Nelson Mandela had been careful to emphasise the 'central role' of the private sector in 'achieving significantly high and sustainable rates of economic growth'.[68]

Many people told us to change our name. But we didn't want to jettison the goodwill built up over 65 years. From Moscow to Washington, from Lusaka to London, from Canberra to Rome, and all over South Africa, people knew us and they knew of our track record of opposition to apartheid. This was a priceless asset instantly conveyed by that name. It gave us a legitimacy for our work in the post-apartheid era which few other organisations could claim. We also suspected that affirmative action would become a euphemism for racial quotas.[69]

There was another formidable obstacle in the way of any name change. 'Over my dead body,' declared Helen Suzman whenever the issue was raised. That tended to shut most people up, including me. I had enough on my plate without wanting to battle her about this.

Helen was always a delight. Although I had known her since my student days, I didn't try to get her actively involved in the Institute until after her retirement from Parliament in 1989. But she agreed to run for president in that same year, in which capacity she served for three years, thereafter becoming one of our vice presidents and remaining a vice president until her death in 2009. She had in fact begun her long fight against apartheid at the Institute, which commissioned her to help prepare its submission to the Native Laws Commission set up under Mr Justice Fagan in 1946 to examine the pass and other laws affecting Africans. She later wrote that her work on that submission (with Ellison Kahn) had alerted her to the 'appalling' effects of these laws, which she spent the rest of her life fighting.[70]

I was flattered to be invited to deliver the opening address at an exhibition on Helen's life's work which was staged in Johannesburg in 2006, and also to preside at a memorial gathering held in the Wits Great Hall some months after she died. It was also a treat to get phone calls from her – usually before seven in the morning – after I'd written an article or made a speech that she liked. On one occasion she rang with a tongue-in-cheek complaint. Malegapuru Makgoba, vice-chancellor of the University of KwaZulu-Natal, had written an article attacking white South Africans who were dissatisfied with the new order as 'dethroned male baboons' – 'depressed' and 'quarrelsome'.[71] I wrote an article taking issue with him,[72] following which Helen sent me a message to the effect that I had ignored 'dethroned female baboons' and was therefore guilty of sexism.[73]

When she first came to dinner at our house, Pierre was terrified that something might go wrong. As she sat down our cat jumped onto her lap, to his consternation. I'd forgotten to tell him that she adored cats, and the said cat spent the whole evening on Helen's lap. She also never forgot the small things: once I had to leave one of her lunches early because my mother was ill; I was not surprised that Helen rang a day or two later to find out how she was.

She attended not only Institute board and council meetings, but also other functions, after most of which we served only wine and beer, apart from soft drinks. Helen always came prepared with a miniature of Johnny Walker Red Label in her handbag. Queenie Nkuna, who looked after our catering on these occasions, would then pour her a glass of soda to go with the Scotch.

Towards the end of her life it was clear to me that Helen was far more disillusioned than she let on in public. 'John, our democracy is dying,' she said on one occasion.[74] But she didn't lose her sense of humour. Once when I did an hour-long radio interview with her to mark her ninetieth birthday in 2007, I asked her how she felt about the forthcoming presidency of Jacob Zuma.

'I won't be here,' she replied.

'Why, are you planning to emigrate?'

'No, darling, I'm planning to be dead.'

I do not think she would have been surprised at the armed robbery of the headquarters of the Helen Suzman Foundation in Johannesburg on 20 March 2016 during which computers were stolen by people who knew exactly what they were looking for and where to find it. The robbery took place only a few days after the foundation launched an application in the high court for an interdict preventing the head of the Hawks – a special police unit – from exercising any of his powers pending the outcome of a review questioning his fitness for office.[75]

CHAPTER 12

Revolution under the rainbow

As the various parties geared up for the 1994 election, I had two approaches to run for Parliament. One was from the Democratic Party, whom I turned down. The other was from Leon Louw of the Free Market Foundation, who wanted to launch a new Federal Party with me as a candidate. I turned that down too. I didn't think I could toe a party line. Parliament soon began to go wrong anyway. With the connivance of the first Speaker, Frene Ginwala, attempts by the parliamentary standing committee on public accounts (Scopa) to investigate the questionable R47-billion arms acquisition deal announced in November 1999 were torpedoed by the ANC and the then president, Thabo Mbeki.[1] Parliament has never recovered from this attack on its vital function of holding the executive branch of government to account. President Jacob Zuma's refusal to account to Parliament for the expenditure on his private homestead in Nkandla follows an established precedent.

Perhaps naïvely, I accepted an invitation from Speaker Baleka Mbete in 2006 to join an independent panel to assess the performance of Parliament.[2] Two and a half years later the panel produced an anodyne document to which I wanted to attach a minority report with more robust recommendations. One of these was that Parliament should call for a judicial commission of enquiry into the arms deal. Another was that MPs should be made to repay money arising from their irregular use of travel vouchers in the 'Travelgate' affair. I further proposed that anyone elected as speaker should be obliged to relinquish any office they held in a political party.[3]

The rest of the 12-member panel refused to allow me to attach a minority report. Max Sisulu, one of its members and himself a subsequent speaker, told me such a report would undermine the 'collective' view of the panel. So I declined to sign the main document and gave my minority report to the press. I told them that the panel – among whose other members were two former opposition leaders, Frederik van Zyl Slabbert and Colin Eglin, who should have known better than to help block my report – had 'ducked' the arms deal, Travelgate, and the issue of presiding officers' conflicts of interest.[4] Given the mockery that the ANC, and Ms Mbete as both speaker and party chairman, have made of Parliament, I'm thankful that I am not a member.

Becoming an MP would have entailed leaving the Institute. The same applied to an earlier invitation I'd had from Jan Steyn, chief executive of the Urban Foundation, to join that organisation with a view to becoming his successor. Although the salary was almost double what I was earning at the Institute,[5] I declined the offer as I would not be comfortable running an organisation so closely linked to business. My independence was too important. So was the ability to speak my mind. This I had at the Institute. But it came at a price – it was my job to find the money to keep going. Although I'd been able to avoid shipwreck in 1983, keeping afloat was never plain sailing. Often we had to budget for deficits. More than once I feared we might not survive, but I could not reveal this fear to anyone. However, by the time I retired as CEO at the end of February 2014, we had just over R60 million in assets under our control, of which R18 million was in bursary funds.[6]

Our first battle was to retain our independence. It was scarcely believable that this challenge confronted us so soon in the democratic era, but in August 1995 an organisation calling itself the Development Resources Centre produced draft legislation to give the government control of all non-profit organisations. The draft provided for the establishment of a 25-member commission all but two of whose members would be appointed by one or another minister. This body would have the power to remove trustees from the boards of NPOs and replace them with its own nominees.[7]

We immediately alerted the NPO sector to this threat and mobilised a campaign against it. Organisations ranging from the Save the Children's Fund and the Salvation Army to the Union of Jewish Women and the Institute of Directors joined the Helen Suzman Foundation and ourselves in opposing the draft bill.[8] We lobbied all the parties in Parliament. Fortunately, I knew Cassim Saloojee, one of the ANC MPs who would have been responsible for processing it. He had himself run a welfare organisation and had also once served on the Institute's board. He shared our objections.

Geraldine Fraser-Moleketi, the minister who would have been responsible for introducing the bill, then contacted us and said, well, if we didn't like the draft bill, what kind of bill would we like? Our public affairs manager, Paul Pereira, who had organised our campaign, set to work with her department producing a liberal alternative. The resulting Non-Profit Organisations Act of 1997, an excellent example of light-handed regulation, remains on the Statute Book. Thanks largely to the Institute's vigilance, the 85 000 registered NPOs in South Africa are as free as any in the world. We were especially pleased to have got a liberal law enacted despite an attack on critical institutions that Nelson Mandela had launched in a speech in Mafikeng in the same year – evidence, we said, of the ANC's 'split democratic personality'.[9]

The lesson I drew from this was clear. If something is wrong in principle you oppose it in principle. And you fight to win. You don't accept the premise of government interference and then bargain for the best deal you can get. But we did not rest on our laurels. When Mandela and Thabo Mbeki a few years later said civil society should not think it was 'needed to curb government', I retorted that independent organisations in civil society were one of the hallmarks distinguishing free from totalitarian societies.[10] When the ANC attacked Cosatu as 'oppositionist and dangerous' for organising a meeting of trade unionists and members of various NPOs, I issued a statement defending Cosatu's rights[11] even though I'd been highly critical of the violence which some of its members and officials all too frequently used to enforce strikes.

It was no surprise that Blade Nzimande, one of the leading communists in the Cabinet, said that an 'autonomous and vibrant civil society' could be 'a dangerous shift away from the perspective of a National Democratic Revolution to that of bourgeois democracy'. He was right to fear this, and he was in good company. Independent NPOs in recent years have come under attack from people who included Yoweri Museveni of Uganda, Vladimir Putin of Russia, Robert Mugabe of Zimbabwe, and Hugo Chavez of Venezuela.[12]

Having beaten off the challenge to our own independence, I made sure that we sprang to the defence of the judiciary, whose 'collective mindset' the ANC said it wished to change, while also making judges more accountable to 'the masses'. Five draft bills calculated to undermine the independence of the judiciary were published in 2005. We fought them in principle and from the start. Although judges had made it clear to the government that they opposed the draft legislation, they were reluctant to speak out in public and some therefore strongly encouraged us to do so. Two who did speak out at lectures hosted by the Institute were Bob Nugent and Carole Lewis, judges on the Supreme Court of Appeal.[13] I also arranged for Johann Kriegler, a former judge on the Constitutional Court, to address a meeting of the 1926 Club, a 'town and gown' dining club that met monthly at the Rand Club and of which I'd once been chairman.

The Institute's campaign helped force the government to defend its legislation. My colleague Anthea Jeffery and I dissected and rebutted all these attempts in our own publications and in newspaper columns. President Mbeki eventually promised that no legislation would be enacted without the support of the judiciary and the bills were with-drawn in 2006. One senior judge told us we had played a 'significant role' in causing the government not to proceed. Another told me we had 'given heart' to him and many of his colleagues by speaking out so strongly when legal academia had been silent.[14] Yet another joked when I met him on an aeroplane that I would always be welcomed as a litigant in the High Court.

Some of the proposals in the five bills were subsequently enacted, though in a less objectionable form.[15] We were less successful in our efforts to defend the independence of the legal profession. Throughout the apartheid years, that profession had regulated itself through bar councils and law societies accountable to their members. Its independ-ence had enabled many lawyers to take on cases defending 'treason trialists, communists, revolutionaries,' and 'many of the other people now running South Africa'.[16] These same people now wanted to under-mine the very institution which had so often fought for them in the courts against the apartheid state.

Draft legislation published in 2012 provided for these independent bodies to be replaced by a council accountable to the minister of justice. The new council would also be entitled to take over all the assets of the previously independent bodies. The chairman of the General Council of the Bar of South Africa, Gerrit Pretorius, wrote to thank me for oppos-ing the draft bill. He had 'little doubt that it is the thin end of the wedge that will quickly lead to the loss of the legal profession's independence', which would 'take decades to reclaim'.[17]

Although some aspects of the proposed government control were watered down, in the end the lawyers were unable to present a united front against the legislation, which came into operation in 2015. My father had come up against a similar problem many years before when Ruth Hayman, an attorney who was a member of the Liberal Party and who had handled a lot of political cases, was banned and house-arrested in 1966. He tried to get the organised legal profession to take up her case and protest to the minister of justice, only to be told that doing so would split that profession.[18] Nevertheless, although a number of lawyers were picked off by the NP government, the independence of the profession as a whole was not attacked as the ANC was now attacking it.

Attacks on independent institutions were not merely the outcome of anger on the part of the ANC at what they might have said or done, but part of a wider plan – the National Democratic Revolution to which Dr Nzimande had referred. Although they differ on other issues, this is one on which the ANC, Cosatu, and the SACP agree. I gave a number of lectures about this revolutionary strategy in various parts of the country, as well as in Berlin and Brussels. Responses both in South Africa and abroad were mixed: some of those who heard me grasped at once what I was talking about and said that for the first time they understood policy developments that previously seemed so confusing. Others simply did not want to hear.

The first component of the National Democratic Revolution is to deploy loyal cadres and party apparatchiks to capture control of as many 'centres of power' as possible. The second is to use affirmative action to bring about demographic proportionality in the racial make-up of both public and private institutions. The third is to bring about radical redistribution of wealth, income, and land from white to black on the grounds that all white assets are the proceeds of colonial exploitation and apartheid. The fourth is to win the 'battle of ideas' against 'ultra-leftism' and 'neo-liberalism'. The ultimate objectives are to turn South Africa into a socialist and then a communist state.

The SACP adopted the National Democratic Revolution in 1962, and the ANC adopted it in 1969. But 25 years after coming to power, it was still talking about 'capturing the state to advance the purposes of the revolutionary forces'. There was talk of exercising 'hegemony' over policy institutes, transforming the ideological orientation of civil servants, and fighting against the liberal concept of 'less government'.

Yet, although the ANC reaffirms it from time to time – most recently

246

at its conference in Mangaung in December 2012 and at its national general council meeting in October 2015 – the National Democratic Revolution receives scant media attention. This is despite the fact that cadre deployment and affirmative action have been implemented throughout the civil service and state-owned enterprises, despite the increasing interventionist powers the state has been assuming for itself, and despite the blurring of the distinction between party and state. When the ANC and the government adopted the National Development Plan at the end of 2012, I suggested that this was the perfect smokescreen under which the organisation's real agenda, the National Democratic Revolution, could be implemented.[19] Many political columnists claim to be 'baffled' by the ANC's failure to implement the NDP. But if they paid a bit more attention to the National Democratic Revolution, they might be less so. Nor does the ANC's revolutionary agenda receive much attention from academia. One university vice-chancellor indeed told one of his professors to lay off the National Democratic Revolution and teach 'transformation' instead.[20]

The Institute, the FW de Klerk Foundation, Accountability Now, and the Solidarity trade union are the only organisations paying the National Democratic Revolution the attention it necessitates. When I spoke about it at a conference organised by the foundation at the Johannesburg Country Club in 2012, some of the businessmen in the audience suggested I was looking for 'reds under the bed'. They presumably felt this because I explained that the National Democratic Revolution had its origins in Lenin's theory of imperialism, adapted for South African circumstances as 'colonialism of a special type'. However, the reds in South Africa are not under the bed, they are on top of the government.[21]

Not only has the ANC committed itself to a strategy devised by the SACP, but many members of the SACP are in key positions in the ANC, in the Cabinet, and in Parliament. According to research done for the Institute, possibly as many as 40 per cent of the current three dozen Cabinet ministers and deputy ministers are SACP members, as is the secretary general of the ANC, Gwede Mantashe. Prominent communists in the Cabinet include Jeff Radebe and two ministers with key economic responsibilities, Rob Davies at the Department of Trade and Industry and Ebrahim Patel at the Department of Economic Development.

Lenin's theory of imperialism claimed that the wealth of imperial powers was derived solely from the exploitation of their colonies. South Africa, however, didn't fit the standard Leninist model because its colonial/settler/white population was both large and as firmly settled in South Africa as were blacks.[22] They couldn't 'return' to a putative 'mother' country which most of them had never seen anyway. The model therefore had to be adapted: hence 'colonialism of a special type'. This meant that whites became the equivalent of the imperial power and blacks the colony. 'On this analysis, white wealth is never the result of enterprise but always of exploitation and is therefore illegitimate.'

Despite this view of white wealth, it could not easily be confiscated. The collapse of the Berlin Wall in 1989 and the subsequent implosion of the Soviet Union undermined prospects for revolutionary liberation in South Africa. What emerged in 1993 from the multiparty talks that replaced Codesa after the ANC walkout was a compromise. Its key components included a sovereign constitution based on the separation of powers plus an independent judiciary charged with the protection of a long list of rights, including property rights. 'Right from the start, people described by the ANC as "ultra-leftists" have accused the organisation of betraying the revolution by agreeing to a constitution that supposedly tried to freeze for all time an unjust pattern of property ownership.'[23]

But did the ANC abandon the revolution in 1994? As it came to power, the ANC inherited a budget deficit which had reached an unprecedented 7.3 per cent. Public debt was climbing towards 50 per cent. The organisation had no choice but to bring both borrowing and spending under control. The alternative was possible subordination to the demands of the International Monetary Fund. The ANC also inherited a mixed economy with a large private sector. The organisation recognised that it could not simply 'seize the means of production'. Hence Nelson Mandela's repudiation of nationalisation. Since property was 'at the core of all social systems', tensions about redistribution had to be managed via 'dexterity in tact and firmness in principle'. Implementation depended on the 'balance of forces' prevailing at any given time.

> Perhaps confusingly, the National Democratic Revolution is not being pursued come hell or high water as an immediate objective. Implementation is not via the storming of the Bastille or the Winter Palace but is incremental. As one ANC document put it, you advance when next an opportunity arises to 'move the struggle decisively forward'. The collapse of communism was a setback, but the ANC believes that the current global financial crisis has helped it by demonstrating what it calls 'the bankruptcy of neo-liberalism'.

I made this point in several speeches in 2011.[24] One of the reasons why Thabo Mbeki was unseated at the end of 2007 was his apparent lack of enthusiasm for the National Democratic Revolution. Even so, key elements had already been implemented. Affirmative action, in the form of the Employment Equity and Broad-based Black Economic Empowerment Acts, was adopted in 1998 and 2003 respectively. Nothing has been formally nationalised, but mineral and water rights are now in the gift of the government, while a new 'right to farm' is in the offing via legislation that will take all land into the 'custodianship' of the state. Also in the pipeline is legislation that will entitle the state to expropriate property without compensation. The new controlling body for lawyers is but one example of how independent regulatory bodies are being replaced by statutory ones as the ANC seeks to consolidate control of all 'centres of power'. Many company boards in the private sector have appointed prominent ANC members as chairmen or to other positions, testifying to the organisation's ability to influence these other 'centres of power'. More licensing bodies are being established, giving the state more influence over business. The financial sector is also facing demands for 'transformation'. Although land reform is supposedly designed to transfer white-owned agricultural land to blacks, in practice ownership goes to the state.

The market-orientated Growth, Employment, and Redistribution (Gear) strategy of 1996 – stigmatised by the Left as 'neo-liberalism' – has been replaced by various plans providing for greater state intervention, including the NDP of 2012: although this emphasises the importance of entrepreneurship in generating employment, it also envisages a 'developmental state' with the power to 'bring about rapid transformation in [the] country's economic and/or social conditions through active, intensive, and effective intervention in the structural causes of economic or social underdevelopment'.[25] There is a widespread belief that the NDP is not being implemented, but more and more 'active and intensive' intervention in the economy is actually taking place. This may seem haphazard, but if you connect the dots the pattern that emerges is the National Democratic Revolution.

Following Mr Mbeki's departure, the Soviet-style supremacy of party headquarters at Luthuli House has been re-established. The cadre deployment policy is well entrenched. Supposedly independent institutions, among them the police, the intelligence services, and the prosecuting authorities, are subject to political control. The same applies to major and many minor state-owned enterprises. The independent Public Protector was the focus of repeated attack during her seven-year term of office, which expired in October 2016. Government and party spokesmen regularly express hostile attitudes to the press, the judiciary, non-profit organisations, and business. They also make no secret of their irritation at the constraints imposed upon them by the Constitution. Foreign policy shows increasing hostility towards the Western liberal democracies and growing preference for Russia and China. Disdain for Parliament and accountability complete the picture.

I several times pointed out that although President Zuma's government was widely believed to be so mired in corruption and factionalism that it was not doing very much, it was actually putting through a series of major laws shifting power and property ownership away from the private sector and towards the state. Critics who failed to recognise this were, I said, 'sleeping through the revolution'.[26]

'Once upon a time' there had been a NP minister who dedicated himself to carrying out Dr Verwoerd's promise to reverse the flow of Africans from the homelands to the cities by 1978. 'His name was Blaar Coetzee and he was the butt of many jokes. Yet his government spared no effort to implement its policy.' As this book has shown, that policy, although widely ridiculed, with many a reference to King Canute, was remorselessly implemented. It was abandoned only when it failed and exposure of its cruelties eventually aroused the consciences of the ruling Afrikaners. Describing the National Democratic Revolution as a programme of 'racial, social, and economic engineering' similar to that of the NP, I suggested that it was time the commentariat, business, and foreign diplomats paid it attention[27] instead of shrugging it off as mere rhetoric. I also pointed out that the print media had ignored President Zuma's statement at the ANC's national general council meeting in October 2015 that his party and the 'vanguard' SACP were partners facing in the 'same direction' towards a 'socialist revolution' and a 'communist society'.[28]

However, the media paid far less attention to the silent revolution than it deserved, while underplaying the violence of the people's war and the ANC's role in it. So it is not surprising that they pay little attention to the ruling alliance's declared revolutionary aims. Perhaps the reason is reluctance to acknowledge the possibility that the post-apartheid South Africa is ruled not by a civil rights movement made good but by a nationalist-communist alliance committed to using the state to effect a revolution from above and to promote a black nationalist agenda.

President John F Kennedy once spoke of the need for vigilance against 'an intrusive and officious state'. The Institute under my leadership played a key role in highlighting all these trends and tendencies, including the slow strangulation of the economy.[29] Others have also highlighted many of them, along with the growing problem of lawlessness on the part of the state itself, not to mention rampant corruption and the 'capture' of state institutions to subordinate them to the interests of particular politicians and their business associates. But we have been one of the very few organisations to connect all the dots between these various developments, and to show their connection to the overriding policy of bringing about a National Democratic Revolution.

As CEO of the Institute I spent a great deal of time on racial policy – and probably far more after the formal demise of the apartheid system than before it. I never anticipated the extent to which racial policy would come to dominate the post-apartheid South Africa. As the next chapter will show, it went far beyond the affirmative action measures contemplated in the final post-apartheid constitution. Whereas my own and the Institute's opposition to the previous government's racial policies were in line with global opinion, we now found ourselves in a tiny minority openly opposing the racial policies of the new government. Some of those who agreed with us had supported the previous government's racial policies, and we didn't particularly wish to be in their company. Many liberals who had opposed the old racial policies supported the new government's, and didn't particularly want to be in our company. Some who did agree with our opposition to affirmative action and black economic empowerment policies regarded it as opportune to keep silent.

Other people were surprised at our attitude. They seemed to think that the job of liberals was to be pro-black. Given the fact that liberalism and white opposition to apartheid had been so closely intertwined for so many years, this was understandable. But it was a misunderstanding of liberalism. We'd been fighting for a liberal political system, not one based on a new kind of racial ideology.

Some people found us confusing because of our name. If you rang up to make an appointment to visit a particular company, they would assume you wanted to check on their 'diversity' profile and refer you to the human resources department. Others would hasten to tell you how well they were doing on affirmative action. One day a CEO who'd met one of my senior staff telephoned to congratulate me on my own successful affirmative action policy. 'I don't have any such policy,' I replied in puzzlement. Only then did I realise that the CEO had assumed that the (black) manager he met had been put there because he was black and not because he was the best man for the job. Fortunately, I burned my fingers with affirmative action at an early stage with the one and only appointment I'd made on racial grounds. Everybody in the building suspected this was a racial appointment and they all resented the person in question. Fortunately the incumbent misbehaved and I was able to dismiss him. I never again hired, or promoted, anybody on grounds of race – or sex for that matter.

Although I've read plenty about revolution in various places, my main interest during my very first trip to Leningrad, as it still was, was not revolutionary sites but the city's wonderful collections of paintings. My guides drove me one morning to the Hermitage, the former Winter Palace which houses one of the world's richest art collections, and said they would be back to fetch me in two hours to go on a sightseeing tour of the city. 'What time does the Hermitage close?' I asked. 'At six this evening.' 'Well, please come back then,' I replied.

I spent as much time there as I could, as well as in the Pushkin Museum in Moscow, awestruck by their collections of Rembrandts, Van Dycks, Picassos, and other masters. Some of the European paintings in Russia were bought by the czars from the British royal collection after the puritans had decided to get rid of them. Others were bought privately in Paris and elsewhere by Russian collectors, and were then nationalised by the Bolsheviks after the revolution. I went back twice to Russia to see some of these treasures again, and also to look at some of the glorious Russian paintings in the State Russian Museum in St Petersburg that are almost unknown in the West. The Hermitage is full of Western European art, from Leonardo da Vinci to Matisse, but in the 50 or so art museums Pierre and I have visited in the UK, Europe, and the US we have only very occasionally seen a Russian painting (except once in a special exhibition at the Guggenheim in New York). Galleries in Berlin and Munich also house paintings by German artists that you seldom see in Western galleries.

Pierre, who has an encyclopaedic knowledge of art, taught me how to look at paintings. A visit to a particular gallery can take anything up to three days: the first to see what there is to see, the second to look at all the paintings in detail, and the third to visit favourites for another look. If there's not enough time to see everything properly, we plan another visit. We thus paid return visits to both Munich and Dresden, which have fine collections. You can't rush through these galleries like a tourist taking snapshots – although you have to dodge many of those. You need time to savour what there is to see, to have frequent breaks for coffee, and to call it a day when you're suffering from what Pierre calls visual indigestion. On our last trip to St Petersburg we spent four days in the Hermitage and another four in the State Russian Museum. The former is full of tourists from all over the world, but only Russians seem to go to see Russian paintings.

Sometimes it can be very exciting to see a famous painting for the first time. Something you've seen only in catalogues or magazines is suddenly right there in front of you. On one occasion I was doubly excited to see in a travelling exhibition in Leningrad, as it still was, a Raphael that I'd seen a few months previously in Florence. A visit to London is not complete without dropping into the National Gallery, even if only for a minute or two, to say hello to Von Honthorst's *Christ Before the High Priests* or George Stubbs's great portrait of the horse Whistlejacket. Nor is a visit to Washington complete without stopping to pay one's respects to Rembrandt's Polish nobleman in a hat. It's taken me several years to see everything in Washington's magnificent National Gallery of Art, which I've done by snatching a Sunday morning or afternoon at the beginning or end of an Institute business trip. One of the great joys of visits to Italy is that you come across magnificent Caravaggios or other paintings in ordinary churches all over Rome – if there is such a thing as an ordinary church in Italy. When the *Queen Victoria* docked for a day in Malta, we were thrilled to see Caravaggio's great *Execution of John the Baptist* in the cathedral vestry.

It can also be marvellous to discover in a gallery or museum paintings by people you've never heard of. In Edinburgh we came across an exhibition of great watercolours of Naples by a man called Lusieri. Collections of works by particular painters can also be especially interesting: Rembrandt self-portraits, or Courbet, Poussin, or the Fontainebleau School, or Sisley, or Pisarro, or Van Gogh. Borrowed for a few months from museums and private collections in dozens of different countries, there they all are in the same room. And from what I've seen on a couple of tours of Buckingham Palace, the Queen's Gallery at the palace, Windsor Castle, and various special exhibitions, the Queen has one of the finest collections of paintings anywhere.

One of the things I always found striking about paintings was how even the greatest artists were often unable to depict children's faces, even – or especially – Christ or John the Baptist. One brilliant exception is the two little angels in the bottom corners of Raphael's Sistine Madonna in the Zwinger gallery in Dresden.

If we can't visit the world's great art museums, South Africa's game parks are the next best thing, especially the Kruger National Park. I remember how exciting it was for me as a small boy to get up at four in the morning to drive there with my grandparents from Lowlands to arrive just as the gates opened. Over the years we've been there a dozen times. Even if we drive for days on end without seeing very much, we will soon be back for another visit. First out of the gates as the sun rises, drive slowly all day to get to the next camp if necessary, and then a braai at night. And we stop for pretty much everything. We'd much rather park for half an hour in the middle of a herd of impala than sit for an hour in a traffic jam straining one's binoculars to look for a single leopard's paw supposedly hanging from a branch of a tree 100 metres away. We once stopped to look at a huge golden orb spider whose web was shining brilliantly in the setting sun. A car crawled up beside us and the occupants asked excitedly where the lion was – '*Waar's die leeuw? Waar's die leeuw?*' When we pointed to the spider, the driver looked at us in disgust, swore, and drove off. They'd probably have been even more disgusted if they'd seen us stop to allow a chameleon or a tortoise to cross the road. Elephants are my favourite: they are huge and can be hugely destructive, but they move so quietly through the bush that you will scarcely know they are there.

Sometimes when we go out early to watch the sun slowly light up the landscape, I'm reminded of an orchestra coming to life instrument by instrument in a Mahler symphony. As this tuft of grass lights up, that's like the French horns softly starting up. Then the sun catches a big bush, and the cellos strike up. Then it catches the trunk of a wild fig, and muted trumpets sound. Then it is a few twigs on various other trees, and the clarinets make themselves known. Then the harp as the light catches the eye of an impala, hitherto unnoticed. Finally as the whole landscape lights up, the entire orchestra comes to life. Now when I hear a great Mahler movement building up in a concert hall as the conductor beckons each group of instruments into action, I can visualise the dawn gently breaking over the Kruger bush.

On one occasion, when we were staying at the Augrabies National Park, I went out before dawn to test some lines from Arthur Hugh Clough's wonderful poem 'Say not the struggle Naught Availeth'. He wrote in the fourth stanza:

> And not by eastern windows only
> When daylight comes, comes in the light
> In front, the sun climbs slow, how slowly
> But westward look, the land is bright!

256

I had to see for myself whether this was true. The Augrabies camp was on an outcrop from which I could see 360 degrees of horizon with nothing to block my view. So I stood on a rock to see whether the western sky did indeed light up before the eastern. Determined not to miss anything, I went out in the dark about an hour before dawn. But it was very cold, and by the time I had discovered that the poem was right I was almost frozen solid.

Thanks to speaking invitations at conferences there, I have visited some of the upmarket game reserves that adjoin Kruger. Apart from being much cheaper, I think Kruger is nicer. This is because you have the sense that it belongs to the animals, not to the visitors. Once at Mala Mala we crashed through the bush at night in a Land Rover with the searchlight chasing after two leopards who were trying to mate. I thought this a gross invasion of their privacy.

CHAPTER 13

Race and redress

I had celebrated the success of the silent revolution against apartheid. I was delighted also when Peter Randall, a former assistant director of the Institute, wrote that school integration was progressing much better than had been expected.[1] Others had also reported to us the success of model C schools as 'melting pots of racial integration'.[2] I had visited my old headmaster Deane Yates when he was running the Maru a Pula school in Gaborone, Botswana. There too racial integration had been so successful that he'd founded the New Era Schools Trust to promote it in South Africa. There was every reason to suppose that race would simply disappear in the 'new' South Africa once described by Desmond Tutu as the 'rainbow nation'. Had the white supremacists not subordinated themselves to majority rule?

Themba Sono, who was our president between 1996 and 2003, wrote that if a small minority of whites hankered after white supremacy, this was nothing that we should spend sleepless nights about. Even though whites might harbour feelings that the 'bantus' were not yet ready to govern, the proper response was not a fusillade of denunciations but simply to continue governing well.[3] Colin 'Jiggs' Smuts, who had once run the Institute's youth programme, wrote that white racists were a 'pathetic spent force, pain in the neck though they are'.[4] We ran these articles in *Frontiers of Freedom*, a quarterly journal we launched the year after the 1994 election; edited by Jill Wentzel, it took its title from Nelson Mandela's statement that the purpose of his government 'shall be the continuous expansion of the frontiers of human fulfilment and of the frontiers of freedom'.[5]

But Colin also wrote an article criticising Mandela for using racial labels: 'I am very fond of Madiba and of hearing him speak except when he addresses people with "you whites", or "you coloureds", or "you Indians". I shout at the TV and say, "Piss off, Madiba. I'm a citizen you know, a South African, an African, just like you, not some other sub-species."' Colin wrote that he always tried to live his life in a non-racial way, but that he 'never felt so coloured in my life as under our new democratic government'. The UDF had been 'relatively non-racial', but former Islanders and exiles in the ANC had missed out on the non-racial nation-building that took place in the 1970s and 1980s 'right under the nose of apartheid'. They either didn't understand this process, or feared it because it was not of their own making. So it had to be destroyed by retaining race classification under the guise of 'transformation'.[6]

Apartheid was so pervasive and so destructive, as I myself had described in countless articles and speeches over so many years, that there was powerful appeal in the argument that only interventions by the state on a similar scale in the name of 'transformation' could reverse its effects. But even before the change of government and constitution in 1994 I questioned this. The real alternative to apartheid, we said, was not another form of social and racial engineering, but a society which prized economic as well as political freedom and which was founded on equality before the law. This ruled out racial discrimination in the form of affirmative action. Given the Institute's history and who we were, the decision to oppose affirmative action and other racial legislation was the most important taken while I was running the organisation. Nothing has altered my conviction that this was the right decision.

That conviction has been strengthened as it has become clear that the racial policies being pursued by the ANC go far beyond the affirmative action contemplated in the Constitution. The National Democratic Revolution described in the previous chapter of this memoir seeks not merely redress for the past, but to impose an entirely new doctrine of demographic proportionality on the country. Cyril Ramaphosa, deputy president of both the country and the ANC, has thus said that 'race will remain an issue until all echelons of our society are demographically representative'. I commented: 'Given the country's human needs and its skills profile, this can only have dire consequences.'[7]

We opposed affirmative action legislation in its entirety, including the two most important statutes, the Employment Equity Act of 1998 and the Broad-Based Black Economic Empowerment Act of 2003. The main objective of the first was to require employers to use 'preferential treatment' for blacks (as well as women and disabled people) to bring about 'equitable representation' at all levels and in all occupations in companies with more than 50 employees or annual turnovers above certain thresholds (R10 million in manufacturing, for example) within successive five-year periods.[8] The two main purposes of the second were to get companies to hand over 26 per cent of their equity to blacks and procure 70 per cent of their goods and services from firms which had done the same.

The first of these was gazetted as a bill in 1997. When we denounced it the labour minister, Tito Mboweni, accused us of orchestrating public confusion.[9] When my colleague Anthea Jeffery spoke against it at a labour law conference in Durban, several delegates called her a racist and walked out.[10] Themba Sono said the bill would give lawyers a 'field day'.[11] Helen Suzman objected that it would deter foreign investment.[12] Some of our corporate members praised our 'solo stance' against the bill and our 'incisive and courageous critique' thereof;[13] Solly Tucker of the Institute of Directors told me our work on it had been 'magnificent'.[14]

Press reaction was mixed. *Finance Week* criticised human resources practitioners for failing to understand how 'malevolent' the bill was,[15] but *Business Day* in an editorial dismissed our criticism of the 'unobtrusive bill' as 'hysterical'.[16] One of the assistant editors of the *Financial Mail* attacked us for 'ignoring its spirit' – although it wasn't long before that paper was writing about its 'hidden horrors'.[17]

Our opposition to the Employment Equity Act meant that from very early on we were fundamentally at odds with the ANC on a key component of its package of policies. We were also at odds with Cosatu and the SACP, as well as with most business chambers, the media, and civil society. We still are.

Right from the start we took the view that racial discrimination, even if now supposedly designed to promote equality rather than maintain white supremacy, was still wrong in principle. It also violated the maxim of equality before the law. But I had also described how the industrial colour bar had broken down during the 'silent revolution' when shortages of white skills forced employers to train and promote blacks despite the apartheid laws designed to prevent this. The way to speed up this process of erosion in the post-apartheid era was to speed up the rate of economic growth. If there were not more blacks in skilled and managerial jobs, this was the result not of a shortage of demand for them but a shortage of supply. This in turn would have to be remedied by repairing the country's education and training system.[18]

A survey had shown that nearly two thirds of companies experienced 'poaching' of black professionals, while salary premiums paid to such professionals were further evidence of both their scarcity and the demand for them. Even before the employment equity legislation was enacted, a firm of human resources consultants had said a third of companies were already paying up to 50 per cent premiums on white salaries to get top black personnel.[19] We said it was absurd to require that Africans should comprise 50 per cent or more of top management when only 3 per cent of Africans had tertiary qualifications and only 25 per cent fell within the 35 to 64 age cohort from which managers were usually drawn.[20]

We also argued that the philosophy underlying the Employment Equity

Act was illogical in assuming that if the proportion of Africans in any occupation was smaller than their proportion in the country's workforce, this was the result of racial discrimination. Although the Department of Labour sometimes tried to defuse our criticism by obfuscating what it meant by 'employment equity', its stated goal was 'full demographic representation across all levels'.[21] And although nobody liked to talk about 'quotas', we said that there was little difference between a quota and a 'numerical goal' designed to correct 'under-representation' within a specified period on pain of a fine of R500 000 for a first offence, rising to R900 000 for a fifth.[22]

The Act came into operation in 1999. Since then it has been criticised more and more for benefiting a black middle class to the detriment of the interests of poorer people, including the unemployed. Despite the criticism, amending legislation with tougher penalties – including fines of up to R2.7 million or 10 per cent of turnover for repeated failure to implement racial targets at management levels – came into operation in 2014.

Though we criticised the legislation right from the start, we actually underestimated the harm affirmative action would do to the public as opposed to the private sector. The latter operated under the constraint that poor appointments risked damaging businesses. No such constraints applied in the public sector, where affirmative action has been applied without regard to costs or consequences. Large numbers of skilled whites, including teachers, have been retrenched, posts left vacant rather than filled with whites, and plenty of people promoted or appointed for reasons of race alone. The police, the defence force, provincial education departments, public hospitals, local authorities, sewerage systems, and Eskom are among dozens upon dozens of public entities that fail to work properly. The ANC has eviscerated large parts of the civil service on which it relies to implement its policies. This has done as much damage to the state and to the ANC's own supporters as to the whites who have lost or been denied jobs.

Our critique of BEE was essentially twofold. In the first place the funding of BEE deals would come at the cost of funding new investment in plant and equipment, and so be detrimental to growth. The second problem involved a paradox. Instead of promoting black entrepreneurship, BEE required white companies to do things for blacks. What was being measured was not black success but white success. This was a strange form of liberation.

As long as this approach continued, BEE would fail to capture the critical component of entrepreneurial success.[23] Twelve years later, the ANC itself bewails the absence of black industrialists – but fails to acknowledge that BEE created the wrong incentives.

One day I had lunch with Stephen Mulholland, one of my former editors on the *FM*. He said that BEE was a very good thing because it gave black people role models. I disputed this, and we couldn't reach agreement, so we decided to let our waiter at the restaurant settle the matter. 'Who is the businessman that you most admire?', we asked him. Quick as a flash came the reply, 'Harry Oppenheimer'.

Our critique of all of the new racial legislation was summed up in a talk I gave to the Johannesburg Rotary Club in November 2009 entitled 'Empowerment which disempowers':

> About 10 years ago the Institute hosted a panel discussion about affirmative action. One of the speakers was Temba Nolutshungu of the Free Market Foundation. He predicted that the main beneficiaries would be whites. Formerly protected white youth who found that the Employment Equity Act limited their job prospects would be forced to turn to the technical trades or become entrepreneurs. Young blacks, on the other hand, would be channelled into 'low-risk soft-option' positions. This would reinforce white dominance and blunt the entrepreneurial spirit among young blacks.
>
> Another factor undermining black entrepreneurship relative to white is that so many blacks have been absorbed into the public service. Whites

displaced to make way for them have been forced to set up their own businesses. Professor Lawrence Schlemmer, a vice president of the Institute, observed in April 2007 that the number of small businesses owned by whites had increased very rapidly because of the exodus from the public service. Anecdotal evidence has it that former white policemen who have become private security agents are happier – and better off – than blacks who displaced them.

BEE is more about white than black achievement. White-owned companies are given ratings for doing things for blacks. BEE empowers white firms to get contracts from the black government. Black individuals benefit, but do they have to perform in a competitive marketplace? What are the government's priorities: making blacks independent or whites compliant?

Brian Molefe, CEO of the Public Investment Corporation, complained in August 2007 that whites were not doing enough to develop black talent. But how much are blacks doing to develop it? Given its record in education, the government is certainly not doing very much. Nor is 'transformation' doing much. This is because the focus is on making white companies harness blacks, rather than on creating new black or non-racial institutions.

I wonder what Steve Biko would have thought. Professor Sipho Seepe, at the time president of the Institute, wrote in September 2007: 'Given Biko's emphasis on self-reliance, it is reasonable to assume that he would have great discomfort with affirmative action and the current form of BEE. These forms of intervention discourage self-reliance and self-actualisation. They perpetuate the victim mentality and discourage an enterprising spirit. They also encourage a debilitating sense of entitlement.'

It is sometimes suggested that BEE requirements are not very different from the policies used by Afrikaners to build up their economic power. But there is a difference: in the 1930s the savings of tens of thousands of individual Afrikaners were mobilised to start financial institutions. Why have the savings of the burgeoning black middle class not been similarly mobilised to create black financial institutions?

Joel Netshitenzhe, until recently a top man in the president's office, said that apartheid had crushed the entrepreneurial spirit among blacks. But the present government's policies are doing little to liberate that spirit. Quite the reverse. Vincent Maphai, chairman of BHP Billiton, commented in July 2009: 'Under apartheid, people were most creative and the community flourished. People did not sit back and think what will the state do for me? They were empowered by apartheid but ironically disempowered by liberation.'

BEE requirements have almost certainly deterred foreign direct investment (FDI), in the mining industry in particular. Lower FDI has meant lower rates of economic growth, so BEE has retarded the generation of jobs. So we can re-configure President Thabo Mbeki's old 'two-nations' divide. Instead of rich-and-white versus poor-and-black, we have a growing divide between whites who have to look after themselves and blacks who are becoming increasingly dependent on the state. This is profoundly disempowering. As Professor Achille Mbembe of Wits wrote in April 2007, 'It risks codifying within the law and in the minds of its beneficiaries the very powerlessness it aims to redress.'

What will all this mean for race relations? In May 2002, Tim Modise wrote, 'One problem with seeing ourselves as permanent victims is that it makes those who believe they are racially superior feel vindicated.' In August 2008 Professor Jonathan Jansen, now rector and vice-chancellor of the University of the Free State and also president of the Institute, said that affirmative action 'perpetuates the myth among white people that black people are inferior'.

That speech was made more than six years ago. Since then criticism of BEE from blacks in particular has intensified. So has the policy, now to be backed by fines and even prison sentences.

Our critique of the ANC's racial policies went beyond their content. It was based on a different idea of what racism actually was. We saw it as a question of actions, laws, and attitudes. Racially discriminatory treatment could be prohibited by law and the courts should hand down heavier sentences if racism was found to be an aggravating factor in crime.[24]

For the ANC, however, racism was also something embedded in institutions and socio-economic conditions. This became clear at a national conference on racism in Sandton in August and September 2000 which was opened by President Thabo Mbeki and attended by numerous cabinet ministers. Afterwards I wrote that the conference had been so busy blaming racism for poverty and unemployment that there was very little discussion of what could be done about them. I had in fact chaired a working group of which Essop Pahad, minister in the Presidency, was also a member. There had been an embarrassed silence when one of the other participants reported that his grandmother had dismissed the conference as a talkshop irrelevant to a person struggling with poverty.[25]

The conference was also something of a paradox. It was attended not only by half the Cabinet but by hundreds of well-dressed members of the emerging black middle class. Afterwards Rian Malan described how he had watched a succession of glamorous and self-confident black yuppies lamenting black helplessness.[26]

About a year after the Sandton conference we published the results of a comprehensive survey of racial attitudes conducted for the Institute by Lawrence Schlemmer, who had become one of our vice presidents after serving out his term as president. He found that for every person who thought race relations were deteriorating, two thought they were improving. The only pessimists on this issue were white Afrikaners, whose pessimism Professor Schlemmer attributed to affirmative action.

However, the most interesting finding of the survey was that 55 per cent of South Africans thought that unemployment was the biggest problem in the country. 'Race issues' were identified as a problem by only 8 per cent. Crime, housing, lack of water and sanitation, education, poor health services, streets and infrastructure, and lack of electricity were all seen as more serious problems than race. The answers were not prompted: respondents were simply asked to specify the 'serious problems not resolved since 1994'. We did not suggest unemployment might be a problem; they brought it up.

These results did not mean, Schlemmer said, that ordinary South Africans were not 'deeply conscious of racism and the latter-day consequences of apartheid'. They were, however, 'also aware of other factors in the complexity of the causes of poverty and disadvantage', so they did not 'oversimplify' these issues. 'Educational differences' were thus seen as the dominant cause of inequality, while education was seen by Africans in particular as the key to progress in a career. Education and unemployment, rather than race, were blamed for the growing inequality in the country.[27]

Professor Schlemmer commented: 'Since 1991 popular concerns about racism have subsided, which is heartening news in a formerly deeply divided society.' However, 'since about 1997, political leadership has tried to put racism back on the popular agenda by labelling more and more of what it does not like as racist – the most recent being criticism of irregularities in the massive arms deal. Happily the results of the survey suggest that the population will not fall for the use of race as a constant scapegoat.' This was true even of government supporters. But he also warned that if political leaders and many analysts worked hard enough to 're-politicise race', they might succeed.[28]

The results of our survey were widely reported, prompting Essop Pahad to dismiss us as 'foolish' when he spoke a few days later at a United Nations 'world conference against racism' in Durban in August and September 2001. 'How the hell can you say jobs are more important than racism? Unemployment is the consequence of racism.'[29]

Pahad's view was echoed by *The Economist*. Citing the finding in our survey that crime, housing, and jobs mattered more to South Africans than race, the paper immediately dismissed it with the words 'but these issues are racial too'.[30] Schlemmer said in his published reply that the Institute knew very well that unemployment and most of South Africa's other problems were substantially due to apartheid. But he warned against promoting the view that various forms of racism were currently still the major cause of inequality in the country. 'South Africa,' he wrote, 'is a brittle society and if race antagonism is rekindled its people will pay a terrible price in loss of investor confidence and economic growth.'[31]

Racism had to be resolutely combated, he said, but he also warned against defining problems so broadly that they became 'too large or too complex to solve'.[32] If virtually all social and economic problems affecting a category of people were equated with 'institutional racism', opportunities for dealing with other causes of these problems and finding solutions to them might be overlooked.

On an earlier occasion, while he was working at the Institute as a visiting fellow, Schlemmer had warned that it was 'vital to protect the perception that people should be responsible for their own progress'. Apartheid had dealt this perception an enormous injury and affirmative action would perpetuate the malaise: 'A person appointed on merit tends to see a new occupation as an opportunity to perform, whereas a person who enjoys an allocated appointment more easily sees the job as a privilege to be enjoyed. In other words, the values which racial entitlement encourages are simply not compatible with the competitive demands of the global economy of today.'[33] These were wise, courageous, and prescient words, and I was proud of the fact that Schlemmer spoke them from an Institute platform. Very few people dared to speak the truth in this way.

Once again, we had adopted a contrarian position. Fifteen years previously, as the silent revolution progressed, I had written that apartheid was on the way out and that the country was teetering on the brink of negotiations. Lots of people refused to believe this. Now all the apartheid laws had been repealed, the negotiations had taken place, the Nats were out and the ANC was in. Our survey showed that most South Africans, though well aware of the legacy of apartheid, no longer saw racism as the country's most serious problem, but wanted issues such as unemployment to be addressed. These ordinary people were way ahead of the political elites in their thinking. They were both more realistic and less intellectually hidebound. Ignoring them, policy-makers risk perpetuating unemployment by blaming it on apartheid rather than on current policies.

Lawrence Schlemmer's death in 2011 deprived the country of one of its finest and bravest social scientists. How have his findings in the 2001 survey stood the test of time? A survey by another agency, Ipsos, in 2014 found that unemployment remained by far the most serious concern of South African voters. Other concerns were crime, poverty, corruption, lack of development, education, health, land, and the brain drain. Race was not even mentioned as an issue to be addressed.[34] As we have seen, however, racial legislation is being more strictly enforced. It seems as if the government chooses its priorities in inverse proportion to what voters think is important.

As Nelson Mandela's life drew to a close towards the end of 2013, several foreign journalists suggested to us that his death might mean the end of racial harmony. As one paper put it, 'Now that the moderating influence of Nelson Mandela is gone, the delicate social harmony of the past 20 years could be torn apart.'[35] I disputed this, and expressed confidence that his death would not undermine racial harmony. I wrote in *Business Day* that the Institute's criticism of racial legislation was less because of any threat to racial harmony than because of the risk to growth. By repudiating nationalisation even before the ANC came to power, Mandela had made the ANC respectable in business circles. 'Like the prodigal son, South Africa was rewarded with inflows of investment and successful reintegration into the global economy from which it had [largely] been barred. Most people thought the country's economic future was as promising as its political future.' This was now at risk. But the risk came not from Julius Malema and his Economic Freedom Fighters (EFF) with their threats of nationalisation. It came rather from ministers dealing with mining, business, local and foreign investment, labour, intellectual and other property rights, and land reform, who were bent on measures that would undermine investment and growth.

Some of these measures were only to be expected given that a number of the ministers concerned were members of the SACP. Others arose from attempts to implement aspects of the National Democratic Revolution. Another factor driving policy – especially the tougher racial laws – was the widespread commitment in South Africa to 'redress'. Critics of 'redress' were accused of attempting to preserve white privilege. But the real damage was to the economy:

> This is because redress involves redistribution of some kind, or interference in the allocation of capital or human resources, or additional uncertainties in the administration of licences, or new threats to various kinds of property rights, or additional discretionary powers for ministers and officials. Among the results is slower growth, which translates into fewer jobs. Redress, in other words, however appealing or justified it might appear to be, comes at a price. The conventional wisdom is that whites are paying it. It is also argued that it is only fair that they should be forced to pay it. But a bigger price is being paid by all those who are denied jobs they would have had if the economy had grown faster.[36]

A few weeks later, as the twentieth anniversary of the ANC's assumption of power approached, I wrote that one of its greatest successes had been getting its racial policies endorsed beyond its own electoral support base. Those who had swung into line behind these racial policies included business, the media, most political commentators, non-governmental organisations, most of the donor community, the official opposition, churches, academia, and most other parliamentary parties. Although these policies were designed to promote the overarching ideology of the National Democratic Revolution, they had been successfully marketed to this wider constituency as little more than necessary 'redress' – something which few people would want to oppose.[37]

Martin Williams, editor of *The Citizen*, captured the dilemma neatly: 'Thanks to apartheid, there is an overwhelmingly strong moral argument for socio-economic transformation policies and programmes, but the accompanying state control and interference are economically ruinous.'[38] They were ruinous in other ways too. We argued that the deaths of three babies from diarrhoea in the town of Bloemhof in the North West province were due in part to crumbling public health care and crumbling municipal infrastructure. These in turn were the result of the implementation of affirmative action and cadre deployment policies throughout the public service, where, to make matters worse, there was no accountability for failure.[39]

'Vintage JKB' was one e-mail response to my article, which reported that contamination of the town's water supply had been caused by sewage spilling into it, leading to several hundred cases of diarrhoea. Nor was Bloemhof an isolated case. The South African Institution of Civil Engineering had reported numerous problems around the country with poor sanitation, 'leading to people dying'. The training system designed to produce artisans was failing to do so. A third of municipalities had no civil engineers, technologists, or technicians on their staff. Hundreds of professionals had been forced out and replaced with managers without the necessary skills. Not only was there a lack of skill throughout the public sector, but posts were often left vacant if the only person available to fill them was white. Managers had even been given incentives to keep whites out for racial reasons. This might hurt the whites in question, but, I said, it also hurts 'countless numbers of people dependent on the public service'. The health minister had admitted to having been 'appalled' at the very poor state of the country's health services. The country's entire system of government, I wrote, was 'poisoned by a toxic mix of affirmative action, cadre deployment, and impunity'.[40]

These were strong words, but justified by what has happened: if you appoint people on grounds of race and political loyalty and then fail to hold them accountable for failure, there is little incentive for them

271

to do their jobs properly. The critical links between performance and pay, performance and promotion, and performance and pride in your work are broken. It is now rare to pick up a newspaper in South Africa without finding several reports about a crisis in some or other branch of government or agency of state at national, provincial, or local level: corruption, theft, incompetence, negligence, neglect, and sheer callousness. Problems fester for years on end. Incompetent or corrupt officials get paid big dollops of hush money to make them quit quietly.

We drew a parallel between the fate of the Bloemhof babies and that of babies whom the previous government had dumped in the homelands in the course of its policies of ethnic cleansing. Just as my provocative *Financial Mail* article and cover had outraged Prime Minister John Vorster in 1973, so in 2014 our articles about the Bloemhof babies led the secretary general of the ANC, Gwede Mantashe, to telephone in to a radio station to attack us – although Cyril Ramaphosa said the press should condemn the government when children died from contaminated water.[41] Condemnation is easy. What we were concerned to do was to trace the problem to its roots. We had wanted to show John Vorster that his ethnic cleansing policies could have tragic consequences for infants. Similarly we wanted to alert the ANC to the tragic consequences of subordinating local government to its affirmative action and cadre deployment policies.

During my time on the *Financial Mail* and later writing for foreign papers, I had described the impact of the then government's grand policy designs on ordinary people, each of them an individual. I was doing the same with the new government's designs. And the more reading I did about the two world wars, the more I realised that the statistics of casualties in their millions somehow concealed the fact that they were all individuals.

Pierre and I had visited First World War cemeteries in Flanders and France, as well as some of the battlefields and museums. Graveyards seemed to be everywhere. You could be driving along a small country

272

lane, and suddenly there would be a signpost and a walled enclosure with a score or two of graves. We happened to arrive at the Thiepval memorial on the ninety-first anniversary of the opening of the Battle of the Somme on 1 July 1916. Overlooking the battlefield, the memorial lists the names of the 'missing of the Somme' – more than 73 000 soldiers 'who have no known graves'. We joined in the requiem mass, as regimental flags were dipped and the Last Post was sounded. Others in the congregation included Ian Paisley, prime minister of Northern Ireland. Having visited one of the Irish memorials in the area, we knew why he was there.

In Ypres, at the Menin gate opening on to the road down which so many men marched to battle only to be drowned in mud or otherwise lost, we stood in silence as two buglers from the local fire brigade sounded the Last Post as part of a ritual at 8 pm every evening. A couple of buses discharged British schoolchildren, who proceeded to lay wreaths below the panels bearing the names of nearly 55 000 missing soldiers. We thought it a very good thing that visits to these memorials were part of the tourism industry. This would help to ensure that the sacrifices they commemorated would not be forgotten. In one little Anglican Church in Ypres there were tablets on the walls listing the names of all the boys from particular British schools who had died in that war. Go into a church or cathedral somewhere else in France, and there would be plaques with the names of South Africans and others who had died there.

We visited Ypres, Passchendaele, and other places with our friend Reina Steenwijk, who lives in Amsterdam and represented overseas members on the Institute's Council for several years. On our return to South Africa, one of our other friends was rather taken aback when we said we'd spent part of our holiday visiting battlefields and cemeteries. Her remark dismayed me, and I didn't quite know what to say. But it seems to me that visiting these places should be part of one's education. In many war cemeteries the graves carry the name, regiment, rank, and dates of the person buried there, but also a brief message from his wife, fiancée, parents, brother, or sisters. Some of those lying there or whose names are listed at Thiepval and other memorials are South Africans, who fought and died under a flag which so many of their countrymen now spurn.

Yet, perhaps it is inevitable that some should spurn it. One day in 2011 I got a phone call from the Belgian ambassador in Pretoria. He wanted to know whether his government could rely upon South Africa to participate in ceremonies in Flanders commemorating the First World War. Given that black South Africans who joined up were treated as second-class soldiers, he thought the ANC government might want to distance itself from the commemorations, due to take place on the centenary of the war between 2014 and 2018. After making a few phone calls to various people, I was able to pass on a message that South Africa would participate. Among other things, there were plans to send a naval detachment to float wreaths upon that part of the English Channel where the *SS Mendi* sank in 1917 after being accidentally rammed by another ship.

Altogether 616 black members of the South African Native Labour Corps perished in this tragedy. Although they wore uniforms they were not allowed to bear arms but were confined to menial work, including digging trenches, laying railway track, and carrying stretchers. In a typical piece of South African contradictory nonsense, the (all-white) Parliament rose to pay tribute to the victims of the *Mendi* disaster when the news reached Cape Town, but black servicemen were denied war medals. Many years later the Institute took it upon itself to start a campaign for black ex-servicemen to receive the same war pensions as whites. Eventually, this was successful. But it was sad that it had to be launched in the first place. Thank God that there were a handful of whites willing to take up such causes. Never mind the politics, decency and common humanity required no less.

Pierre and I also visited some of the Commonwealth war cemeteries and military museums in Normandy. We clambered down from the American cemetery onto Omaha Beach, on which so many soldiers perished during the Allied D-Day landings on 6 June 1944. We also visited the Commonwealth war cemetery at Monte Cassino, as well as the German and Polish cemeteries nearby. On that same day, a Sunday, we drove up the mountain to the famous abbey which had been reduced to rubble by Allied bombing in 1944. We arrived just in time for a performance of Verdi's requiem to mark the reconsecration of the abbey church. On another occasion we visited the military museum and Commonwealth war cemetery at Alamein, with its rather sad little memorial on the perimeter to the South African soldiers who had 'outspanned' there.

With Rudolf and Sheila Gruber we visited Nuremberg, Dachau, and the Obersalzberg, Hitler's retreat above the village of Berchtesgaden in Bavaria. I had once been waiting for a train in Germany somewhere and had an eerie feeling when I saw 'Berchtesgaden' on its front as the destination, although I got off at another stop. Now we drove through this village to where Hitler had built his Berghof house with its huge picture window in the Obersalzberg, once described as the 'holy mountain' of national socialism, on the Austrian border.⁴² Close by were the houses of other top Nazis, among them Hermann Goering, Martin Bormann, Rudolf Hess, and Albert Speer. Here Hitler took his dogs for walks, here Eva Braun presided as lady of the house, and here Neville Chamberlain had the first of his three meetings with Hitler in September 1938. Hitler spent much of the war here – although it was at Wolf's Lair, his military headquarters in East Prussia when he was fighting the Russians, that he narrowly escaped assassination in the bomb plot in July 1944.

From the Berghof you take a winding road and then a leather padded lift up to the Kehlsteinhaus ('Eagle's Nest'), built for Hitler on what seems to be the roof of the world, although he seldom went there because he was afraid of heights. As Rudolf could not see, I helped him to the lavatory, where he carefully traced his fingers over the dull brass lettering on the door, HERREN. He said this was exactly the style of lettering they would have had when the building was put up. It was a strange sensation to think that these self-same lavatories must have been used by some of the top Nazis. Stranger still to recall that so much evil had been planned in so beautiful a natural setting. The Berghof was damaged by Allied bombing in April 1945, but Eagle's Nest survived. Today it is a restaurant and beer garden, and from the site you look down on hang gliders drifting across the Austrian Alps.

CHAPTER 14

Liberalism for all seasons

While running the Institute in the post-apartheid era I was variously accused of being right-wing, neo-liberal, neo-conservative, or whatever. I was also described as one of the 'old lefties' who'd become 'new righties', people who read Paul Johnson, Thomas Sowell, PJ O'Rourke, *Commentary* and *The Spectator* (guilty on all counts).[1] We ran one or two articles in *Frontiers* pointing out that the 'right-wing slur' was designed to cow people into silence, but it never worked with us. A columnist on the *Cape Times* wrote that the Institute's 'increasingly outspoken brand of liberalism under the leadership of John Kane-Berman has put it very much at odds with the ANC and its academic supporters'.[2] This was true, and it didn't bother me either. We knew that criticism from liberals would be especially resented because they had always been part of the broad anti-apartheid family, which would give our opinions more weight. But we shouldn't feel too much self-pity if we got more than our fair share of criticism, because we handed out plenty ourselves. We noted with amusement that some of the previous government's supporters had eagerly thrown in their lot with the new one; *Beeld,* for example, had become the most politically correct newspaper in the country.[3] Many people who had dismissed liberals as left wing now said they were the New Right.

On one occasion, Aggrey Klaaste, a prominent journalist, said I was a 'right-wing racist'. Our honorary legal adviser, Raymond Tucker, said he would love to sue Klaaste on my behalf, but I couldn't be bothered. Although there was a widely held politically correct view that it was impossible for blacks to be racists we had no hesitation in hitting back when necessary. After Barney Mthombothi, editor of the *Financial Mail*, launched a personal attack on my colleague Anthea Jeffery for some of her writing on political violence, I replied that his article was a 'racist and repugnant character assassination'.[4]

A magazine called *De Kat* said that I was a 'pedigree' liberal if ever there was one, but that I and my 'salon of preppie researchers' had shifted the Institute to the Right and were writing the New Right's 'position papers'.[5] This was quite flattering: most of us were too old to qualify as 'preppies'; the said 'salon' usually had only one 'preppie' in it.

I had in fact unleashed one of the 'preppies' on Ken Owen, at the time editor of the *Sunday Times,* after he described us as the intellectual mainspring of the New Right. We were happy to regard this as a compliment. Owen, however, had attacked an article by Paul Pereira in which Paul had said one of the components of liberalism was an economic system that provided ample scope for economic freedom and private enterprise. This, said Owen, was 'grotesque'. But Paul replied that the new generation of liberals was sceptical of the state's ability to bring about lasting upliftment through welfare, protectionism, and the like. The *Sunday Times*, Paul wrote, had described the Labour Relations Act of 1995 as 'enlightened legislation' even though it protected big business and trade unions at the expense of less powerful people.[6] This 'enlightened' piece of legislation has helped to keep millions out of work. We have been its foremost and most consistent critic – just as we were the only liberal critic of the racial legislation described in the previous chapter. Along with the Free Market Foundation, we were also the most consistent critic of interventionist legislation.

On this we parted company with many people who regard themselves as liberal, especially in their support of affirmative action laws. We therefore sometimes described ourselves as 'classical liberals' or even as 'libertarians'. This was to distinguish ourselves from those espousing the far more interventionist brand of 'liberalism' imported from the US, where 'liberal' is often a synonym for 'social democrat' or even 'socialist'. Left and Right both wanted state power to achieve their objectives. Classical liberals, we said, were in the middle: they cherished individual liberty over state power. They were as far from the Left as they were from the Right.

Long before 1994, in fact, it was clear to me that once apartheid legislation had been repealed, there would be less difference between the ANC and the NP than between either of them and liberalism. The main thing they had in common was their belief in an interventionist state. We, on the other hand, believed that the powers of the state should be limited, irrespective of whether the Left or the Right was in power. Although President Mandela had promised to expand the 'frontiers of freedom', we noted that governments 'were generally in the business of expanding the frontiers of government'.[7] So we were not surprised when Steve Tshwete, minister of sport and recreation, said 'there is going to be interference by government in every sphere of life in South Africa'. I greeted this with an article headed 'Government on the march'.[8] And Alfred Nkungu and I opened a file on the topic. It's been getting steadily thicker, almost by the day.

One of the biggest challenges liberals face is to counter the belief that defending economic freedom, private enterprise, and private property is to defend only big business or the rich. One day many years ago one of our staff, Lindsey Morton, was walking along the pavement in Braamfontein near our offices when she witnessed a raid on pavement hawkers. Outraged, she tried to prevent the confiscation of their goods, only to be bundled into a police van and carted off to the Hillbrow police station. With the help of Raymond Tucker, I managed to get her speedily released. Seizing goods from hawkers is not unusual in South Africa. In fact these people, many of them very poor, face a threefold threat: when striking workers go on the rampage in city centres, they invariably lay waste to hawkers' stalls; hawkers who are foreign nationals are frequently the targets of violent, and even lethal, attack; and the police are able to confiscate their goods lawlessly and with impunity.

Many years later the 'Arab Spring' in 2011 was sparked off in Tunisia by a similar incident when Mohamed Bouazizi set himself alight in December 2010 in a desperate act of protest after officials seized the fruit and vegetables he was selling from his barrow. The Institute's defence of property rights recognised that 'the protection of property from illegal seizure is something that benefits everyone from the mightiest to the humblest'.[9] But we also challenged the assumption that you can hammer business without harming people whose livelihoods depend on a thriving private sector. The main victims of the ANC's increasingly hostile policies towards business are not captains of industry, but all the people who have failed to find jobs. Since the ANC came to power the number of jobless people has more than doubled from 3.7 million to 8.9 million.[10] Unemployment, at 36 per cent, has risen to its highest level yet.

The unemployment numbers may be huge, but they are merely statistics. Each jobless person, however, is an individual. So too are all the members of their families. These millions of people personally experience unemployment daily at first hand. High unemployment, especially high unemployment among young people, has long been routinely described as a 'ticking time bomb'. Time bomb or not, it is morally unacceptable. A study produced for the government in 2008 said that if South Africa had an unemployment rate equivalent to those of other countries at our stage of economic development, we would have another six million people in jobs: 'They would be predominantly African, women, young, and with no post-matric education.'[11] Think of all the lost production arising from the fact that these millions are not working. But think also of the denial of opportunity, the lost human endeavour, and the waste of human potential.

One of the reasons I was an enthusiastic supporter of the government's

Growth, Employment, and Redistribution programme announced in 1996 was that it attached so much importance to growth as the means of combating unemployment. I praised the ANC for adopting Gear despite the opposition of Cosatu and the SACP. The government had come to power promising to create 2.5 million jobs over the next 10 years through a public works programme. But now it had recognised that its role was not to do the job-creating itself but to create an environment in which the private sector could make profitable investments of which jobs would be the spin off. The deputy minister of finance, Gill Marcus, had been correct to state that the greatest redistribution took place when people were earning their own wages.[12]

We were the ANC's strongest critics on most issues, but on Gear we were its strongest supporters. It needed to be 'fearlessly implemented to cope with the human tragedy of rising unemployment'.[13] The ANC's adoption of Gear had been a 'seminal achievement'. One reason why the NP had run up such huge budget deficits was that it thought it could spend its way out of political trouble. 'The ANC, showing political courage and a sound grasp of the issues at stake for public finance, resisted this temptation.' But Mbeki's liberal economic policies had been 'contradicted by dirigiste labour and racial policies'.[14]

Gear was also undermined by incessant attack from the Left. This scared business into silence or equivocation. And the government itself undermined Gear by ever-increasing restriction on the labour market and on small business. Nearly 10 years later, Jabu Moleketi, one of Ms Marcus's successors as deputy minister of finance under President Thabo Mbeki, wrote a paper emphasising the need for labour market liberalisation. 'All strength to Mbeki as he tackles labour laws,' I wrote in *Business Day*.[15] But Moleketi's proposals ran into so much opposition from within the ruling alliance that they were dropped. And in December 2007 Cosatu, the SACP, and others on the Left joined forces to replace Mbeki with Jacob Zuma as party leader, so enabling him to become president of the country in 2009.

Throughout my time as CEO I seldom let slip an opportunity to argue the case for labour market liberalisation, whether in print or in speeches. The Institute was easily the leader in this battle of ideas. Not that there was much competition: South Africa's interventionist labour laws were backed by a consensus that included the media, academia, most of civil society, labour lawyers, and organised business. With the support of a grant from USAID, I visited the US, the UK, and New Zealand to find out if there was anything we could learn from their labour policy. There was plenty, and I wrote it all up or spoke about it to various gatherings.[16]

But our starting point was the property rights of the poor. In 1776, the same year in which the Americans proclaimed the God-given and 'unalienable' rights of man, Adam Smith wrote the following in *The Wealth of Nations:*

> The property which every man has is his own labour. As it is the original foundation of all other property, so it is the most sacred and inviolable. The patrimony of a poor man lies in the strength and dexterity of his hands; and to hinder him from employing this ... in what manner he thinks proper without injury to his neighbour, is a plain violation of this most sacred property. It is a manifest encroachment upon the just liberty both of the workman, and of those who might be disposed to employ him.[17]

What flows from this moving passage is that without capital or education, the poor have nothing to exploit but their own willingness to work. Yet South Africa's industrial relations system denies them this opportunity. We condemn slavery because we don't think any man should be able to confiscate another man's labour. But then we pass laws restricting his right to sell their labour. Either way, he earns no money. He is consigned to permanent poverty. Our labour market has been configured to protect organised labour and big business to the detriment of small business and the unemployed.

Our Constitution contains just about every right anyone could wish for, but it omits one of the most fundamental: the right to embark upon employment free of restrictions laid down by trade unions, employer organisations, or labour ministers. So we need to add such a right to our Bill of Rights. A second new right would guarantee the right to earn money. This is so taken for granted that we do not stop to think that our labour laws make it impossible for millions of people by erecting barriers to market entry. Few human rights activists complain about these barriers, but they are one of the worst human rights violations committed by governments in South Africa and elsewhere. We tax the unemployed on the little they can afford to buy. We urge them to vote and so help to choose governments. But we don't allow them to choose to work for a wage unless we think it's 'decent'.

My proposed two constitutional amendments are designed to make it unlawful for ministers to impose minimum or 'decent' wages or other restrictions that price unemployed people out of jobs. The amendments would also bring about a fairer balance between the collective rights of unions and employer organisations guaranteed in the Constitution and those of individuals wishing to operate outside this framework of collective rights.

In many rich countries, social security systems look after the unemployed. But in South Africa unemployment insurance covers only those who lose their jobs, and then only for a limited time. A third of unemployed people have never worked, so they are not eligible for unemployment insurance payouts anyway. And two thirds of the unemployed have been unemployed for more than a year, so they are unlikely ever to get jobs. Some will be supported by family members, pensioners included. Some will depend on social grants paid to their own children. Millions will be dependent on subsistence agriculture to feed themselves and their families. Some may turn to stock theft and other types of crime.

Rather than allow this state of affairs to continue, we must enable the poor to find work, and so take the first step out of poverty through their own efforts. For most individuals, holding down their first paying job is the foundation of upward mobility. They will learn skills on the job, and become contributors to national output. Nothing else will help as much in reducing crime, restoring dignity, promoting self-esteem, and fostering family life. Having one's own money is one of the most liberating things of all. It helps to free young people from dependency on their parents. It frees women from dependency on their husbands. You can go out and buy shoes or clothes without having to ask a family member for the money.

Unlike the more interventionist brand of liberalism, classical liberalism sees no walls between economics and politics. Freedom of contract, freedom to trade, and freedom to engage in economic activity are logical extensions of individual liberty, as are property rights. If I may speak freely and worship freely, why may I not trade freely or work freely? If there can be a free market in ideas, why not in goods and services, including labour? The individual, indeed, should be free to do as he pleases subject to the constraint that in exercising his rights and enjoying his freedoms he does not undermine the ability of others to do the same. These rights and freedoms are in the nature of man as a sentient being with free will and the ability to imagine, reason, and create. These in turn are God-given faculties which man is not entitled to take away. The role of the state is to protect my rights and freedoms from invasion by others just as I must be prevented from invading theirs.

This has numerous implications. One is that the freedom of the individual is the natural state of affairs, all derogations requiring justification. The second is that an individual *is* an individual, entitled to be treated as such rather than as a member of any particular group or class. His personal rights, liberties, dignity, and freedoms are fundamental. So is the principle of equality before the law. Legislation that discriminates against an individual on grounds of race violates both the principle of equality before the law and his dignity. As we learnt during apartheid days, laws designed to give privileges to chosen groups always have as their victims individual human beings.

Apart from being illiberal, post-apartheid racial laws are unnecessary: if you want to help the disadvantaged, there are better ways of doing so that also have the attraction of being colour-blind. Obviously, many people may not actually be blind to colour or race. The point, however, is that the law should be.

Classical liberalism also holds that the individual is a better judge of his own interests than a state which might claim to be promoting the common good but which in practice is more likely to be promoting particular interests. There is accordingly a conflict between the state as an agent for social engineering and the liberal concept of the state. The interventionist state, confident of its own wisdom, will intervene in the economy whenever it feels intervention is desirable or politically expedient. The liberal state, sceptical about its own wisdom, will be cautious about using its power and will regulate and intervene only where absolutely necessary. The liberal state is also frugal. Recognising the right of the individual to enjoy the fruits of his labours, it will take away in taxes only as much as it needs to perform its limited core functions of protecting life, liberty, and property.

Freedom to become an entrepreneur by starting a business is a logical extension of individual freedom. Just as we need to liberalise the labour market, we need to create a much friendlier climate for entrepreneurship. Profit-seeking, risk-taking entrepreneurship is the key to growth and therefore to the generation of jobs. We must encourage it in all sectors, from the low-wage labour intensive to the high-wage capital intensive. Instead of empowering ministers to pick 'winners', we must encourage businesses of all shapes and sizes all over the country, from micro-businesses run by individuals and families to multi-million-rand corporations run by professional managers. We must make it easier for established businesses to expand, but we must also encourage start-ups. We must encourage innovation, creativity, and human ingenuity. We must allow the informal sector and self-employment to flourish.

An important spin-off of giving priority to promoting employment and entrepreneurship is that the state's endeavours can be colour-blind: most of the unemployed, the poor, the illiterate, and the sick are black. In terms of numbers, black former victims of apartheid will accordingly be the main beneficiaries of employment-creating policies, even though the same policies will apply to everyone irrespective of race. As employment rises, so will tax revenues, while the dependency burden on the state will be reduced. This will free resources for the truly needy: our hundreds of thousands of orphaned children, the elderly poor, and those too sick or disabled to work.

I first used some of these arguments back in 2002 in a booklet written for the Friedrich Naumann Foundation for Liberty, the German political foundation which is the Institute's closest soul-mate.[18] Most recently I used them in the Zach de Beer Memorial Lecture I delivered in March 2016 in honour of one of the former leaders of the Progressive Federal Party; Dr De Beer had also been one of the liberal MPs who broke away from the United Party with Helen Suzman in 1959. The lecture received many accolades, and I was invited to repeat it to the Free Market Foundation a month later.[19]

Although these audiences loved what I said as much as I enjoyed saying it, it's not always easy to argue the case for classical liberalism. Socialists and other interventionists have long since captured the moral high ground with their arguments that the way to deal with poverty is for a 'caring' state to act against it rather than leave people to the mercies of an 'impersonal' market or a hand that one cannot even see. But the 'caring' state comes at the price of rising government debt in many rich countries that are saddling subsequent generations with the burden of paying it off. The huge liabilities of the American and European social security systems are a warning to South Africa to pull back before it becomes politically impossible to do so.

Fifteen years ago there were 312 people employed in South Africa for every 100 on social grants. Now, because we have extended social security faster than we have generated jobs, there are only 86 people employed for every 100 on social grants. The solution is not to stop the grants, but to get more people into work. Apart from removing barriers to market entry, this necessitates revitalising a culture in which everyone able to work feels both moral obligation and peer pressure to do so.

Just as it is easy to argue for a 'caring' state, so it is also easy to urge the adoption of a minimum wage. Those who oppose minimum wage laws are accused of having a 'devil-take-the-hindmost' attitude to people struggling on low wages. But actually it is those making this accusation who have adopted precisely that attitude towards all the people who would be priced out of jobs. Markets can of course be harsh. But the best hope for South Africa's jobless is to enable them to enter those markets so that they can do something about their poverty rather than to shut them out of markets and then blame their plight on 'market failure'.

Given our high unemployment, and the low education levels of most of the jobless, their earnings in a deregulated labour market are likely to be low. This of course conjures up the spectre of 'sweatshops'. I was indeed once accused of advocating them. But a sweatshop is the bottom rung of the ladder of upward mobility. And low-wage jobs in cities and towns allow poor people to escape rural drudgery. Better to spin or weave cotton in the shade than pick it in the blazing sun, half the time bent double. The government wants to create 300 000 black peasant farmers, but poor people continue to leave the rural areas for cities and small towns. Many have clearly decided that life even in a shack settlement is better than rural hardship where they have to walk maybe half a mile to the nearest dam or spring with a plastic container on their head to collect water. The present devastating drought will accelerate the urbanising trend. This makes it more urgent than ever to liberalise our labour market so that employers in our cities can satisfy the demand for jobs by entering into private voluntary contracts with workers, free of external interference.

There is much hostility both in South Africa and elsewhere to economic freedom, especially among academics and other intellectuals. But evidence from around the world shows a powerful link between economic freedom and economic growth on the one hand and wealth and high living standards on the other. According to data compiled by Neil Emerick for the Free Market Foundation and the Institute,[20] between 1990 and 2010 the 'least free' countries experienced growth in GDP per head at an annual average rate of 1.6 per cent. The 'most free' clocked up 3.6 per cent – more than double. As a result of these different growth performances the least free countries recorded GDP per head in 2010 of $5 200, while the most free recorded almost $38 000 – more than seven times as much. Moreover, the average per capita income of the poorest 10 per cent of the population in the least free countries was $1 200, whereas in the most free it was nearly $12 000 – almost 10 times as much. Poor people are better off in rich than in poor countries. So poor countries must make themselves rich. It's as simple as that. Economic growth is sometimes denigrated, but it is the process by which poor countries and the people in them become richer.

Whenever the opportunity arose, whether in speeches or newspaper articles or research reports, I argued that economic policy in South Africa should aim first and foremost at pushing up the country's growth rate. Not only was this the only way to deal with poverty, it was also more important than tackling inequality, even though that was 'the current intellectual fad'.[21]

The form of inequality with the most damaging long-term impact is that in our schooling system. In 2015 the matric maths pass rate for Africans was 26 per cent and for whites 85 per cent. More and more black parents are voting with their children's feet against dysfunctional township schools and sending their children to former model C schools or independent schools. This is a movement that should be strengthened. One way of enabling more parents to choose independent schools over failing state schools is for the state to provide them with vouchers to pay the fees. The state would keep paying for school education, but it would gradually stop running the schools itself as private providers take over. Vouchers would be a means of empowering poorer families to exercise the choice about their children's schooling which is now available only to the middle class.[22]

Vouchers could also be explored as a means of enabling more people to buy private health care. The proportion of the population covered by medical aid schemes has been stuck at around 16 per cent for nearly 20 years. Vouchers provided by the state would enable everyone to buy private health care. They would do so via an expanded medical aid system offering more low-cost options than is currently permissible. This would promote entrepreneurship and give poor people more choice.

Where does this leave the state? It must enforce contracts, prevent cartels from manipulating markets, combat inflation, enact rules to ensure road safety and occupational health, and combat crime – in short, do all the things associated with the notion of the 'nightwatchman' state. But it must also divest itself of airlines and all the other enterprises and functions the private sector can take over.[23] The fewer regulatory and licensing powers the state possesses, the fewer will be the opportunities for 'state capture' and other forms of malfeasance. The more that can be left to the market, the better. Markets can quickly correct themselves. Government bureaucracies cannot. They are run by people as fallible as the rest of us. The only difference is that these fallible, ordinary, people have extraordinary power. And some of them clearly enjoy using it, sometimes regardless of the consequences.

Some of these ideas were first put forward in a 'twelve-point plan for prosperity' we published in February 2014, a fortnight before I retired as chief executive of the Institute.[24] Some of them I later developed in greater detail. I argued not only for economic liberalisation, but also for a fundamentally different system of government, one in which power was dispersed instead of centralised. Why, for example, should local communities not be empowered to elect their own police chief, set his performance indicators, and then dismiss him if he fails to bring down the crime rate? To make Parliament more accountable to voters and less to party headquarters, the National Council of Provinces could be replaced by a chamber elected on a constituency basis. In short, we needed not merely different policies, but a whole new paradigm.

I used this anecdote to illustrate my point:

> There was a delightful news report in *The Star* a few weeks ago about three armed robbers who stormed a church in Berea in Johannesburg. Two pointed their firearms at the congregation and ordered it to sit, while the third went round collecting cellphones and money. A woman worshipper suddenly stood up and shouted 'This can't happen in the house of God!' Others joined her in earnest prayer. This confused the robbers. One fled. The worshippers then grabbed the second man's gun, pushed him over and laid into him. The third man, busy collecting the money and cellphones, was unarmed but they hit him too. Said one of the congregation, 'I've never seen women angry like that. We beat them up and threw chairs at them. We had to do what we had to do.' When the police arrived they found two injured and bleeding thugs on the floor, and arrested them. 'Church robbers given an unholy thrashing,' said the headline on the article. To this one can only add, 'Hallelujah!'
>
> Few crime stories have happy endings. The relevance of this one is that the women in that church did things in a fundamentally different way. So, too, fixing the future in this country means that we must do things in a fundamentally different way, according to fundamentally different ideas.[25]

Many people applauded me for putting forward ideas so different from those currently being pursued by the government. 'Great stuff! We need fresh thinking, so desperately!' said an e-mail from a professor at the University of the Free State. Others dismissed them: 'The establishment is dead set against each and every point of this pie-in-the-sky plan as far-fetched.' Maybe, I retorted. 'However, it is not unusual for governments to adopt plans and ideas they once dismissed.' In South Africa the National Party did this. In the United Kingdom, the British Labour Party under Tony Blair abandoned its historical commitment to social-ism and all but embraced Thatcherism. Under Mikhail Gorbachev the Communist Party of the Soviet Union embarked on *glasnost* and *pere-stroika* policies designed to reform Communism but which destroyed it. Under Deng Xiaoping's policy of 'communism with Chinese character-istics', that country also started to liberalise economically.[26]

To win the policy battle it is necessary to fight in the realm of ideas as well. Victor Hugo said that an idea whose time had come was more powerful than all the armies in the world. When Harold Macmillan was asked what dominated politics, his answer was 'events, dear boy, events'. Though apparently contradictory, both are right. When crises occur and governments have run out of ideas as to how to deal with them, the smart ones seek different ideas. So we have to do our home-work with ideas. One of the biggest battles ahead is to push liberal ideas into the economic sphere. This means showing how liberal economic policies work better for the jobless and for the poor.

In promoting alternative ideas, the same principles apply to both Right and Left. The free-market ideas of Milton Friedman and of Friedrich Hayek, which became so influential after the stagflation of the 1970s, had long since been promoted by various think-tanks in the UK and the US. The strategy also worked for socialism. The British Fabian Society, founded in 1884, waged a battle of ideas to pave the way for the rise to power of the Labour Party 40 years later.

The Institute has always been in this business. One of the reasons the post-apartheid Constitution contains so many liberal ideas is that organ-isations such as the Institute, individuals such as Helen Suzman, liberal opposition parties, and newspapers such as the *Rand Daily Mail* and the *Financial Mail* spent so much time fighting for them, sometimes against odds that seemed pretty hopeless. The outcome would have been very different if we'd abandoned that battle to the Marxists.

Both the ANC and the SACP have several times expressed the fear that they might be losing the 'battle of ideas' against 'neo-liberalism'. We must make sure that they do lose it. Among other things, this necessitates dogged propagation of the liberal alternatives. Drawing on various talks I gave to Institute members and others from 2011 onwards,[27] the final chapter of this book sets out a strategy for a liberal victory in the battle of ideas.

But before I venture into the future I want to take a look back. Ever since my school days I had spoken my mind, but when I took over the Institute in 1983 I was responsible no longer just for myself but also for the organisation and its survival. The well-being of its staff and their families was also in my hands. 'Telling the truth without fear or favour', as the Institute had always believed, was noble but also risky, especially after the ANC came to power and some of the companies on whose membership subscriptions we relied were anxious to keep on the right side of it.

Yet if we dug out the facts, as the Institute had been doing since before I was born, there was really no choice but to point out the truths that arose from them. Robert Birley had spelt out the consequences when people did not speak out. And my father had always said that silence was not an option.

So the die was pretty much cast when I took the job. Even though it's not always clear what the truth actually is, speaking one's mind is not only liberating but much easier than trying to figure out what is the most expedient thing to say to a particular audience. Few audiences – whether listening to you or reading what you say – are all of like mind anyway. I once gave a talk to the South Africa German Chamber of Commerce and Industry which elicited comment such as 'how admirable it is the way you always speak out' but also a long lecture during question time from the German ambassador which could have been written in Luthuli House.

I got plenty of other feedback – once or twice literally when people turned their backs on me. One judge was irritated to find me at a New

Year's Eve party at another judge's house. One of my board members told me there had been a 'horrified' reaction to his suggestion that I give lectures at a business school.[28] One bank gave the Institute a donation on condition it was kept anonymous because of the 'reputational risk' if they were known to have sent a cheque to an 'untouchable' organisation that was 'too conservative and too outspoken'.[29] When a big law firm was asked to help us act as *amicus curiae* in a case before the Constitutional Court we were told by one of their partners that they could have nothing to do with a 'counter-revolutionary' organisation.[30] It was both amazing and amusing to hear this standard communist smear being echoed to us from the very heart of corporate Sandton.

Since we were often asked to compile political forecasts, one of the most gratifying comments was that we had got things right. A member in New York who was forever telling us not to be harsh on the ANC wrote that we had been 'correct on most calls in the past decade'.[31] The staff of a big embassy in Pretoria brought one of my *Business Day* columns to a meeting with our marketing team and said that more than anyone else I had been accurate about what was going to happen in South Africa.[32] The man in charge of corporate social investment in a big insurance company said I had been vindicated in almost everything where I had given an opinion.[33] Once again, telling the truth is best: you are more likely to get your forecasts correct if you look at the facts and say what you think rather than what you think your audience might wish to hear.

When my retirement was announced, Solidarity, the trade union which grew out of the old Mine Workers' Union headed by Arrie Paulus, asked me to visit them so that they could 'convey their sincere appreciation for [my] huge inputs'.[34] At the meeting Flip Buys, founder and CEO of Solidarity, thanked me for my 'lifetime of integrity'. I was touched by this. We had come from opposite sides of the political spectrum, but now we often found ourselves taking the same stance against the ANC's affirmative action policies. Flip was one of the first people to recognise that there was a racial wolf lurking inside the ANC's non-racial clothing.

Andrew Kenny, one of our Council members, said in his column in *The Citizen* that I was a 'hero' who had spoken truth to the power of apartheid as well as to the ANC. Also, however, I had been 'scrupulously accurate and fair towards the ANC government, acknowledging its successes and condemning its failures'.[35] David Gleason wrote in his column in *Business Day* that I had turned the Institute into a 'remarkable think-tank brimming with ideas', and that my 'fearlessness' excused my 'grumpiness'.[36] A senior official of the South African Reserve Bank praised my 'visionary leadership'.[37] And Rudolf Gruber wrote that the Institute would have folded by 1984/1985: 'Then you came.'[38]

The chairman of a large investment company wrote to me that our achievements far outweighed 'those of us in the business world who are merely measured in terms of financial statements'.[39] One banking economist told other economists that the Institute 'gets away with saying exactly what they think when no one else dares'. He wished he could also speak so freely, 'but the bank would not allow it'.[40] Others wrote in to commend us for 'our ability to see through politically correct claptrap',[41] to say 'thank you for telling the truth',[42] and to express 'joy that at last someone with credibility is speaking out'.[43] I was frequently complimented for 'raising issues that no one else does'. I was 'legendary', said the chairman of a big investment house, for 'saying things as they are'.[44]

We were complimented so often for thus speaking our minds that I realised there must be a great many people who thought as we did but could not say what they thought. A *Business Day* column under the headline 'ANC setting SA on path towards failed statehood'[45] under Jacob Zuma elicited an excited phone call from a judge to thank me for being bold enough to write it and to tell me a number of other judges thought the same.[46] It also caused Xolela Mangcu, a journalist and academic, to write an article in another paper saying he rarely agreed with me, but that on this occasion 'I'd written the column of my life'.[47]

JKB with Cyril Ramaphosa and Jeff Nemeth, president of the American Chamber of Commerce in South Africa.

Photo courtesy Amcham.

Our marketing staff sometimes reported to me that we were seen as 'anti-transformation' and 'anti-ANC'. One of our board members told me that a former ambassador from one of South Africa's major economic partners had told him after seeing various cabinet ministers that they were 'incensed' by my *Business Day* column – so much so that the ambassador thought the government's intolerance of criticism was a great threat to democracy. 'Jeepers!' I replied to the board member, but 'at least they read my column.'[48]

Some years before this the chairman of a bank who regularly invited me to give briefings to his board over dinner rang to ask me to be 'more upbeat than negative' at the forthcoming meeting because many of his board were strong ANC supporters. One leading ANC member on his board always sprang to the defence of the ANC. At the dinner I sat next to this same ANC member, who had the week before expressed great anger to one of my colleagues at the current state of the ANC and its leadership while being very complimentary about the Institute and saying that when we spoke people listened.[49]

About a year after being told about the bank that regarded us as 'untouchable' because it was afraid of the ANC, I was invited by the American Chamber of Commerce to receive its 2013 leadership award for the Institute's 'independence and courage' in 'disseminating powerful ideas' and being willing to 'stand on the wrong side of public opinion'.[50] When I was called up at the thanksgiving dinner in the Sandton Convention Centre for the Amcham president to present the award to me, Cyril Ramaphosa, who was the guest speaker, asked if he could also go up on the dais to be 'associated with' the presentation and accompanying photograph. Big smiles all round. So perhaps not so 'untouchable' after all.[51]

CHAPTER 15

The way forward

As I write this final chapter South Africa has for the moment nar-rowly escaped downgrade of its government debt to sub-investment status, business confidence is waning, corruption and violent crime are rampant, the state has itself become increasingly lawless,[1] growth is shrinking, and our own companies are decamping elsewhere as fast as they can. Books asking how long the country can survive have been flying off the shelves. In December 2015 President Jacob Zuma sent shock-waves across the country and even beyond when he fired a respected finance minister who had apparently refused to support an unaffordable and murky deal with Russia to build nuclear power stations. At the end of March 2016 Mr Zuma was found by the Constitutional Court to have 'failed to uphold, defend, and respect the Constitution' in his handling of the public protector after she had found that he was liable to repay some of the public funds spent on his private estate at Nkandla in KwaZulu-Natal. At the end of April 2016 the High Court effectively ordered the National Prosecuting Authority to reinstate 18 charges com-prising 783 counts of fraud, racketeering, and corruption against him arising from the controversial arms deal announced at the end of 2000; the charges had been withdrawn in 2009 by a compliant official who had put loyalty to Mr Zuma above his legal duties.

This is all a tragedy. The ANC was launched into power with goodwill unprecedented in modern history. Few governments anywhere can have started off so widely acclaimed by political parties of both Left and Right across the world. Right-wing resistance, limited as it was, had already been crushed, never seriously to be tried again. Foreign television crews who had come to film a bloodbath during the election in April 1994 packed up in disgust and went home. The handover of power from the National Party to the African National Congress in the amphitheatre of the Union Buildings was as orderly as the one that occurs every four or eight years in front of the Capitol in Washington DC. South Africa had the largest non-oil mineral reserves in the world, and the best infrastructure on the African continent. I myself said that it could be the continent's political and economic success story. Much of this has been squandered.

Various journalists have described Mr Zuma as a 'one-man wrecking ball' – reminding me of what Prime Minister Jan Smuts wrote to a friend in 1942: 'What will it profit the country if justice is done to the underdog and the whole caboodle then, including the underdog, is handed over to the wreckers?'[2] Not only has Mr Zuma's government done immense harm to the economy and to the underdog, he has also undermined one state institution after another. As school education and public health services fail so many pupils and patients, and unemployment mounts, more and more people fear that South Africa will become yet another failed African state. The despair among writers who support the ANC is as great as among those who don't. Although some journalists and academics dismiss critics as malcontents or 'doomsayers' suffering from 'whiteness', many of the most trenchant critics are black. If Alan Paton were alive today he would no doubt write a book entitled *Loot the Beloved Country*. It too would be a best-seller.

A few on the Right point fingers at the Institute and say, 'We told you so. You naïve liberals have got what you want. This is all your fault. Is it not time to say you're sorry?'

'Actually, no,' is the answer. 'If you had listened to us a long time ago, we wouldn't now be in this mess. There would have been decent education for the whole population, not just the whites. We wouldn't have lost all those lives, or all that investment, and the economy would be much larger; there would be less poverty, less inequality, and less unemployment. In any event, the real issue is not political stability or economic efficiency, vital though they are, but human dignity. On that score alone, apartheid had to go.'

As this book has shown, dignity was violated day in and day out in ways ranging from denial of the franchise through the cruelty of the pass laws to supposedly 'petty apartheid' in the form of social segregation. One day during my first spell at the Institute in 1971 I went out for a cup of coffee with my friend and colleague Robin Margo. We found a table at a café on the pavement in Braamfontein a few blocks away. As a waiter brought our coffee, a senior Institute staff member whom we knew as 'Mr Nkonyane' walked by. He ran the print room and he called the two of us – half his age – 'Robin' and 'John'. Perhaps we should have caused an incident by inviting him to join us, but we didn't. He greeted us and walked on, as we wished the pavement would open up and swallow us. Robin and I looked at one another and said as with one voice, 'This is a disgusting country.'

The *Financial Mail*, which I joined a few years later, had offices in the Carlton Centre, then the most glamorous part of the city. The centre included a pond called the 'Rondehof' which was turned into an ice-rink in winter for children to skate. It was overlooked by a circular gallery. The white children would strap on their skates and swing around on the ice, while the black children and their parents watched them from the gallery. I often wondered what black parents would say when their children asked whether they too could go and skate.

At about this time one of my *FM* colleagues, Stewart Carlyle, and I drove from Durban to Nongoma to interview Mangosuthu Buthelezi in what was then his temporary capital before he moved to Ulundi. The interview over, we stopped for a drink in the local hotel, which was forbidden territory even for the chief minister of the KwaZulu homeland.

Even today when I see people of all races happily mixing in restaurants and elsewhere I often recall these experiences and the daily humiliations that black people had to endure in their own native land. Their money was welcome in all the shops in the Carlton Centre, but they couldn't sit down there for a cup of coffee or allow their children to whizz round on the ice.

Another colleague on the *FM*, Nic Stathakis, shaking his head at something or other the government had done, declared that blacks were living under an army of occupation. He was right. The pass laws alone, which meant that 80 per cent of the population could not move freely about their own country, justified this description. Despite the risks of going the way of Africa, FW de Klerk was right to take the steps he did in February 1990. And liberals who fought the injustice, insanity, and cruelty of apartheid for decades should have no regrets either.

The question now facing South Africa is whether the ANC can reform itself as the NP reformed itself. Does it have an FW de Klerk? Does it even have a John Vorster or a PW Botha? As this memoir has shown, they too played a role in dismantling apartheid. The NP was under immense pressure from all sides. The ANC is not – not yet anyway. Although pressure for Mr Zuma to resign has been growing following the strictures by the courts and the unceasing flow of reports of malfeasance on his part, there is little pressure for fundamental change in ANC policy.

People sometimes ask me whether South Africa is going the way of Zimbabwe. I ask them whether they want it to. And if not, what are they doing to stop it? So the rest of this chapter will put forward ideas on what needs to be done. Better that we should ourselves reverse the country's downward slide before we have policy change forced upon us by the International Monetary Fund after a financial crisis. This means subjecting the ANC – and the SACP – to both deeper scrutiny and more pressure for fundamental change. How can this be done?

The first necessity is to do a proper analysis of our problems. Although it is fashionable to say South Africa has 'great policies but poor implementation', the truth is that we have a great many thoroughly bad policies. Understanding how they all fit together necessitates understanding what drives the ruling party. Countering a revolutionary agenda is harder than dealing with pragmatism, but the starting point is to recognise its existence. The ANC makes no secret of its revolutionary agenda, but the main response to it is denial. 'It cannot happen here!' is the unspoken refrain.

Getting one's analysis correct also means connecting the dots. Trevor Manuel said in 2015 that it was a 'tragedy' that management at Eskom and other state-owned enterprises had deteriorated.[3] It is more than a tragedy. The fate of these institutions is the predictable result of the policy governing appointments to them.

Let's make some other connections. Why is the ANC bent on replacing self-regulation with regulation by statutory bodies? In each case a pretext peculiar to a particular industry is cited: newspapers which don't give the government fair coverage, for example. But the capture of all centres of power is also a stated ideological objective. It was well under way long before anybody had heard of the Gupta family or of the problem of 'state capture'. It must be recognised for what it is: a threat to democracy with its origins in totalitarian ideology.

The second necessity is to build alliances. Newspapers often support the establishment of regulatory bodies in other sectors – supposedly to keep down medicine prices, for example – but complain when they themselves are threatened with regulation. They support racial quotas in sport and business, without thinking that such quotas may one day be imposed on newsrooms. They seem to have forgotten that freedom is indivisible. The government is able to pick off independent institutions one by one. So these institutions should form an 'alliance for independence' to counter further encroachment by the state. This is how the Institute defeated plans to capture control of NPOs.

Thirdly, we must defend vital assets. Many people have already sprung to the defence of the Constitution, the judiciary, the press, and the public protector. They should keep their powder dry. A party unscrupulous enough to use violence to gain power is likely to be unscrupulous in trying to retain it. The Independent Electoral Commission will require watchful scrutiny lest it be hijacked as the prosecution and intelligence services have been.

Resistance to frontal attack was wonderfully on display in December 2015 in defence of the National Treasury – of all institutions! People from the EFF to the banks leapt to its defence when President Zuma fired his finance minister, Nhlanhla Nene, causing international markets to dump South African shares, rands, and government bonds, with potentially catastrophic consequences. This compelled business to intervene with the ANC. The ANC then forced Mr Zuma to undo the damage by restoring a former finance minister, Pravin Gordhan, to the treasury.

This was an astonishing turnaround. And the lesson is that countervailing forces are themselves a powerful asset. They distinguish democracies from totalitarian societies. Lobby groups, newspapers, social media, politicians, churches, the entire non-profit sector, business, and outspoken individuals can all be mobilised against abuses of power. Democracy works. So does freedom. The proviso is that people are willing to make use of them, not leave them to rust.

Nor must we be afraid to defend the institutions and processes of wealth creation. One reason for the country's downward slide is that there has for too long been too little opposition to policies damaging to investment and growth. Business in particular has been too prone to appease and too reluctant to criticise. This was true for most of the apartheid era, and it has been true of the entire post-apartheid era. Renewed threats to Mr Gordhan in the form of trumped-up charges in October 2016 prompted numerous normally reticent business leaders to declare their support for legality. Rather than face the humiliation of having the charges thrown out by the courts, the National Prosecuting Authority dropped them. The criticism from business may have contributed to this decision. But it remains to be seen whether business has the conviction and the guts to speak up for the fundamental changes in policy necessary to enable South Africa to start generating wealth again.

The fourth necessity is to expose contradictions. The ANC's claim to be 'non-racist' is incompatible with all its legislation requiring discrimination on racial grounds. It wants an efficient developmental state, but it also wants affirmative action and cadre deployment. We can't have high rates of economic growth if we play fast and loose with property rights. We can't have the promised 'better life for all' if we cannot offer hope to the jobless. Or to the millions dependent on failing schools and hospitals. Relentless exposure of these contradictions will generate greater demand for changes in policy – as happened with apartheid.

Nor should the moral dimension be ignored. Never-ending exposés of the human misery and cruelty inflicted by apartheid helped to end that system. We must seek likewise to prick the consciences of people in the ANC with continuing exposés of the human costs of current policy failures, such as the Bloemhof babies or the child drowned in a school lavatory[4] – just two examples of the tragic consequences of the callous neglect so prevalent in this country. We must also challenge all those people who joined the ANC for idealistic reasons rather than to support a revolutionary agenda or participate in the looting of the state. They sat silent while Thabo Mbeki sent AIDS victims to their deaths. Until the ANC lost control of Johannesburg, and also of the metropolitan councils that include Pretoria and Port Elizabeth in the nationwide municipal elections on 3 August 2016, it was remarkably tolerant of Jacob Zuma and of his disdain for Parliament, the Constitution, the public purse, and the rule of law. Where will it stop?

Number five is to put forward alternatives. Take the initiative. Seize the gap. Almost daily now, business leaders, journalists, and economists call upon the government to provide 'leadership' or come forward with new ideas. This is a cop-out. Any ideas the present political leadership comes up with are likely to be bad ones. None of the ANC leaders suggested as possible successors to Mr Zuma has suggested any fundamental changes in racial, economic, or interventionist policy. People who want change must put forward new ideas themselves. Imagine, for example, the power of a package of policies designed to put South Africa at the very top of the Fraser index of attractiveness for mining investment instead of leaving us to languish at number 53. Or of policies aimed at pulling us steadily up from number 132 (out of 144) in the global rankings of health and primary education.[5]

The sixth essential is to launch the necessary intellectual battle to get the liberal state back on to the public agenda. Embark on a new crusade for economic freedom. This will require stamina, courage, resources, and marketing. It will provide a new vision to which the country can aspire. Get this vision accepted, and policy change will follow.

Number seven is public education. We need to build up critical mass for both alternative ideas and alternative policies. The press must be both a vehicle and a target. The target market must also include politicians of all parties and civil servants. Many ideas will fall upon stony ground, but some will fall upon fertile soil, including members of the ruling elite increasingly aware of the failures of their own policies. This is what happened in the 1970s and 1980s. It can be made to happen again.

The eighth and final essential is to fight on your own ground. Don't say you favour 'transformation', because you thereby give the government a blank cheque. Opposition parties seeking to attract votes away from the ANC must be especially vigilant lest they move onto the ANC's ideological ground instead of holding up clear alternatives. This destroyed the old official opposition, the United Party. In the end, the liberal Progressive Party was far more successful because it told the truth and stuck to principle. Its successor, the Democratic Alliance, needs to remember this.

Part of sticking to principle is playing with a straight bat instead of going along with harmful policies. It was not difficult to foresee the consequences of harmful policies when they were being discussed prior to enactment. The Institute and others spelt them out very clearly. If more people had spoken out at the time, less damage would have been done. The country would be much higher up global rankings. Unemployment would be lower. GDP – and GDP per head – would be higher.

South Africa's future is not preordained. The country has choices. It can continue on its present path. Or it can change course. In one sense this will be easier now than when the NP did so, because although the ANC can intimidate its critics, it cannot ban them. But in another sense it will be harder because the ANC is heavily influenced by Marxist economic ideas, whereas the NP was not. Although the capitalist and free-market systems were undermined by its racial legislation, the NP was not ideologically opposed to them.

The country's plight is compounded by the fact that there are too few warriors in the battle to propagate liberal ideas, including the virtues of the capitalist and free-market systems. Business is absent from that debate, leaving the field wide open for the EFF and like-minded non-profit organisations, some of them financed by business.

The media are not doing much to promote capitalism and free markets either – even though without them we would have no independent newspapers. Much of what appears in the press from academics is in line with ANC thinking on economic and racial issues. There is no longer an organised liberal voice on the campuses, although one or two groups are trying to get one going again. It is left to a handful of newspaper and on-line columnists and a couple of under-resourced think-tanks to promote the alternatives.

But there are factors working to our advantage. One is the growing awareness of policy failure. The public knows it, and the ANC and the SACP know it. This makes them increasingly vulnerable to the influence of different ideas. Also to our advantage is the waning moral authority of the ANC, a party with which the whole world was in love 20 years ago. Pennies are dropping everywhere as corruption, criminality, and incompetence consume the organisation. It seems powerless to stamp out whistle-blowing within its own ranks. The party's image as the voice of the poor is crumbling under the suspicion that it has been captured by rich elites of dubious probity. All of the resulting disillusionment and despair should be harnessed to promote the new paradigm.

More than 50 years ago, when I joined the battle of ideas as a schoolboy, the ruling party and prevailing ideology seemed monolithic and impregnable. But they were not. The NP was compelled to abandon its own ideology. The ANC will have to do likewise. It will eventually have to liberalise economically, just as the NP had to liberalise. Even the communists in the ANC and the government will find themselves having to search for pragmatic solutions. The question is whether they can be prevented from doing more damage before they begin the retreat from revolutionary ideology into liberal pragmatism. South Africans who want to hasten that day can do so by joining the battle of ideas. Democracy provides the opportunity and free speech the weapon.

NOTES

The regular publications of the South African Institute of Race Relations (SAIRR) are cited as follows:

Annual Report Annual reports to Institute members, cited by serial number

@Liberty The occasional policy bulletin, cited by date

Fast Facts The monthly bulletin, cited by date

Frontiers The quarterly publication *Frontiers of Freedom* is cited as *Frontiers* plus serial number

Survey The annual survey of the state of the nation (originally *A Survey of Race Relations in South Africa*, then *Race Relations Survey*, now *South Africa Survey*) is cited as *Survey* plus the relevant year.

Chapter 1 Home, school, army

1 *The World English Bible.*
2 Jaap Steyn, *Penvegter: Piet Cillié van die Burger*, Tafelberg, 2001, pp 131, 357. Reference kindly supplied by Hermann Giliomee by e-mail to JKB dated 31 October 2016.
3 1959–1960 *Survey*, pp 278–281.
4 *Rand Daily Mail*, 9 March 1963.
5 Letter from me to my grandparents, 15 October 1963.
6 Shireen Motala, *Behind Closed Doors – A Study of Deaths in Detention in South Africa*, SAIRR, Johannesburg, 1987.
7 Letter from Alan Paton to JKB, 10 September 1964.

8 Letter from Alan Paton to JKB, 25 January 1965.

9 Letter from Alan Paton to JKB, 10 April 1978.

10 Exchange of letters Alan Paton/JKB, 9 July, 4 October 1984.

11 Maritz van den Berg, PoliticsWeb, 5 October 2015.

12 Maritz van den Berg, PoliticsWeb, 13 September 2015.

13 Muriel Horrell, *Action, Reaction, and Counter-action – A Brief Review of Non-white Political Movements in South Africa*, SAIRR, Johannesburg, 1971, p 70.

14 *Rand Daily Mail,* 16 September 1972.

15 Ann Beverley Coltman, A Comparative Study of the Breretons of Wisconsin and the Breretons of South Africa, senior thesis, University of Texas, Austin, 1977–1979.

16 Jocelyne Kane-Berman, 'The Kane-Berman Family History', unpublished, 2006.

17 Claire Robertson (ed.), *Remembering Old Johannesburg*, Ad Donker, Johannesburg, 1986.

18 These words from Field Marshal JC Smuts appear on her tombstone in the Brixton Cemetery in Johannesburg.

19 Muriel Horrell, *South Africa – Basic Facts and Figures*, SAIRR, Johannesburg, 1973, p 10.

20 JKB interview with Louis Kane-Berman, *Frontline,* June 1982.

21 Muriel Horrell, *Legislation and Race Relations*, SAIRR, Johannesburg, 1971, pp 2, 15–16.

22 1955–1956 *Survey*, p 4.

23 MM Corbett, *The Truth about the Constitutional Crisis*, War Veterans' Torch Commando, Cape Town, 1952.

24 Louis Kane-Berman, 'The Torch Commando – Its Beginning and End', unpublished paper, undated; JKB interview with Louis Kane-Berman, *Frontline,* June 1982.

25 Gwendolen Carter, *The Politics of Inequality – South Africa since 1948*, third ed., Thames & Hudson, London, 1962, p 330.

26 Louis Kane-Berman, 'The Torch Commando – Its Beginning and End', pp 317–318.

27 1952–1953 *Survey*, pp 5–6.

28 JKB interview with Louis Kane-Berman, *Frontline,* June 1982.

29 John Kane-Berman, *Contract Labour in South West Africa,* SAIRR, Johannesburg, 1972.

30 *Assembly Hansard* 10, 13 April 1972, columns 4854–4855.

31 Louis Kane-Berman, 'The Torch Commando – Its Beginning and End', p 22.

32 Card sent by Transhaven Seaside Fund to JKB, November 2012.

33 E-mail from Ruth Spector to JKB, 7 November 2012.

Chapter 2 Wits

1 *Wits Student*, 12 August 1966.

2 Letter from Harold Wilson to JKB, 6 July 1970.

3 *The Times*, 26 August 1982.

4 Letter from Elinor Birley to JKB, 28 September 1982.

5 Robert Birley, *Universities and Utopia*, The Chancellor's Lecture, University of the Witwatersrand, 4 May 1960.

6 Robert Birley, The Seventh Richard Feetham Lecture, SRC, University of the Witwatersrand, 6 August 1970.

7 Arthur Hearnden, *Red Robert – A Life of Robert Birley*, London, 1984, p 202.

8 Tamsanqa Wilkinson Kambule in the Festschrift in honour of Robert Birley, undated.

9 Muriel Horrell, *Bantu Education to 1968*, SAIRR, Johannesburg, 1968, p 116.

10 1970 *Survey*, p 243.

11 *Rand Daily Mail*, undated clipping.

12 Lawrence Schlemmer, *The Negro Ghetto Riots and South African Cities*, SAIRR, Johannesburg, undated but probably 1968.

13 Exchange of letters Charles Simkins/JKB, 5 October, 14 November 1985.

14 Charles Simkins, *Reconstructing South African Liberalism*, SAIRR, Johannesburg, 1986.

15 ID MacCrone, Excerpt from the address given by the vice-chancellor and principal in Wits Great Hall on the occasion of the summer graduation ceremony, 3 April 1965.

16 *The Star*, 12 October 1967.

17 *Wits Student*, 2 June 1967.

18 Steve Biko, *I Write What I Like*, A Selection of His Writings Edited with a Personal Memoir by Aelred Stubbs CR, The Bowerdean Press, London, 1978, p 11.

19 Ibid, p 13.

20 John Kane-Berman, 'Some thoughts on recent protests,' in *Individual – Nusas Local Quarterly*, October 1968, p 16.

21 *Rand Daily Mail*, 14 June 1968; *Wits Student*, 21 June 1968.

22 1968 *Survey*, p 254.

23 Alan Paton, *Save the Beloved Country*, Hans Strydom Publishers, Melville, 1987, pp 223–224; Helen Suzman, *In No Uncertain Terms – Memoirs*, Jonathan Ball, Parklands, 1993, p 182.

24 *Wits Student*, 13 June, 26 August 1968.

25 *New Frontier*, Journal of the Houghton Young Progressives, March 1966.

26 Suzman, *In No Uncertain Terms*, pp 61–62.

27 *Rand Daily Mail*, 15 August 1968.

28 *The Star*, 17 August 1968.

29 *The Star*, 19 August 1968.

30 *Rand Daily Mail*, 20 August 1968.
31 *Rand Daily Mail*, 25 August 1968.
32 *The Times*, 21 August 1968.
33 *Rand Daily Mail*, 25 August 1968.
34 *Rand Daily Mail*, 26 August 1968.
35 *Rand Daily Mail*, 29 August 1968.
36 *The Star*, 30 August 1968.
37 *Rand Daily Mail*, 31 August 1968.
38 Letter from Raymond Tucker to JKB, 20 August 1968.
39 *Wits Student*, 15 March 1968.
40 Alan Paton, Address given at Darragh Hall, Johannesburg, 24 April 1968.
41 Randolph Vigne, *Liberals against Apartheid – A History of the Liberal Party of South Africa 1953–1968*, Macmillan, London, 1997, p 222.
42 1970 *Survey*, p 278.
43 1969 *Survey*, pp 4–5.
44 FW de Klerk, *The Last Trek, A New Beginning – The Autobiography*, Macmillan, London, 1998, pp 231–234.
45 Leo Marquard, *The Peoples and Policies of South Africa*, third ed., Oxford University Press, London, 1962, p 9.
46 HR Hahlo and Ellison Kahn, *The Union of South Africa – The Development of its Laws and Constitution*, Juta and Company, Cape Town, 1960, p 54.
47 Janet Robertson, *Liberalism in South Africa 1948 to 1963*, Oxford University Press, London, 1971, pp 3–4.
48 Liberal Party of South Africa, *Non-racial Democracy – The Policies of the Liberal Party of South Africa*, Pietermaritzburg, Liberal Party, undated.
49 RF Alfred Hoernlé, *South African Native Policy and the Liberal Spirit*, Witwatersrand University Press, Johannesburg, 1945, p viii.
50 Suzman, *In No Uncertain Terms*, p 181.

Chapter 3 Oxford

1 *The Memoirs of Field Marshal Viscount Montgomery of Alamein*, Collins, London, 1958, pp 120, 132, 167.
2 *The Times*, 4 November 1969.
3 *New Nation*, November and December 1970.
4 Shireen Motala, *Behind Closed Doors*, pp 40–44.
5 John Kane-Berman, *Soweto: Black Revolt, White Reaction*, Ravan Press, Johannesburg, 1978.
6 John Kane-Berman, 'South Africa's Marxist Myth', *Reality*, March 1971.
7 *Wits Student*, 3 September 1971.
8 John Kane-Berman, *South Africa's Silent Revolution*, SAIRR and Southern Book Publishers, Johannesburg and Halfway House, 1990.

9 Letters to JKB from JJ Kruger, 25 August, 26 October, 30 November 1971.
10 Milton Mayer, *They Thought They Were Free – The Germans 1933 to 1945*, University of Chicago Press, Chicago and London, 1965.
11 William Sheridan Allen, *The Nazi Seizure of Power – The Experience of a Single German Town, 1922–1945*, Franklin Watts, New York, 1965.
12 For example, 'Nazism – A Question of Perception', *Nusas Newsletter*, 29 September 1972, and 'Remember the Nazism Method', *Pro Veritate*, October 1972.
13 Mayer, *They Thought They Were Free*, pp 166–167.
14 JKB at Durban SRC seminar, 27 November 1976.
15 Julius Ebbinghaus, *Zu Deutschlands Schicksalswende*, Frankfurt am Main, 1946, as quoted in F Lilge, *The Abuse of Learning*, New York, 1948, p 170, as quoted by Robert Birley in *Universities and Utopia, The Chancellor's Lecture*, 4 May 1965, Witwatersrand University Press, Johannesburg, 1965, p 18.
16 JKB at Wits 4 April 1989, and at UCT 15 December 1989.
17 *The Citizen*, 10 October 1986.
18 Letters to JKB, 18 April 1989, 1 January 1990.

Chapter 4 Truth to power

1 Joel Mervis, *The Fourth Estate: A Newspaper Story*, Jonathan Ball, Johannesburg, 1989, p 338.
2 Ibid, p 356.
3 Ibid, pp 423–424.
4 Letter from the Directorate of Publications to the Students' Representative Council at the University of Cape Town, 27 May 1977.
5 CF Beyers Naudé, Wolfgang Thomas *et al*, *Management Responsibility and African Employment in South Africa – Report of a Panel Investigation*, Ravan Press, Johannesburg, 1973.
6 *Financial Mail*, 30 May 1973; *Rand Daily Mail*, 30 May 1973; *Die Vaderland*, 30 May 1973; *Rapport*, 3 June 1973.
7 1973 *Survey*, p 288.
8 Institute for Industrial Education, *The Durban Strikes 1973*, Ravan Press, Johannesburg, 1974, pp 105–106.
9 *Financial Mail*, 8 February 1974.
10 *The Citizen*, 17 May 1977.
11 John Kane-Berman, *Soweto: Black Revolt, White Reaction*, Ravan Press, Johannesburg, 1978.
12 Letter from Sheena Duncan to JKB, 6 September 1979.
13 *Financial Mail*, 10 December 1976.
14 Steven Friedman, *Why Radicals Read the FM*, www.fm.co.za, 4 November 1999.
15 *Financial Mail*, 1 November 1974.

16 *The Star, Rand Daily Mail*, 21 November; *Sunday Times*, 24 November 1974.
17 John Kane-Berman, 'The Crisis Over the Land', *Diakonia*, Durban, 27
    February 1979.
18 *Financial Mail*, 27 January 1978; *The Citizen*, 31 January 1978.

Chapter 5 Injustice and absurdity

 1 1973 *Survey*, pp 284–285.
 2 *Financial Mail*, 23 March 1973.
 3 *Financial Mail*, 15 June 1973.
 4 *Financial Mail*, 16, 30 August 1974.
 5 *Financial Mail*, 30 August 1974.
 6 *Financial Mail*, 8 February, 19 July 1974.
 7 *Financial Mail*, 3, 10 December 1976.
 8 *Financial Mail*, 4 March 1977.
 9 *Financial Mail*, 23 September, 7 October 1977.
10 Republic of South Africa, Departments of Labour and of Mines, *Report of the
    Commission of Enquiry into Labour Legislation*, RP 47/1979.
11 *Frontline*, May 1982.
12 *The Times*, 2 June 1982.
13 *The Economist*, 25 June 1983.
14 2014/2015 *Survey*, p 415; *Business Day,* 17 November 2014.
15 South African History Online, viewed 19 December 2014.
16 *Financial Mail*, 23 April 1976.
17 *Financial Mail*, 12 October 1973.
18 *Financial Mail*, 18 April, 6 June 1975, 17, 24 September 1976.
19 *Financial Mail*, 18 June 1976.
20 *Financial Mail*, 3 August 1973.
21 *Financial Mail*, 14 February 1975.
22 *Financial Mail*, 14 December 1973.
23 *Financial Mail*, 21 November 1975.
24 *Financial Mail*, 4 April 1975.
25 *Financial Mail*, 12 October 1973.
26 *Financial Mail*, 12 October 1973.
27 *Financial Mail*, 5 December 1975.
28 *Financial Mail*, 21 November 1975.
29 JKB for *World Business Weekly*, 21 November 1982.
30 JKB for *African Impact*, 2 June 1982.
31 JKB for *Business International*, 3 December 1981.
32 *Financial Mail*, 22, 29 July 1977.
33 *Financial Mail*, 7 October 1977.
34 *Business Day*, 22 June 2006.

Chapter 6 A permit for everything

1 Suzman, *In No Uncertain Terms*, pp 67, 106.
2 *Financial Mail*, 26 October 1973.
3 *Financial Mail*, 26 July 1974.
4 *Financial Mail*, 11 February 1977.
5 *Financial Mail*, 12 November 1976.
6 *Financial Mail*, 16 March 1979.
7 *Financial Mail*, 15 June 1973.
8 Letter to George Palmer from the economic adviser to the prime minister, 22 June 1973.
9 Robin Renwick, *Mission to South Africa – Diary of a Revolution*, Jonathan Ball, Johannesburg and Cape Town, 2015, p 25.
10 *Financial Mail*, 5 July 1974.
11 *Financial Mail*, 26 July 1974.
12 *Financial Mail*, 29 June 1973.
13 *Financial Mail*, 17 February 1978.
14 *Sunday Times*, London, 6 March 1977.
15 *Financial Mail*, 20 February 1976.
16 *The Guardian*, 22 May 1979.
17 *Financial Mail*, 1 June 1979.
18 Quoted in Kane-Berman, 'The crisis over the land', *South African Outlook,* March 1979, p 43.
19 *Financial Mail*, 18 May, 1 June 1979.
20 Kane-Berman, *Silent Revolution,* p 35.
21 *Financial Mail*, 30 March 1979.
22 Republic of South Africa: *Report of the Commission of Enquiry into Legislation Affecting the Utilisation of Manpower [excluding the legislation administered by the departments of labour and mines]*, Pretoria, 1978.
23 *Financial Mail*, 11 May, 18 May, 8 June 1979.
24 Suzman, *In No Uncertain Terms*, p 42.
25 *Financial Mail*, 19 December 1975, 21 May, 10 December 1976.
26 Desmond Tutu, *Rand Daily Mail*, 30 April 1976, as quoted in Kane-Berman, *Soweto*, p 99.
27 *Financial Mail*, 7, 14 January 1977.
28 *The Argus*, 17 April 1996.
29 Colin Smuts, *Staffrider,* vol. 10, no. 2, 1992.
30 *Business Day*, 22 November 1993.
31 Letter from JKB to Tony Bloom, 7 July 1978.
32 Letter from the minister of police to Helen Suzman, 14 June 1978.
33 *The Argus*, 17 April 1996; JKB speech at bursary prize-giving, 5 May 1997.
34 *Financial Mail*, 14 April, 5 May 1978.
35 *Financial Mail*, 1 March 1974.

36 *Financial Mail*, 14 May 1976, 13 July 1979.
37 *Financial Mail*, 26 November 1976.
38 *Financial Mail*, 25 June 1976.
39 *Financial Mail*, 10 December 1976.
40 *Financial Mail*, 16 September 1977.
41 *Irish Times*, 21 January 1981.
42 *Financial Mail*, 13 July 1979.
43 *Financial Mail*, 29 June 1979.
44 *Financial Mail*, 17 August 1979.

Chapter 7 Soweto, apartheid, and business

1 John Kane-Berman, *Soweto: Black Revolt, White Reaction*, Ravan Press, Johannesburg, 1978, p 19.
2 JKB, UCT mass meeting, 4 August 1976.
3 Arnt Spandau and Heinz-Dietrich Ortlieb, *SüdAfrika – Revolution oder Evolution?*, Verlag Weltarchiv, Hamburg, 1977.
4 John Kane-Berman, *South Africa – The Method in the Madness*, Pluto Press, London, 1979.
5 *The Star*, 21 December 1978.
6 *The Voice of Black People*, undated, but handed out on 27 September 1976; *World*, 10 October 1976.
7 *People of South Africa: the African National Congress Calls on You*, undated, but found near Johannesburg station on 8 July 1976.
8 The voice of the ANC (Spear of the Nation): *The War Is On*, undated.
9 Message of the National Executive Committee to all the units of the African National Congress of South Africa on the Current Situation, Dar es Salaam, 14 September 1976.
10 Kane-Berman, *Soweto*, pp 112–113.
11 *Amandla-Matla* (Newsletter of the African National Congress), vol. 5, no. 1, undated.
12 *Sunday Express*, 10 December 1978.
13 *Time Out*, 7–13 September 1979.
14 *Sechaba*, August 1979.
15 1977 *Survey*, p 168.
16 Ian Davidson, *Financial Times*, 4 August 1979.
17 RW Johnson, *New Society*, 12 July 1979.
18 Oscar Wollheim, *The Argus*, 21 February 1979.
19 Letter from Gita Dyzenhaus to JKB, 28 November 1978.
20 Tony Kleu, *The Guardian*, 16 June 1979.
21 June Goodwin, *Christian Science Monitor*, 12 February 1979.
22 Kane-Berman, *Soweto*, pp 103–108, 217–229.

23 *Sunday Times*, 7 March 1982.

24 Republic of South Africa, *Report of the Commission of Inquiry into the Riots at Soweto and Elsewhere from 16 June 1976 to 28 February 1977*, RP 55/1980.

25 *Sunday Times*, 24 May 1981.

26 JKB notes taken at the time.

27 *Apartheid and Business – An Analysis of the Rapidly Evolving Challenges Facing Companies with Investments in South Africa*, Business International, Geneva, 1980.

28 Ibid, p 229.

29 Ibid, p 264.

30 Ibid, p 219.

31 JKB confidential notes, May 1986.

32 Business International, Conclusions from 'Conference on South Africa: The Evolving Challenge to International Companies', 5–6 June 1985, Hilton Hotel, London, 7 June 1985, Plaza Hotel, New York; JKB notes of the meeting; Letter from Angelo Forte of BI to JKB.

33 JKB notes taken at the conference, 27 May 1987.

34 Kane-Berman, *Soweto*, p 241.

35 Wikipedia, printed out 26 September 2014; O'Malley archives, printed out 26 September 2014.

36 John Kane-Berman, *The Erosion of Apartheid*, Testimony before the subcommittees on Africa and international economic policy and trade of the committee on foreign affairs of the House of Representatives of the 100th congress of the United States of America by John Kane-Berman, Washington DC, 23 March 1988, Times Media Limited, undated, *passim*.

37 John Kane-Berman, 'Grave Allegations and Flimsy Evidence', Address to the Swiss South African Association in Zurich on 4 June and to Institute members in Johannesburg on 29 July 2003; *Fast Facts*, August 2003.

38 *Business Report*, 1 September 2014.

Chapter 8 Dreams and nightmares

1 *Investors' Chronicle*, 5 December 1976.

2 Telexes back and forth between JKB and *Business Week*, 18, 22 January; 6, 11 February 1980.

3 *Financial Times Worldwide News-Features*, 28 September 1979.

4 *The Guardian*, 7 February 1980.

5 *De Volkskrant*, 7 February 1980.

6 *The Atlanta Constitution*, 3 July 1980.

7 *The Australian*, September/October 1979.

8 *The Guardian*, 5 March 1980.

9 *The Australian*, March 1980.
10 *Times Educational Supplement*, 15 July 1983.
11 *Financial Mail*, 16 March 1973.
12 *New York Times*, 31 March 1983.
13 *The Australian*, September/October 1979; *The Atlanta Constitution*, 3 July 1980.
14 *The Atlanta Constitution*, 4 December 1980; *The Guardian*, 15 December 1980.
15 *The Guardian*, 1 September 1981.
16 *De Volkskrant*, 28 March 1983.
17 *The Guardian*, 31 August 1981.
18 *Irish Times*, 13 August 1981, 1 April 1982; *New Statesman*, 2 April 1982.
19 *Irish Times*, 13, 21 August 1981, 1 April 1982.
20 *Irish Times*, 1 April 1982.
21 *The Atlanta Constitution*, 28 March 1982.
22 *Irish Times*, 22 August 1981.
23 *New York Times*, 20 August 1982; *The Guardian*, 28 August 1982.
24 *South*, October 1982.
25 *The Guardian*, 28 August 1982.
26 *De Volkskrant*, 28 March 1983.
27 *Rand Daily Mail*, 10 February 1983; *New Statesman*, 18 February 1983; *New York Times*, 6 March 1983; London *Sunday Times*, 10 April 1983.
28 JKB address, 21 April 1983.
29 *The Guardian*, 1 September 1981.
30 *The Guardian*, 28 September 1981; *Washington Post*, 31 May 1983.
31 *Frontline*, February 1980.
32 *De Volkskrant*, 30 May 1983.
33 *Irish Times*, 22 March 1982.
34 *The Atlanta Constitution*, 16 May 1982.
35 *Irish Times*, 4 March 1982.
36 *Irish Times*, 5 July 1983.
37 *The Australian*, 25 August 1981.
38 *South*, July 1981.
39 *The Guardian*, 21 April 1981.
40 *Irish Times*, 18 February 1981.
41 *The Guardian*, 23 September 1980.
42 *Irish Times, The Guardian*, 23 April 1981.
43 *The Australian*, 25 April 1981.
44 *Irish Times*, 24 April 1981.
45 *The Guardian*, 21 April 1981.
46 *Irish Times*, 29 January 1981.
47 *The Guardian*, 5 May 1981.

48 *Times Educational Supplement*, 7 October 1981, 18 February 1983.
49 *Times Educational Supplement*, 11 February 1983.
50 *Times Educational Supplement*, 15 April 1983.
51 1981 *Survey*, p 1.
52 *South*, July 1981.
53 *Irish Times*, 9 March 1982.
54 1983 *Survey*, p 567.
55 *New York Times*, 18 February 1983.
56 *Financial Post*, 4 June 1983; *Irish Times*, 23 June 1983.
57 *The Guardian*, 26 May 1983.
58 *South*, June 1983.
59 *The Guardian*, 24 May 1983.
60 *Irish Times*, 23 June 1983.
61 Kane-Berman, S*oweto*, pp 217–229.
62 Business International, 3 December 1981.
63 *Dagens Industri*, 9 June 1983.
64 *Africa Guide*, 17 September 1982.
65 *The Guardian*, 18 November 1982.
66 *De Volkskrant*, 24 March 1980.
67 *Times Educational Supplement*, 22 July 1980.
68 *Irish Times*, 22 June 1981.
69 *The Guardian*, 28 October 1982.
70 1983 *Survey*, p 220; *Rand Daily Mail*, 19 April 1983; *The Guardian*, 14 April 1983; London *Sunday Times*, 15 April 1983.
71 *De Volkskrant*, 8 April 1980.
72 *Dagens Nyheter* and *de Volkskrant*, 6 April 1982.
73 E-mail from Rudolf Gruber to JKB, 20 March 2014.

Chapter 9 Survival

1 *Annual Report* 53.
2 Ellen Hellmann, *The South African Institute of Race Relations 1929 to 1979 – A Short History*, SAIRR, Johannesburg, 2000, p 4.
3 Hoernlé, *South African Native Policy and the Liberal Spirit*, p vii.
4 *SAIRR, Go Forward in Faith*, undated.
5 *SAIRR, The Road Ahead*, 1972.
6 Ellen Hellmann, *The South African Institute of Race Relations 1929 to 1979*, p 9.
7 Tribute by Sue Krige, 22 December 2011.
8 *The Star*, 18 May 1994.
9 Ken Owen, *Business Day*, 7 November 1988.
10 *Annual Report* 83.

11 Neil Jacobsohn, *Business Day,* 4 March 1988.
12 Jill Wentzel, *The Liberal Slideaway,* SAIRR, Johannesburg, 1995, p xi.
13 *Annual Report* 56.
14 *Annual Report* 57.
15 Letter from Harry Barker to JKB, 25 February 1991.
16 *Citizen,* 6 May 1987.
17 *Sunday Star* and *Sunday Tribune,* 14 April 1985.
18 *Annual Report* 55.
19 *Financial Times,* 4 December 1985.
20 Letter to JKB from Professor Valerie Moller, 9 March 2006.
21 *Fast Facts,* April 2011.
22 2014/15 *Survey,* p 65.

Chapter 10 The silent revolution

1 JKB speeches, October 1983.
2 1983 *Survey,* p 88.
3 JKB, *The Crumbling of Apartheid – Crisis, Confusion, and Opportunity,* Chicago, 11 June 1985.
4 SAIRR, *Towards a Climate for Negotiation,* Johannesburg, 1984.
5 Steven Friedman, *Understanding Reform,* SAIRR, Johannesburg, 1986.
6 *American Business and Political Change,* SAIRR, April 1985.
7 *Time,* 14 July 1986.
8 JKB, *The Politics of Negotiation, with special reference to the KwaZulu-Natal Indaba,* Saint-Paul-de-Vence, 16 September 1987.
9 Letter from JC Heunis, minister of constitutional development and planning, to OD Dhlomo, 24 May 1989.
10 Nelson Mandela, *Long Walk to Freedom,* Macdonald Purnell, Randburg, 1994, pp 512, 522.
11 JKB, *Current Research and Policy Objectives of the Institute,* Johannesburg, 9 March 1988.
12 Speech by JKB to the AGM of Women for Peace, 21 May 1988.
13 Letter to JKB, 27 May 1988.
14 Memo from Jill Wentzel to JKB, 15 July 1988.
15 Wentzel, *Slideaway,* p 29.
16 John Kane-Berman *et al, Beating Apartheid and Building the Future,* SAIRR, Johannesburg, 1990.
17 JKB speech at Deane Yates's eightieth birthday, 17 February 2002.
18 Address to the Institute of Personnel Management, 27 November 1985.
19 *City Press Prospects,* 15 December 1985.
20 JKB, Address to the 72nd annual conference of the Natal Teachers Society, 6 July 1987.

21 1993/94 *Survey*, p 695.

22 *Business Day*, 9 July 2012.

23 John Kane-Berman, *Südafrikas verschwiegener Wandel*, Verlag A Fromm, Osnabrück, 1992.

24 *South Africa International*, July 1990.

25 *Ilanga*, 23–25 August 1990.

26 Clive Keegan, *Leadership*, September 1990.

27 Jeremy Cronin, *Work in Progress*, September 1990.

28 *Mail & Guardian*, 4–10 March 1994.

29 Ronnie Kasrils, *African Communist*, Third Quarter 1995.

30 John Kane-Berman, *Political Violence in South Africa*, SAIRR, Johannesburg, 1993, p 67.

31 Memo to JKB from Jill Wentzel, 22 July 1989.

32 JKB lecture to the Union of Jewish Women, 1 February 1988.

33 JKB lecture to Barlow Rand, 2 June 1988.

34 Letter from the Institute for African Studies of the Academy of Sciences of the USSR, 7 October 1985.

35 JKB confidential report to the Council of the Institute, January 1990.

36 Ibid.

37 JKB lecture to African Students for Liberty, University of Pretoria, 16 March 2015.

Chapter 11 Turmoil in the townships

1 JKB notes of interviews with Sam de Beer, Adriaan Vlok, Stoffel van der Merwe, and Roelf Meyer, 31 January to 2 February 1990.

2 1996/97 *Survey*, p 600.

3 *Annual Report* 55.

4 *Annual Report* 57.

5 Thami Mazwai *et al*, *Mau-Mauing the Media: New Censorship for the New South Africa*, SAIRR, Johannesburg, 1991, pp v–vi, 63.

6 Wentzel, *The Liberal Slideaway*, pp 139–147.

7 John Kane-Berman, *Political Violence in South Africa*, SAIRR, Johannesburg, 1993, pp 33, 37, 39, 41–44, 55.

8 JKB notes of BI conference, Meridien Hotel, London, 20 September 1990.

9 JKB report to the executive committee of the Institute, 21 November 1990.

10 Wentzel, *The Liberal Slideaway*, p 179.

11 JKB, *Political Violence*, pp 33, 43.

12 Ibid, pp 41–44, 48, 55.

13 Ibid, pp 37–39.

14 *The Times*, 3 December 2015.

15 JKB speech to the Tribute Forum, 24 October 1990.

16 JKB to Inyandza National Movement, 30 September 1990.

17 Undated conversation with Dr Mabuza as mentioned to FW de Klerk in an interview on 12 April 1991.

18 JKB, *Political Violence*, pp 44, 86–88.

19 Memo from the South Africa Foundation, 9 December 1993.

20 JKB, *Political Violence*, p 58.

21 JKB, *Violence in Perspective and the Road Ahead*, Johannesburg, 9 November 1992.

22 Nick Howarth, *War in Peace – The Truth about the South African Police's East Rand Riot Unit 1986 to 1994*, Galago, Alberton, 2012, p 258.

23 *Business Day*, 24 July 1992.

24 FW de Klerk, *The Last Trek – A New Beginning, The Autobiography*, Macmillan, London, 1998, pp 258–267.

25 *Business Day*, 15 April 1994.

26 JKB speech to the Security Association of South Africa, 20 September 1995.

27 Letter to JKB, 27 August 1992.

28 *Fast Facts*, November 2011.

29 De Klerk, *The Last Trek*, pp 208–209.

30 JKB, *Political Violence*, p 83.

31 Ibid, pp 61–70.

32 Press statement dated 4 February 1991.

33 *The Citizen*, 6 February 1991.

34 Letter from Bruce Evans to JKB, 23 August 1991.

35 Phone call from Tom Stanage to JKB, 20 August 1991.

36 Letter from Bill Burnett to JKB, 16 February 1991.

37 *The Spectator*, 4 July 1992.

38 Rachel Tingle, *Revolution or Reconciliation? The Struggle in the Church in South Africa*, Christian Studies Centre, London, 1992.

39 Methodist Church, exchange of letters with JKB, 22 July, 11 August, 23 August, 3 September 1993.

40 *Mail & Guardian*, 1–7 October 1993.

41 *The Salisbury Review*, December 1993.

42 Alan Fine, *Business Day*, 20 September 1993.

43 Patrick Laurence, *The Star,* 20 August 1993.

44 Patrick Laurence, *The Star,* 7 December 2010.

45 JKB, *Political Violence*, pp 74–75.

46 Anthea Jeffery, *Forum on Mass Mobilisation*, SAIRR, Johannesburg, 1991.

47 *The Star,* 13 September 1991.

48 Anthea Jeffery, *People's War: New Light on the Struggle for South Africa*, Jonathan Ball Publishers, Jeppestown, 2009.

49 *Business Day*, 20 August 1993.

50 Rian Malan, *Frontiers* 20; Anthea Jeffery, *Frontiers* 27.

51 Curt Reiss, *Joseph Goebbels*, Fonthill, undated, 2013?, p 206.

52 Hermann Giliomee, *Frontiers* 23.
53 Circular letter from Helen Suzman to members, 16 October 1992.
54 Confidential note from Jill Wentzel to JKB, 4 February 1996.
55 Letter from Kader Asmal to the Institute, 20 June 1995.
56 Exchange of letters between JKB and Dr Rudolf Gruber, 6 January and
    10 February 1992.
57 Letter from Jan Steyn to JKB, 24 August 1993.
58 Letter from Mary Mathews to JKB, 6 August 1993.
59 Letter from Pat Flemmer to JKB, 23 December 1990.
60 Letter from Ina Perlman to JKB, 18 November 1992.
61 JKB confidential statement to Council, 21 August 1993.
62 *Mail & Guardian*, 4–10 February 1994.
63 JKB, 'Whither South Africa and Whither the Institute', Pietermaritzburg,
    21 February 1991.
64 JKB to Richards Bay Minerals, 8 December 1993.
65 *Annual Report* 65.
66 *Natal Witness*, 17 May 1995.
67 JKB to the International Society for Human Rights, Frankfurt, 12 March 1994.
68 *Frontiers* 1/95.
69 JKB to South African Breweries, 19 July 1994.
70 Suzman, *In No Uncertain Terms*, p 14.
71 Malegapuru Makgoba, *Mail & Guardian*, 24–31 March 2005.
72 *Business Day*, 7 April 2005.
73 Message from Helen Suzman, 7 April 2005.
74 *Fast Facts*, February 2009.
75 *Daily Maverick*, 20 March 2016; *PoliticsWeb*, 21 March 2016.

Chapter 12 Revolution under the rainbow

 1 *Business Day*, 9 February 2001, 11 March, 26 August 2003.
 2 Letter from Baleka Mbete to JKB, 4 July 2006.
 3 Parliament of the Republic of South Africa, Report of the Independent Panel
    Assessment of Parliament, January 2009; and John Kane-Berman: Draft
    Minority Report, 12 November 2008.
 4 *Mail & Guardian Online*, 14 January 2009.
 5 Letter from the Urban Foundation to JKB, 19 January 1987.
 6 *Annual Report* 84.
 7 *Business Day*, 27 October 1995.
 8 Memo from Paul Pereira to JKB, 23 April 1996.
 9 *Annual Reports* 66, 67, 68.
10 *Annual Report* 71.
11 *Annual Report* 81.

12 *Business Day*, 13 September 2010.
13 *Fast Facts*, June 2006; *PoliticsWeb*, 15 October 2008.
14 Messages by phone and e-mail.
15 *Annual Reports* 75, 76, 77.
16 *Business Day*, 28 May 2012.
17 Letter from Gerrit Pretorius to JKB, 28 May 2012.
18 JKB, *Political Violence*, pp 72, 102.
19 *Fast Facts,* July 2013.
20 Private conversation, 23 September 2011.
21 *Business Day*, 7 September 2015.
22 JKB addresses to members in Cape Town and Johannesburg, 19 and 28 September 2011.
23 Point made in numerous JKB speeches to different audiences, among them Lombard Insurance Group, Johannesburg, 5 September 2011; University of the Third Age, Hermanus, 16 February 2012; Highveld Forum, Bryanston, 28 February 2012; SA Water and Energy Forum, Sandton, 19 April 2012.
24 For example to the Milk Producers' Organisation, KwaZulu-Natal, 21 September 2011; Institute members, Johannesburg, 28 September 2011; Friedrich Naumann for Liberty, Berlin and Brussels, 5 and 6 December 2011.
25 *Fast Facts*, July 2013.
26 *Business Day,* 2 June 2014.
27 Ibid.
28 *Business Day*, 19 October 2015.
29 *Business Day*, 24 August 2015.

Chapter 13 Race and redress

1 *Frontiers* 4.
2 *Frontiers* 25.
3 *Frontiers* 18.
4 *Frontiers* 26.
5 *Frontiers* 1/95.
6 *Frontiers* 22.
7 *@Liberty*, 24 June 2014.
8 *Fast Facts*, August 1998.
9 Ministry of Labour, Press statement by the minister of labour on the Employment Equity Bill, 12 March 1998.
10 *Sunday Argus*, 12 July 1998.
11 *Bedfordview and Edenvale News*, 29 July 1998.
12 Notes of a conference taken by Anthea Jeffery, 11 September 1998.
13 Reports to JKB, 15 and 16 November 1998.
14 JKB notes dated 12 August 1998.

15 *Finance Week,* 16–22 April 1998.
16 *Business Day,* 12 February 1998.
17 *Financial Mail,* 13, 27 February, 9 October 1998.
18 Anthea Jeffery, *Chasing the Rainbow – South Africa's Move from Mandela to Zuma,* SAIRR, Johannesburg, 2010, p 156.
19 *Frontiers,* September 1994.
20 *Fast Facts,* May 2013.
21 *Sowetan,* 13 February 1998; *Fast Facts,* July 2000.
22 Anthea Jeffery speech to the Development Group, 11 March 1999.
23 *Fast Facts,* March 2003.
24 *Annual Report* 70; *Frontiers* 26.
25 *Frontiers* 26.
26 Jill Wentzel, *Frontiers* 27, citation for a prize awarded to Rian Malan for an article written in *Frontiers* 26.
27 *Fast Facts,* September 2001.
28 *Fast Facts,* December 2001.
29 *Cape Argus,* 27 August 2001.
30 *The Economist,* 1 September 2001.
31 Lawrence Schlemmer, reply to *The Economist,* 9 September 2001.
32 Lawrence Schlemmer, *Fast Facts,* December 2001.
33 Lawrence Schlemmer, *Frontiers* 10.
34 Ipsos South Africa, www.ipsos.co.za, accessed 28 July 2014.
35 Barry D Wood, *USA Today,* 5 December 2013.
36 *Business Day,* 13 December 2013.
37 *Business Day,* 10 February 2014.
38 Martin Williams, *The Citizen,* 26 February 2014.
39 *@Liberty,* 24 June 2014.
40 *PoliticsWeb,* 25 June 2014.
41 *@Liberty,* 24 June 2014.
42 Ernst Hanisch, *Obersalzberg – The Eagle's Nest and Adolf Hitler,* Berchtesgadener Landesstiftung, Berchtesgaden, 1998.

Chapter 14 Liberalism for all seasons

1 *Leadership,* vol. 13, no. 1, 1994.
2 *Cape Times,* 9 April 1996.
3 *Frontiers* 9.
4 *Financial Mail,* 13, 20 August 1999.
5 *De Kat,* 1997.
6 *Frontiers* 7.
7 *Frontiers* 1/95.
8 *Fast Facts,* November 1998.

9 JKB to the Free Market Foundation, 30 March 2011.

10 *Fast Facts,* December 2015.

11 Ricardo Hausmann, *Final Recommendations of the International Panel on Asgisa,* Centre for International Development, Harvard, May 2008.

12 JKB to the South African financial markets conference hosted by Standard Corporate and Merchant Bank, 25 October 1996.

13 *Fast Facts*, May 1999.

14 *Fast Facts*, July 2001.

15 *Business Day*, 23 February 2005.

16 *Frontiers* 14 and 15.

17 Adam Smith, *An Inquiry into the Nature and Causes of the Wealth of Nations*, fith ed., vol. 1, Methuen, London, 1904, p 67.

18 John Kane-Berman, *Empowerment – The Need for a Liberal Strategy*, Friedrich Naumann Foundation, Rosebank, 2002.

19 John Kane-Berman, *A Liberal Alternative*, Zach de Beer Memorial Lecture, 10 March 2016; *The Liberal Way Out – And Up*, Free Market Foundation, 6 April 2016.

20 Neil Emerick, 'Economic Freedom – The Key to Prosperity', *@Liberty*, SAIRR,14 October 2014, p 5. Mr Emerick is a contributor to the *Economic Freedom of the World*, a report published annually by the Fraser Institute, the South African edition of which is published in conjunction with the Free Market Foundation.

21 *@Liberty*, 13 May 2014.

22 *@Liberty*, 9 September 2014.

23 *@Liberty*, 20 September 2016.

24 *@Liberty*, 13 February 2014.

25 *The Star*, September 2014.

26 *Saturday Star*, 8 March 2014.

27 For example, Swisscham Southern Africa, 10 March 2011, and Institute members in Johannesburg and Cape Town, 29 September and 1 October 2014.

28 E-mail, 29 November 2013.

29 Letter, 7 September 2012; e-mail 18 July 2012.

30 Message to JKB, April 2011.

31 Fax, 9 March 2000.

32 E-mail, 18 September 2008.

33 Note, 31 August 2012.

34 E-mail, 20 February 2014.

35 Andrew Kenny, *The Citizen*, 4 March 2014.

36 David Gleason, *Business Day*, 17 July 2013.

37 Letter to JKB, 10 January 2014.

38 Letter from Rudolf Gruber to JKB, 20 March 2014.

39 Letter to JKB, 21 December 1999.

40 Private note to JKB, 7 April 2009.
41 Letter, 17 November 2003.
42 E-mail, 24 June 2011.
43 E-mail, 24 June 2011.
44 E-mail, 14 September 2011.
45 *Business Day*, 29 May 2008.
46 Phone messages, 29 May 2008.
47 Xolela Mangcu, *The Weekender*, 31 May–1 June 2008.
48 Exchange of e-mails, 10 August 2014.
49 Phone message, 9 September 2008; e-mail message, 2 September 2008.
50 Citation, 27 November 2013.
51 Note of conversation with Amcham board member, 29 November 2013.

Chapter 15 The way forward
1 John Kane-Berman, *Going off the Rails: The Slide Towards the Lawless South African State*, SAIRR, Johannesburg, November 2016.
2 Quoted by Sir Louis Blom-Cooper in 'Jan Christiaan Smuts (1870–1950): Middle Templar Extraordinary', *Advocate*, 1 August 2013.
3 Trevor Manuel, *Business Report*, 31 July 2015.
4 *Sunday Independent*, 26 January 2014.
5 2014/2015 *Survey*, pp 378–379, 359.

Index

Page numbers in *italics* refer to photographs.
The abbreviation 'JKB' is used for John Kane-Berman.

327